DIGITAL WORKFLOWS
IN ARCHITECTURE
—

Dear Renee —

Many thanks for your guidance
and mentorship these past two years.
Hope you enjoy the book and keep
pushing the limits —

my best
ADAM.

SCOTT MARBLE (ED.)

DIGITAL WORKFLOWS IN ARCHITECTURE

DESIGNING DESIGN—DESIGNING ASSEMBLY—DESIGNING INDUSTRY

—

BIRKHÄUSER
BASEL

Editor's Assistant: Jason Roberts
Editor for the Publisher: Andreas Müller

Graphic Design: Thumb

A CIP catalogue record for this book is available from the Library of
Congress, Washington D.C., USA.

Bibliographic information published by the German National Library
The German National Library lists this publication in the Deutsche
Nationalbibliografie; detailed bibliographic data are available on the
Internet at http://dnb.d-nb.de.

© 2012 Birkhäuser, Basel
P.O.Box, 4002 Basel, Switzerland
www.birkhauser.ch
Part of De Gruyter

Printed on acid-free paper produced from chlorine-free pulp. TCF ∞
Printed in Germany
ISBN 978-3-0346-0799-5
9 8 7 6 5 4 3 2 1

This book was made possible by the generous support of
Turner Construction Company

FROM PROCESS TO WORKFLOW:
DESIGNING DESIGN, DESIGNING ASSEMBLY, DESIGNING INDUSTRY

—

SCOTT MARBLE

In the late nineties, when computer numerically controlled (CNC) processes were becoming popular in schools of architecture and had already begun to be utilized by ambitious design offices, I began experimenting with this new technology both professionally and academically, with the belief that it would redefine the relationship of architecture to production. Like many architects at that time, I was enamored with the ability of drawings to drive machines and began touring CNC shops of all types—from architectural millwork and metal shops to helicopter manufacturing and auto assembly plants. Upon the recommendation of a fellow machine addict, I contacted a local company that he had recently discovered to schedule a tour for a class I was teaching. From all indications on their website, which advertised a wide range of CNC services for many industries in all types of materials, this was going to provide an unprecedented display of the most advanced machines available. The e-mail response was a bit cryptic, but they offered to host the group with the qualification that there might not be much to see. I followed up with a phone call, only to find out that there were no machines at all at their shop. In fact, there was no shop, only a small office with a small staff of workers who connected online customer orders with a network of the most advanced industrial grade CNC machines in factories around the world. These orders, usually for applications unrelated to the core business of these globally distributed factories, would fill gaps in their daily production schedule to minimize machine downtime. The immediacy of file-to-fabrication processes still resonated with opportunity but was now positioned within the broader potential of digital information to form complex communciation workflows.

Quite simply, the thesis of this book is that the assimilation and synthesis of digital communications among architects, engineers, fabricators and builders is dramatically altering how we work and our relationship to the tools we use. New digital capacities are restructuring the organization and hierarchy of design from autonomous processes to collective workflows. The historical role of the designer as an author, a sole creator, is being replaced with semi-autonomous, algorithmically driven design workflows deeply embedded in a collective digital communication infrastructure. This is creating a number of pressures on the discipline of architecture to reorganize around the opportunities, and risks, of these changes. One of these changes is the role that design itself might play. The Architecture, Engineering and Construction (AEC) industry is in a state of flux fueled by transformative shifts in technology and design. Financial incentives around new economics of production, increased efficiencies afforded by streamlined communication and the automation of labor-intensive processes are already underway. The suggestion of this book is that there is a momentary opportunity to give a direction to this shift that will set the foundation for the next generation of architects.

The logics of digital workflows in architecture have begun to structure the way that architects design, the way that builders build, and the way that industry is reorganizing. These workflows have generally developed around three themes, largely independent of each other, and are now beginning to coalesce into an integrated system The first, Designing Design, is a *procedural* issue and considers how professionally divided design processes are being redefined as integrated design systems. Vast amounts of information, both descriptive and analytical, are now instantaneously available to help define and assess design options. Much, if not all, of this information is filtered through software that, by extension, structures the digital environment in which architects design. Architectural design has become a complex workflow in which geometric, spatial and technical information is filtered through simulation, analysis and optimization processes, with the aim to form integrated, parametric building information models that can generate an array of output ranging from energy usage to manufacturing instructions. With the introduction of parametric and algorithmic design processes, the reliance on the visual as the primary source of design production and evaluation gets supplemented by rules, numbers and other forms of quantitative logic. This logic is placed between creative thinking and calculated output. Designing Design poses design itself as a design problem and foregrounds the ways in which architects are engaging with the broader cultural and technological debate between the open nature of scripting and the closed nature of applications as they begin to define the "design space" in which they work. Beyond the immediate benefits of avoiding constraints by a built-in bias of standard applications, custom scripts open up opportunities for innovation at a core level that extends beyond a single design to the design of design. With this context, the following questions were posed to the contributors as a provocation to formulate their essays:

— How has the increased amount of specialized information relevant to architectural projects today influenced your design process and the composition and dynamic of your design teams?

— The use of computation systems in architectural design ranges from direct representation where the computer is used to visualize a design, to abstract coding where custom algorithms are developed as a design system that generates architectural outputs from numeric inputs. In either case, the tools serve to extend the capabilities and imagination of designers. How are these processes utilized in your work and how do you determine when to use which of these techniques?

— With the increasing need to automate design in the name of efficiency, what do you see as the future relationship between qualitative and quantitative design criteria?

The second theme, <u>Designing Assembly</u>, is a *material* issue and addresses how digital production and material properties influence design concepts. This centers on the development of digital fabrication as an extension of the design process, giving architects a direct link to the tools and techniques used in the manufacturing of building components. Through CNC technologies, architects can reposition design strategically within fabrication and construction processes, such that design information extends beyond the representational to include highly precise sets of instructions used to drive manufacturing processes. Moreover, these instructions can embed the logic of building assemblies into the manufacturing processes, linking design to a new definition of detail that re-establishes the role of craft in the design process. The architectural detail, emblematic of an architect's technique to instill craft into buildings, is largely a product of the relationship of design to industry. If the modernist's detail was based on negotiating tolerances between pre-manufactured material components in order to address the functional problem of connections, today's details are based on the organization of material information, where tolerances and assembly procedures can be numerically controlled and parametrically linked as part of an integrated workflow. Details now consist of parametrically defined relationships of component parts with embedded assembly logics. Designing assembly is the step beyond digital fabrication where the logics of assembling building parts are foregrounded as criteria during design. File-to-factory becomes factory-to-file, creating a reciprocal relationship between design concepts, material properties, methods of production and assembly sequences.[1]

— How does the relationship between architectural design and construction detail get redefined in the context of digital file-to-fabrication processes?

— In the context of your work, how are CNC processes changing the traditional workflow between architects, fabricators and builders?

— Arguably, geometric complexity has been a significant driver of the evolution of CNC technologies in architecture through the need to rationalize this complexity in response to the constraints of materials, manufacturing and cost. Are there other potentials of this technology that might drive design innovation?

The third theme, <u>Designing Industry</u>, is an *organizational* issue with a drive towards integration, where input across multiple disciplines can be collected, modeled and efficiently managed. The amount of relevant and available information for any given architectural project has expanded faster than our ability to process and incorporate it into existing working methods. The range of expertise required to incorporate this information into the design, fabrication and construction of new buildings has led to large multi-disciplinary and highly specialized teams that require new organizational models. While this is certainly a *logistics* issue that is being addressed with new technologies like Building Information Modeling (BIM) and Integrated Project Delivery (IPD) systems, it is also a *design* issue in that any organizational system has inherent biases that either support or obstruct the potential for a culture of collaboration. The question becomes whether the new role of architects is to simply manage this new team of specialists or whether the traditional triangle of practice made up of architects, engineers and contractors merges with these specialists and becomes redefined as a system of design and production. Either scenario puts pressure on architects to sharpen the definition of their core competencies. In the new context of highly specialized knowledge and expertise, what do architects bring to the table? In the very few cases where circumstances, largely beyond their control, elevate them to a brand name, architects can rely on their cultural status to add value to a project, but otherwise, the design of a new professional identity might be in order.

— How can new organizational models expand the capabilities of architects to embed the role of design in all aspects of realizing a building?

— What are the potentials for architects to reposition themselves by taking a more influential role within the current restructuring of industry? Does the fact that digital technology will play a central role in this restructuring give an advantage to architects?

— What are the new models of collaboration in the context of increasing specialized information? Does this lead to a consolidation of expertise into fewer, larger conglomerate firms or to a dispersion of expertise into smaller, more agile and networked practices that come together on a per-project basis?

1. See Menges, A. (2010) Uncomplicated Complexity, Integration of Material, Form, Structure and Performance in Computational Design, *Graz Architecture Magazine* 06, *Nonstandard Structures*.

HOW TO USE THIS BOOK
—

This book presents essays and in-depth case studies from some of the leading voices on the topic of the emerging world of digital workflows. The starting point was the schematization of the industry described above, but the three themes are rarely autonomous in practice and in many cases, contributors move between two and sometimes all three. These themes were also the basis for long exchanges of thoughts and ideas with each contributor to develop the essays that follow. For each essay, Editor's Notes highlight specific points to contextualize the content within the running themes of the book. These comments are not intended to be summaries as much as extensions of the arguments, with the aim to encourage a continuing dialogue and debate about the role of digital technology in the future relationship between architecture and industry.

The case studies included in most of the contributions focus primarily on the design and construction workflows rather than the resulting project. They intentionally vary in their explicit reliance on digital processes. In this sense, they represent a leveling out of the euphoria of digital techniques and a more selective application of these techniques in the service of design ideas. The selection of contributors was based on their unique perspective toward digital technology and in most cases, on their use of digital workflows within an active building practice. This was not to minimize the importance of more speculative research outside of practice; on the contrary, it was intended to take a measure of how the first generation of research has found its way into and affected industry at large. In this regard, this book represents an effort to push the ongoing discourse on digital technology and architecture to a place where the most radical formal experiments, the most integrated processes of material production and the most pragmatic organizational restructuring of industry overlap to form new innovative workflows.

ACKNOWLEDGEMENTS
—

I thought doing a building was difficult until I did this book. It was only upon its completion that I realized how similar these two efforts actually are. You are working against all odds; budget and schedule are always on your mind; it involves design at all scales from the overall concept to the spacing of each letter; it never seems complete; it is intended to be functional and useful to the reader but also inspire unexpected thoughts and new ideas; and it relies on many people, both directly and indirectly, to pull it off. I want to first thank all of the authors for the extended discussions about the book's content and their willingness to work and rework their essays to stay focused on the themes of the book. David Smiley, Adam Marcus, John Nastasi and Nina Rappaport provided valuable feedback on my introduction and editorial comments. My interest in this topic originated in the early 1990's at Columbia GSAPP under Bernard Tschumi's leadership and foresight into the significant impact that digital culture would have on architecture. Mark Wigley has provided unending support for my work, especially over the past three years with the Columbia Building Intelligence Project (CBIP). David Benjamin and Laura Kurgan, my collaborators on CBIP over the last three years, have continually expanded the context for my thinking on digital workflows with their unique insights on the topic. The late night conversations with Michael Bell at the Emerald Inn were a constant source of inspiration about the future of architectural education and practice. Luke Bulman and Jessica Young provided design concepts that were always in sync with the ambitious graphic goals of the book. Quite simply, this book would not have happened without the tireless support and encouragement of Andreas Müller and Jason Roberts. Andreas had an uncanny ability to know exactly when to send an email with precisely the right message to keep me going. And finally, this book is dedicated to Karen and Lukas, who were always understanding during the many evenings and weekends when I was writing.

DESIGNING

DESIGN

BEYOND EFFICIENCY

DAVID BENJAMIN

David Benjamin is Co-Founder of The Living and Assistant Professor of Architecture at Columbia University GSAPP.

EFFICIENCY
—

In 1906, a bearded Italian academic named Vilfredo Pareto published a thick book entitled *Manual of Political Economy*.[1] It was filled with small hand-drawn graphs and with hundreds of equations, the algorithms of this era. It was the author's fifth book, and it represented a retreat into mathematics by a man who had once been so fiery and political that his lectures had to be advertised in secret or risked being raided and shut down by government thugs. Yet Pareto's new math was just as fresh and revolutionary as his old political critiques. And while his book was underappreciated at the time, it is now cited as initiating the study of modern microeconomics.

One of the concepts advanced in the *Manual of Political Economy* was called Pareto efficiency. It referred to a society where nobody can be made better off without somebody else being made worse off. A society in this state of equilibrium was considered to be Pareto efficient, or Pareto optimal, and a series of potential societies could be neatly graphed so that all of the Pareto efficient ones fell on a Pareto frontier, the set of best-performing arrangements. As an example, Pareto imagined a society with a fixed amount of resources for producing bread and wine. One option would be to make a large amount of bread and a small amount of wine. Another option would be the other way around. For each option, if production was efficient, then this version of society would become a

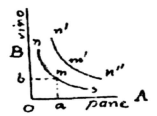

point on the Pareto frontier. And since all of the points on the Pareto frontier were mathematically equivalent—they were all optimal—this frontier could be used to study trade-offs between different options for distributing resources. [Figure 1]

While the principle of Pareto efficiency was developed to describe economics and the design of societies, it can also be applied to design more generally. It can be used for many design problems in many fields. Since engineers often work on problems with two or more clearly defined objectives—such as the design of an analog circuit with the objectives of least footprint and greatest filtering of low frequencies—the Pareto frontier offers a very helpful framework for mapping design permutations and selecting the best ones. And in recent years, architects have used a similar framework with aspects of building design—such as the design of a structural frame with the objectives of least displacement under load and least amount of material required.

In this sense, perhaps Pareto's *Manual*, and the field of economics in general, have provided a foundation for the current interest in performance and optimization in architectural design. Architects today, like economists and engineers, are enchanted by efficient and optimal designs because they can be clearly identified. They are so unambiguous that they seem inevitable. They are so computationally pure that they seem desirable. But as Pareto noted a century ago, efficiency is very narrow. An efficient distribution of resources does not necessarily equal a socially desirable distribution of resources. An optimal design does not necessarily equal a good design. Along these lines, critics of a performance-based approach to complex architectural problems have argued that good design cannot be reduced to mere numbers. For them, judgment and intuition are crucial components of architectural design—with nuances that cannot be quantified or graphed on a Pareto frontier—and they should

Figure 1. Pareto graphed bread production and wine production to derive a simple Pareto frontier. Each point on the graph represents the resource distribution in a different potential society.

not be ignored or diminished. In other words, to rely too heavily on performance and optimization as the drivers of design is to fall under the spell of a dangerous myth of efficiency.

On the other hand, dismissing numbers and optimization may be equally one-sided—especially in the current technological context where almost every daily activity is conditioned by numerical logics. To rely exclusively on judgment and intuition to address complex architectural problems is to fall under the spell of a different dangerous myth—a myth of creativity.

The myth of efficiency is countered by the myth of creativity, and vice versa. But in our current moment of data and digital processes, the issue is not whether to choose one side or the other, but rather how to structure a relationship between the two that balances their different strengths.

EXPLOITATION VERSUS EXPLORATION
—

The field of statistics has developed several robust approaches to achieving this kind of balance between competing demands. One approach offers a mathematical solution for a situation called the multi-armed bandit problem. In this problem, there are two levers on a slot machine and information is known about the performance of one lever but not the other. The question is which lever to pull, and how to determine a sequence of steps that balances two possible moves: utilizing existing information (through pulling the known lever), or searching for new information (through pulling the unknown lever). More generally, this type of problem involves what statisticians refer to as a spectrum between exploitation and exploration.

For design problems, this spectrum may be useful even if designers have different aims than statisticians. In order to be more specific about the balance between efficiency and

creativity in design, it may be helpful to outline these terms on a spectrum between exploitation and exploration. An example of exploitation might be the optimization of the nose cone of a high-speed train for aerodynamic performance. Here, designers want to find the single best-performing design according to only two objectives: least drag and greatest crosswind stability. They want to exploit small differences in inputs to achieve the best output. They use a narrow range of geometric variations with the ultimate goal of achieving an efficient result. [Figure 2] On the other hand, an example of exploration might be the evolution of spanning structures that are high-performing but also unexpected. Here, designers want to find novel designs above a minimum threshold of structural performance. They want to explore completely different sets of inputs that might result in similar outputs (for example, spanning structures with different forms but the same performance under load). They use a wide range of geometric variations with the goal of achieving an innovative result. [Figure 3]

To identify whether a design problem lends itself more to exploitation or to exploration, it may be helpful to draw a map of its potential design space—the space of all possible design permutations. When a design space is visualized in three dimensions, it becomes a topological surface, with the x-axis and the y-axis registering the properties of potential solutions, and the z-axis measuring the performance. By definition, specific design solutions must lie on this topological surface, which then becomes an extremely consequential design constraint.

Designers interested in exploitation prefer a narrow, continuous design space, such as a slanted plane or a topological surface with one or two bumps. In this case, it is possible to quickly hone in on the region of best performance and to locate the single global maximum. The simpler the design space is, the faster they can find the optimal design.

Designers interested in exploration prefer a wide, discontinuous design space, such as a jagged mountain range with multiple peaks. In this case, there are many distinct regions

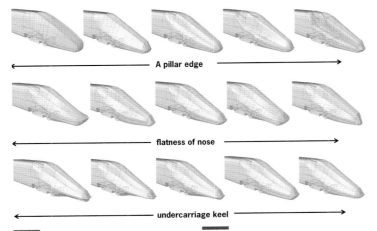

A pillar edge

flatness of nose

undercarriage keel

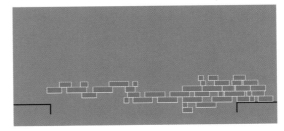

Figure 2 (above left). Each design permutation involves a different geometric form and a different level of aerodynamic performance for the Zefiro train by Bombardier. Over time, the automated process evolves higher-performing designs.

Figure 3 (above right). Simple building blocks are assembled in different arrangements created with EvoCAD by Jordan Pollack and the Dynamic and Evolutionary Machine Organization at Brandeis University, in order to create a structure that

spans from right to left. Over time, the automated process evolves novel designs that meet minimum performance requirements.

of good performance, and it is often possible to find multiple local maximums that are both interesting and high-performing, even if they are not the global maximum. The more complex the design space is, the more likely it is that they will make an unpredictable discovery. [Figure 4]

As architects struggle to balance the power of computation with the need to maintain control, the exploitation/exploration spectrum and the visualization of design space may offer

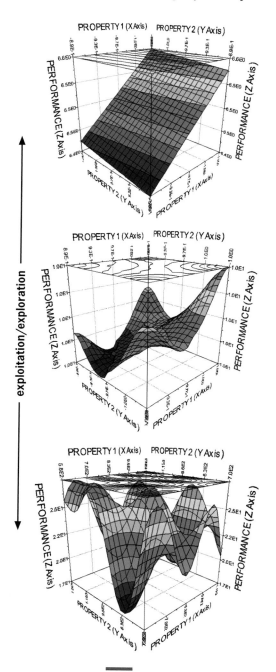

useful frameworks for studying and extending current digital tools and methods. Five potential strategies for designing design can be derived from this context.

DESIGNING THE ALGORITHM
—

It is obvious but worth stating that algorithms have a great influence on the outcome of architectural design processes. Algorithms specify the way a double-curved surface takes its shape from two wavy lines; they define the way complex structural forces are broken down into finite elements; and they perform more complex tasks that may be closer to artificial intelligence. Algorithms written by corporations such as IBM are now able to compete in (and win) the game show Jeopardy, or quickly find pertinent information in mountains of legal documents (a task that would take a human weeks to accomplish). Algorithms written by academics such as Hod Lipson at Cornell University can invent new machines without direct human input, or take any data set and produce a mathematical formula to explain it. [Figures 5a, 5b]

Yet algorithms are not neutral or inevitable. They are designed with assumptions and biases that condition what they produce. And if these assumptions were different, the designs produced through them would be different. In architecture, digital workflows and applications—such as software for parametric modeling, BIM, building simulation and building optimization—push

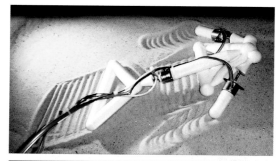

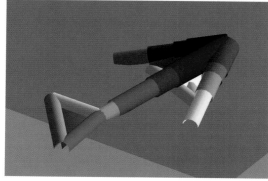

Figure 4 (above). Each graph represents a different design problem. As the problem becomes more complex, the surface describing the design space becomes more complex. Finding the maximum point is relatively straightforward for the problem on the top, but more challenging for the problem on the bottom.

Figures 5a (top), 5b (bottom). With almost no predetermined rules, the algorithm in the Golem Project by Hod Lipson and Jordan Pollack evolves successful but unexpected designs for configurations of robots that move rapidly in a specified direction.

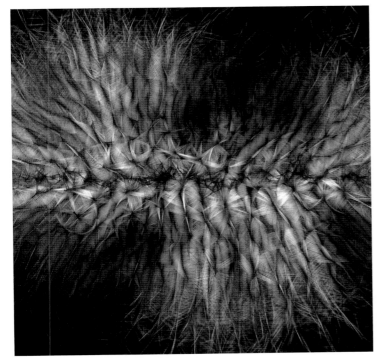

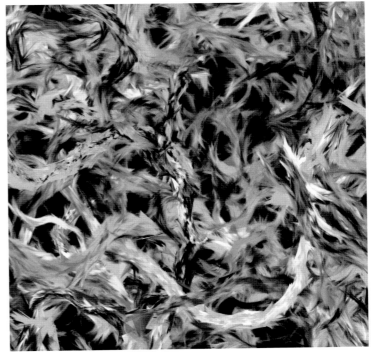

Figures 6a (top left), 6b (top right),
6c (bottom left), 6d (bottom right).
Casey Reas has designed both the
algorithms of the core application
and the algorithms of his individual
projects, using Processing to create
innovative drawings.

us in certain design directions. They play a significant role in architectural design, defining the design space of any project that uses them. Software has an enormous influence on the topological surface that describes any design problem. While end user input affects the features of this topological surface, software defines the type of topological surface. A change in software would mean a change in type. But architectural software, and the algorithms behind it, are usually authored by teams of computer scientists, and they are usually opaque to architects. The assumptions and consequences of the algorithms are often difficult for architects to ascertain. As computer scientist Eitan Grinspun observes: "I think architects have been hijacked! The tools they are working with are written by programmers whose training, by and large, comes from a very scientific, engineering-based mindset. These tools provide the language that architects have to use, and as architects start becoming more proficient with the tools, they start adapting to the engineers' language."[2] In other words, the sheer fact of using architectural software means already to operate like an engineer.

Perhaps this could change. It might be possible for architects to become more proactive in understanding, and even authoring, some of the algorithms that influence their designs. Instead of going through a typical sequence of architects demonstrating creative control through analog processes, and then struggling to maintain control as digital processes are applied, it may be possible for architects to lead these digital processes. In other words, one option for designing design is *designing the algorithm*.

Of course, many young architects are already fluent in developing digital workflows and writing custom scripts within software applications. But the algorithms in these custom scripts may have a limited influence on the design results in comparison to the algorithms in the core software application. In order to avoid being hijacked, as Grinspun described, architects may need to play a more active role in designing the core software. This is no easy feat, but there are a few precedents.

In the film animation industry, software companies often provide early versions of applications to animators and deliberately seek input on core features and uses of the software before it is fixed and frozen. This kind of open-ended input is different from input during typical beta testing of software that simply aims to fix bugs and refine features that have already been finalized by the programmers.

A more profound example involves designers writing entirely new software applications. In 2001, designers Casey Reas and Ben Fry released the first version of a software application called Processing. This programming language was created by designers who also had deep experience with computer science. Processing emphasized interactivity and visualization, and it allowed Reas and Fry to create their own designs that would not have been possible otherwise. [Figures 6a, 6b, 6c, 6d] But it also offered other designers a new, open-ended platform. It was software for designers by designers.[3] Ten years later, there are thousands of diverse design projects created through Processing, and there is also an incredible online community around this tool and these projects. [Figure 7] Yet Processing is just the beginning of what might happen if designers authored their own software and made deliberate decisions about the assumptions embedded in it. For the field of architecture to take control of digital processes by designing the algorithm, it may benefit from a few architects designing a few new software applications like Processing.

COMPUTING THE SOCIAL
—

One aspect of computation that has become increasingly important in architectural design is software for simulating building performance. The design of most complex architectural projects now involves several types of digital simulation, including finite element analysis (FEA) for structure, computational fluid dynamics (CFD)

Figure 7. The Processing website offers tutorials, example projects, a source code, a community of users and free downloads of the software application.

for airflow and environmental/energy analysis for building systems. Simulation software is especially useful when the design problem is complex (when the topological surface of design space is like a jagged mountain range) and when it is difficult to predict the best design based on standard rules of thumb. The process of digital simulation—often combined with digital optimization—has enabled design workflows that produce convincing quantitative results, which in turn have contributed to the trend of performance-based architectural design. In other words, if Pareto's principles provided the foundation for performance-based design, simulation software provides the fuel.

But clearly there are aspects of design that are difficult to digitally simulate and optimize. There are qualitative features of architecture that seem beyond quantification. While quantitative features—such as structural and environmental performance—are typically driven by simulation software, qualitative features—such as aesthetics and atmosphere—are driven by less computational, more open-ended processes. Often this leads to a duality in the design process, a duality which may simply be another version of the efficiency/creativity division or the exploitation/exploration spectrum. Yet this

duality may be too simplistic, and it has been challenged by some recent projects that apply simulation software to new domains.

AnyBody is a software application that simulates "human well-being" and ergonomic comfort. It has been used in the design of automobile foot pedals and wheelchairs. [Figures 8a, 8b, 8c] From the perspective of engineering design, the software is useful since the complexity of human anatomy makes it difficult to compute forces and stresses by hand.[4] From the perspective of architectural design, the software is interesting because it involves a system of metrics for quantifying human comfort, which is normally considered to be a qualitative feature outside the domain of computational analysis.

In a related area, a growing number of software applications now simulate human crowd behavior, including SMART Move by Buro Happold. [Figure 9] These simulations consider the interactive behavior of very large numbers of people, which would be difficult to calculate without computation. In fact, most crowd behavior software simulates the flow of people much like CFD simulates the flow of air, by means of simple rules and mathematical vectors.

Vacate is a crowd behavior application that adds another level of complexity. It simulates human behavior during the emergency evacuation of an airplane, and it computes social interaction and factors of human psychology that include situations like the presence of a group leader, the act of helping a disabled person, panicking, "seat jumping" and competitive vs. cooperative behavior. [Figures 10a, 10b, 10c] With Vacate, critical human behaviors are identified from a computer database known as Aircraft Accident Statistics and Knowledge (AASK)—developed from survivor's accounts of aviation accidents—and then programmed into the software. Since many social and psychological behaviors have been identified

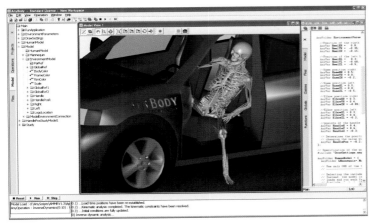

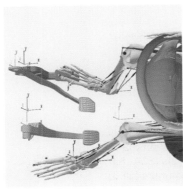

Figures 8a (top), 8b (above left), 8c (above right). In this simulation, AnyBody starts with the geometry of human bones and muscles, adds multiple forces of stress and strain that continually change as the body moves, and identifies a numerical level of comfort for each scenario.

Figure 9 (above). With SMART Move, the crowd behavior simulation produces both performance metrics—such as duration of circulation—and animations for visual representation.

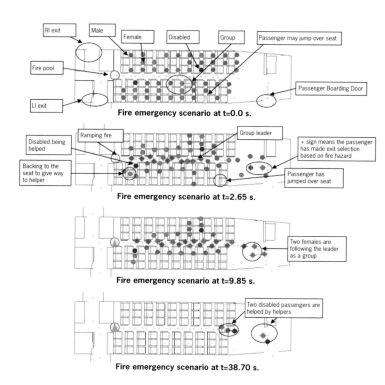

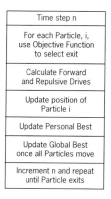

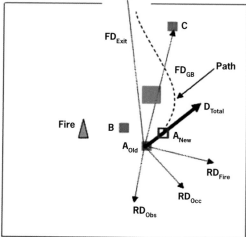

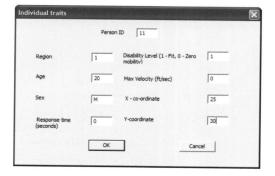

Figures 10a (top), 10b (middle), 10c (bottom). With Vacate, the crowd behavior simulation involves multiple types of passengers, each with different rules, to account for different social and psychological behaviors.

and cataloged in this database, it is possible to integrate them into a computational model and establish an environment for digital simulation. Vacate's simulations provide a unique resource for design, as it is difficult to obtain reliable data from real accidents and also because there are ethical issues involved with conducting physical experiments to generate these data.[5] Vacate offers an example of *computing the social*, and as the category of simulation software expands to include features for predicting "soft" reactions—such as human comfort and human movement in emergencies—the territory of computation in architecture may shift.

DESIGNING THE PROBLEM
—

Airports[6] are complex, and they are also data-driven, so it makes sense that they would be a testing ground for some of today's most complex digital workflows, and an important site for balancing efficiency and creativity. The design of airports already incorporates a wide variety of simulation applications, both for far-reaching topics such as financial models of GDP and simulation of urban growth, and for building-specific topics such as structural and environmental analysis or the flow of planes, cars, baggage and passengers (though the crowd behavior simulations utilized do not typically involve social or psychological behaviors as Vacate does). Each simulation must be performed in a logical sequence. Each expert must be consulted at the right stage of design. Non-quantitative goals and factors must be articulated and balanced with quantitative goals and factors. Generally, each simulation application is run by a different expert, and this brings to the table a large group of diverse players. It is generally understood that architects play the role of director. Architects work with all of the different experts; they synthesize the different simulations into a cohesive design process; they direct multiple digital processes and combine them with the architectural vision for the building. This involves judgment as well as integration of data. The architect must check the setup, constraints and assumptions of each simulation and then negotiate trade-offs between competing demands.

For example, as veteran airport architect Derek Moore explains, in designing passenger flows, one of the first steps is to conduct a low-tech, analog survey in order to determine a "show-up profile" for the expected passengers. This show-up profile involves going to existing airports and observing people as they arrive at the airport and go through the check-in process.

Information from the show-up profile is then fed into a spreadsheet in order to study the flow of passengers. Here, the spreadsheet becomes a simple type of building simulation. Then, once a schematic design is created with a corresponding digital model, more sophisticated simulations of passenger flow are conducted. The design process involves multiple steps, simulations and professionals, which the architect must direct. [Figure 11]

In another example, according to Moore, the process of designing airside movement starts with creating the schedule for a sample day of airport operations called the "design day schedule". [Figure 12] This process involves multiple specialists and types of analysis, and is sometimes conducted before the architect is hired. Utilizing the design day schedule, the architect produces a sketch layout based on human experience and rules of thumb. A digital model is created of the sketch layout and then

a sophisticated simulation application, such as PathPlanner, analyzes local movements at typical gates to identify points of congestion. [Figure 13] After the gate sizes and locations are refined, even more sophisticated and complex simulation applications, such as SIMMOD or TAAM, analyze movements across the entire airfield during crucial periods of the design day schedule.

A third example involves baggage flows. Here, in Moore's summary, there are many factors for the flow and each system has sub-systems. The design must account for check-in, security screening, human baggage handling, automated baggage sorting, airplane loading and unloading as well as carousel delivery. One inter-esting issue is that it is necessary to distinguish between the simulation of machines handling baggage and the simulation of humans handling baggage. Machines and humans both make errors, but the errors of machines are easy to compute, while the errors of humans are difficult

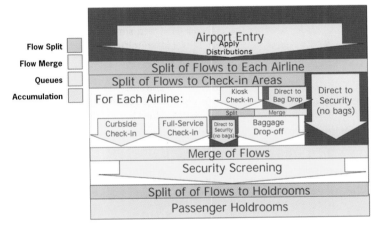

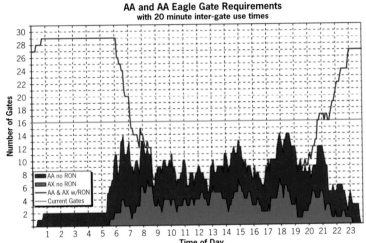

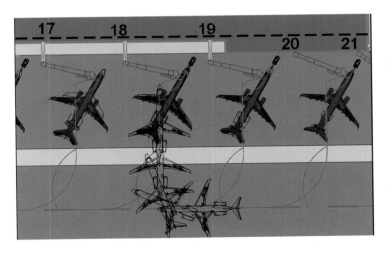

Figure 11 (top left). In this diagram of passenger flow, each step requires input from different specialists, and multiple digital simulations are run to evaluate performance.

Figure 12 (top right). The "design day schedule" incorporates changes in the number of passengers over time.

Figure 13 (bottom left). Based on flight arrival and departure informa-tion, along with data about passenger movement and processing, airplane movement at the gate is simulated and visualized.

Figure 14 (bottom right). The design of baggage flows, like most aspects of airport design, involves numerical inputs, numerical outputs, digital simulations and models such as this graph of passenger flow and baggage flow over time.

to encapsulate in a formula. As with the other processes and examples, it is the role of the architect to synthesize the different simulations and then integrate them into a coherent building design. [Figure 14]

In the architect-as-director model, there is an implicit division of power—or a system of checks and balances—between efficiency and creativity. There is an assumption that human intuition and creativity is separate from computation. The director must monitor and tame the computer, while the computer must verify the choices made by the director.

But perhaps the separate processes could be integrated. Perhaps efficiency and creativity could be part of the same computational model. Perhaps subjective criteria could be introduced into the optimization routines themselves. Instead of optimizing different criteria independently, a single routine could solve for multiple criteria at the same time.

This would involve a well-known approach called multi-objective optimization, common in fields like product design and aircraft design. While this approach seems well-suited for the multiple and diverse demands of architectural design, it is currently under-utilized. Even less explored are digital processes that combine subjective criteria with objective technical criteria in the same optimization routine. In this type of process, multi-objective optimization could be

used to combine objectives such as atmosphere, aesthetics and program with objectives such as structural performance, circulation and baggage-handling efficiency. Here, the algorithm would integrate many of the desired features of the final design, and the creativity of the design process would involve designing objectives and designing experiments rather than simply designing solutions. In other words, the role of the architect would involve designing the problem. Rather than focusing on form and performance in an alternating sequence, the architect could focus on creating the potential design space—the complex topological surface—for the overall project.

OPTIMIZING CREATIVELY
—

Anthony Radford and John Gero, in a book titled *Design Optimization in Architecture, Building, and Construction*, study the application of

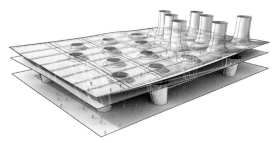

Figures 15a (top), 15b (bottom). In this airport roofscape experiment by GSAPP student John Locke, design permutations are based on precise design objectives, but the results are more open-ended and exploratory than those of typical optimizations.

Pareto efficiency for architectural design. Compared to other optimization techniques, Pareto optimization "is more realistic and useful for design", the authors conclude, "because it allows subjective criteria to be taken into account".[7] Radford and Gero are mainly referring to the way that judgment can be applied to select a single design from the set of optimal designs on the Pareto frontier.

An extension of the argument might involve using optimization to explore rather than to exploit: to search creatively within wide potential design spaces rather than hone in efficiently within narrow potential design spaces. In other words, perhaps we could use algorithms for invention, and not simply for cold-blooded efficiency. We could *optimize creatively*. While optimization is most often used to locate a single global maximum, its fundamental algorithms could be equally proficient at identifying multiple local maximums. So in a workflow for exploration rather than exploitation, the process could search for several novel, high-performing designs rather than searching for a single best-performing design.

For example, in the initial massing design for an airport, an automated optimization routine could be set up to explore different configurations of program, circulation and an all-encompassing space-frame roof. The geometry and the objectives of the optimization process could be calibrated to generate many interesting massing arrangements that meet the design objectives, including a few that are very unusual. [Figures 15a, 15b] Or in the schematic design for mixed-use towers, an automated optimization routine could be created to investigate a very large number of connection configurations. Here, the geometry and objectives could be designed to search for options that are structurally stable, provide striking public sky lobbies, link to one another through bold angles and lack redundancy. Beyond computing all of the complex relationships, the digital process could be helpful to generate a wide variety of geometric options and precisely indicate the benefits of each option. [Figures 16a, 16b]

In both examples, the computational process expands the design options rather than narrows them. Optimization yields results that can be understood as creative solutions to the design problem. More generally, this design process could be valuable in order to navigate design spaces that are not immediately legible, or to step outside of the limitations of linear thinking, or to identify new regions of performance worthy of further study. To put this in terms of the multi-armed bandit problem used by statisticians: pulling the unknown lever may have value in itself, beyond winning the jackpot, because it will provide new information, and information is intrinsically valuable.

DEMOCRATIZING DESIGN
—

Beyond efficiency, and even beyond creativity, we might use algorithms and digital processes to debate values. Any version of multi-objective optimization and any process of evaluating a parametric model reinforces the need for clearly defining design objectives (also called fitness criteria). And design objectives are values: they are the goals and desires of a project that involve judgment and beliefs, outside of efficiency and computation. All algorithms contain values, but this is especially true for the algorithms of design objectives.

The relationships between different values, and the prioritization of these values, are explicitly defined in the digital model, and although they might be buried and hidden, they are there. It is difficult to set up a parametric model without values. And it is impossible to run an optimization process without values. If the values of a project could be exposed and stated in plain language, then the digital model could become a platform for debate and discussion. In many architectural projects, interdisciplinary members of the design team are now finding ways to structure discussions about values around digital parametric models. Perhaps this process could be extended. These discussions could easily encompass a wider audience and a larger collective beyond design professionals. They could involve input from a broader public, in a structured and productive format. Artists, philosophers, residents and citizens of all backgrounds could join the discussion and debate.

In many ways, current digital design processes already lend themselves to this involvement. The process of setting up the digital model could be considered a location for discussion. For example, in the design of a new tower, should the number of floors be fixed, or dependent on the amount of public space at ground level? This question clearly involves values that could be discussed and debated by a wide public, and its answer would clearly affect the digital model. Similarly, the process of tuning the digital model could be considered a location for discussion. For example, through a parametric model, one constituency could argue for increasing environmental performance even if cost also rises. Another constituency could argue for an iconic building entrance even if it decreases environmental performance. The model could be tuned in different ways according to different values. Different design permutations would reflect these different values. The "sliders" of the parametric model could be tools to negotiate between competing demands and competing constituencies. [Figure 17]

In this sense, the digital model becomes a platform for an open and inclusive process of design. It widens participation rather than narrows it. It *democratizes design*.

Pareto may have foreshadowed this in his original example of bread and wine. In this case of a society's distribution of resources, a Pareto "frontier" could be a site for debate about values. It could be a starting point for discussing design permutations and making trade-offs. Since all design permutations on the Pareto frontier are optimal, values and judgment are required to choose between them. The act of selecting a single design from the set of all Pareto-efficient designs could be understood as the exact location where computation meets design—as well as where computation meets society, politics and even culture.

If the objectives of greatest bread and greatest wine were supplemented by a third objective of greatest number of books, then a new Pareto frontier would be established. Thus alternate Pareto frontiers could be generated through different values. The computational model and the multiple possible Pareto frontiers could be a very information-rich site for debate about prioritizing values.

BEYOND
—

In 1916, ten years after his groundbreaking work on economics, Vilfredo Pareto published a completely different book entitled *The Mind and Society: A Treatise on General Sociology*.[8] Pareto had resigned as Chair in Political Economy at the University of Lausanne. He had tired of the over-simplification involved in economic theory and had become disillusioned with the terrible track record of economic

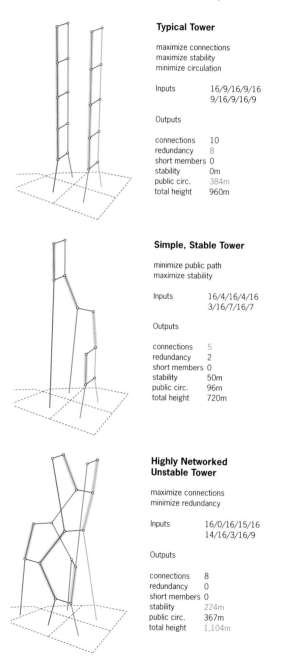

Typical Tower

maximize connections
maximize stability
minimize circulation

Inputs	16/9/16/9/16 9/16/9/16/9

Outputs

connections	10
redundancy	8
short members	0
stability	0m
public circ.	384m
total height	960m

Simple, Stable Tower

minimize public path
maximize stability

Inputs	16/4/16/4/16 3/16/7/16/7

Outputs

connections	5
redundancy	2
short members	0
stability	50m
public circ.	96m
total height	720m

Highly Networked Unstable Tower

maximize connections
minimize redundancy

Inputs	16/0/16/15/16 14/16/3/16/9

Outputs

connections	8
redundancy	0
short members	0
stability	224m
public circ.	367m
total height	1,104m

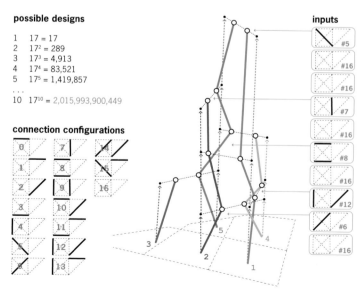

possible designs

1   17 = 17
2   17^2 = 289
3   17^3 = 4,913
4   17^4 = 83,521
5   17^5 = 1,419,857
. . .
10   17^{10} = 2,015,993,900,449

connection configurations

inputs

#5
#16
#16
#7
#16
#8
#16
#12
#6
#16

Figures 16a (above left), 16b (above right). In this mixed-use towers experiment by GSAPP student Danil Nagy, the digital process offers a tool to creatively explore design options: it helps filter an overwhelming number of possible configurations, identifies multiple local maximums and provides geometric and analytical data about each one.

predictions. He had abandoned the fundamental economic tenet that people act logically. Instead, Pareto now believed that people are non-logical but believe they are logical. In his new book, Pareto turned from economics and equations to more complex theories of behavior, and to the field of sociology. It was as if he was saying that his earlier charts and his Pareto frontier needed to be re-evaluated. There needed to be more. Pareto's simple mathematical models were no longer sufficient to bear the weight of a multi-dimensional world. It was clear that the models would have to be transformed.

Perhaps the same is true for our early versions of digital processes in architecture. Perhaps they need to be re-evaluated and transformed. Perhaps there needs to be more. The question is how much of the original model will remain, and whether the new framework will look anything like the one which has been so influential and has taken us so far.

ENDNOTES

1. Pareto, V. (1906) *Manuale di economia politica*, Milan, Società Editrice.
2. Eitan Grinspun, from a transcript of the Columbia Building Intelligence Project Think Tank, New York, February 18, 2011.
3. Maeda, J. (2007) Forword, in Reas, C.; Fry, B. (eds) *Processing: A Programming Handbook for Visual Designers and Artists*, Cambridge, Mass., MIT Press, p. xix.
4. "Design Optimization for Human Well-Being and Overall System Performance", Gino Duffett and Hiram Badillo (APERIO Tecnología en Ingeniería, Barcelona) and Sylvain Carbe and Arne Kiis (AnyBody Technology, Aalborg East, Denmark).
5. Xue, Z.; Bloebaum, C. L. (2009) Human Behavior Effects on Cabin Configuration Design Using VacateAir, 47th AIAA Aerospace Sciences Meeting and Exhibit, Orlando, Florida, AIAA-2009-0042. Also, Xue, Z. (2006) A particle swarm optimization based behavioral and probabilistic fire evacuation model incorporating fire hazards and human behaviors, Master Thesis, Mechanical and Aerospace Engineering, State University of New York at Buffalo.
6. Material for this section is based on discussions with and writing by Derek Moore, Associate at Skidmore, Owings & Merrill, and an expert on the design of airports.
7. Radford, A.; Gero, J. (1988) *Design Optimization in Architecture, Building, and Construction*, New York, Van Nostrand Reinhold.
8. Pareto, V. (1916) *Trattato di sociologia generale*, Florence, G. Barbéra.

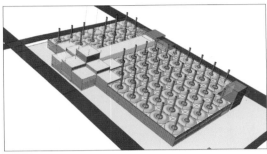

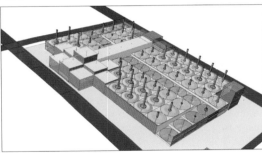

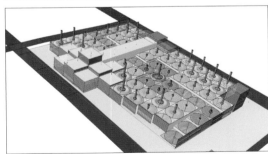

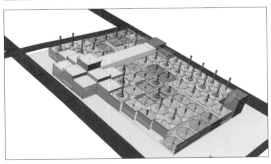

Figure 17. In this hypothetical re-design of the Javits Center in New York by GSAPP students Muchan Park, Patrick Cobb and Miranda Romer, the parametric model structures a trade-off between two competing values: new public space on the roof versus lightwells that provide natural light for the interior.

AUTHORSHIP
—
EDITOR'S NOTES

The identity of the architect is largely built upon her or his ability to author design solutions that satisfy pragmatic concerns while also capturing the imagination by producing unique visual and spatial experiences. Pragmatic concerns are usually well defined and therefore can be solved with a high degree of certainty—the respective design space is relatively narrow, more quantitative, and possible to define algorithmically. The creation of unique experiences, by contrast, is ambiguous, it relies on inference and an indirect connection between an architect's knowledge and own lived experiences and how well they can anticipate responses from users. The result is never fully known or predictable. In this case, the design space is difficult, if not impossible to define algorithmically; it is highly qualitative and therefore better suited to human judgment.

While this portrayal of design space as either quantitative or qualitative is perhaps oversimplified, as these two threads are more typically intertwined, it serves to highlight the challenge of capturing the full range of architectural design intent within digital workflows. With more and more steps in these workflows being driven by design, analysis and performance algorithms authored by anonymous programmers, the identity and authorship of the architect comes into question. If the architect has been increasingly displaced by technologically mediated processes over a long time, the expanded realm of digital workflows transforms this in historically new ways.

David Benjamin embraces the full use of such techniques in his proposition that both qualitative and quantitative criteria be contained within design algorithms. In his five scenarios for designing design, automating the process of design through discrete rules poses no threat to human creativity nor to professional identity and instead offers ways to redirect digital techniques in architecture. Beyond the well-known applications of simulation, analysis and optimization techniques that target the quantitative performance of select parts of buildings like structure and environmental behavior, the examples Benjamin cites cross over to human behavior and comfort. They offer a glimpse into new digital workflows for architecture that integrate qualitative and quantitative design criteria.

Buildings are physically discrete assemblies of parts in which the ultimate decisions that determine which parts to use and the relationships of these parts are unambiguous. As such, the process of decision-making—the design space—can theoretically be defined exclusively through algorithms that quantify and organize what is assumed to be the messy act of creativity.[1] Together with the multi-objective optimization process required to explore the myriad relationships and trade-offs between the outputs of these algorithms, this results in a workflow where all human decisions are filtered through computation. For Benjamin, human intuition and judgment occur when designing the design space of a problem, by choosing the inputs and evaluating the outputs to an algorithm but also by designing the algorithm itself. This, then, is not seen as a reduction of authorship; by focusing exclusively on the design space as the locus for decision-making, algorithms are positioned as creative tools that expand the design capabilities of architects.

By *designing the algorithm*, the relationship between constraints (to control possible design options) and variables (to explore possible design options) can become an integral part of the architect's overall design intent. Several case studies presented in this book demonstrate the emergence and use of architect-authored algorithms. These range from small-scale projects like the the net sculptures presented in the contribution by Craig Schwitter and Ian Keough of Buro Happold, where custom algorithms were used for all aspects of the project development, to large-scale projects like the Museo de Acero presented by Shane Burger of Grimshaw Architects, where custom algorithms were created to refine the design of the façade. By *computing the social*, the complex actions and responses of future users to building program conditions can be assessed through historical data and statistical probability, in order to better inform the heuristic processing skills of human experts. By *designing the problem*, multiple quantitative and qualitative objectives in a complex building can be set up in relation to each other in a single algorithmic process, such as in the above-mentioned multi-objective optimization. This is a process that Benjamin has been exploring in his design research studios at Columbia University over the past several years. As an extension of this work, *optimizing creatively* repurposes optimization procedures. Typically used to refine very specific attributes of a design with regard to narrowly focused,

closely related objectives, these procedures can be adapted to explore more open-ended design possibilities, by juxtaposing seemingly unrelated objectives within a single optimization routine. Far from being random or arbitrary, these juxtapositions express the creative choices of the architect, introducing an aspect of playfulness into an otherwise extremely logical process. They could be seen as part of a lineage of procedural experiments extending from the musical chance operations of John Cage to the drip painting techniques of Jackson Pollock.

Perhaps the most far-reaching of Benjamin's five strategies for designing design is the use of algorithms to *democratize design*—to shift the culture of architecture from prioritizing the value of a single author to placing greater value on the team of authors, who each contribute to the design of any building. As Benjamin notes, design processes that are structured through algorithms require clearly articulated

objectives and parameters that can be understood, discussed and debated by many. These parameters, he suggests, can play the role of agreed-upon design principles that drive possible design solutions. By turning the "black box" of computation inside out and exposing the "myth of creativity" often associated with the most successful architects, the values and biases of both programmers and designers can find a common platform to refine authorship and subsequently evolve the next generation of digital workflows.

—

1. William J. Mitchell, elaborating on the articulation of a specific language of terms and explicit formal grammars, created a theoretical framework for early versions of computer-aided design in anticipation of the impact that computer technology would have on architectural design. See Mitchell, W. J. (1990) *The Logic of Architecture: Design, Computation, and Cognition*, Cambridge, Mass., MIT Press.

PRECISE FORM FOR AN IMPRECISE WORLD

—

NEIL DENARI

Neil Denari is Principal of NMDA in Los Angeles and Professor of Architecture at UCLA.

"Main Entry: pre·ci·sion
Pronunciation: \pri-'si-zhən\
Function: noun
Date: 1740
1 : the quality or state of being precise : exactness
2a : the degree of refinement with which an operation is performed or a measurement stated—compare accuracy[2b]

2b : the accuracy (as in binary or decimal places) with which a number can be represented usually expressed in terms of the number of computer words available for representation <double precision arithmetic permits the representation of an expression by two computer words>"
—*The Merriam-Webster Dictionary*

THE SPECTRUM OF PRECISION: OBLIGATIONS OF THE DISCIPLINE OF ARCHITECTURE
—

Although we are not quite certain exactly when the sweeping changes of the information age made life so materially and experientially different from before, it is safe to say that the last fifteen years of this process have produced the deepest and most radical advances in the production, storage and delivery of data of all kinds. To contend with this warp speed shift in the digital world, whole new languages have been invented, indeed they have been mandated by the powerful capabilities of hardware and software, the elements that make up this ubiquitous, accessible field. Among the many disciplines that have had to contend with irrevocable changes to traditional forms of work, architecture has in this brief era been extended into realms of research and representation that operate as much virtually as they do materially. Indeed, whether one is concerned with bricks and mortar or with the production of simulated design, the digital environment has now more than ever superseded the reliance on manual dexterity in the field of architecture. Less and less debated as a fact of life, the digital world continues, however, to be debated as a phenomenon that has displaced aspects of human intervention in favor of machine-based logics, driven by computational accuracy and precision. As if exiled into a soulless territory, precision today is often so deeply associated with technology it is easy to forget that it is a human ambition first, and a machinic directive second. In fact, the logic of precision with its exacting nature does not necessarily increase in coherence with the implementation of digital technology, rather it becomes simply the clearest and cleanest pathway for the delivery of ideas, whether or not they first emerge from precise thought.

Precision, a term that invokes finitude, uncompromising accuracy and minimum tolerance, is often used to describe a particular quality of a physical artifact. In its essence, precision presumes refinement as an end condition, where the material artifact could not be made any other way: that everything about it is in the right place, whether monolithic or made of many parts. Often driven through obsessive desires, the acts of design, production, assembly and construction of a building are phases in a progressive and comprehensive process of refinement to the *nth* degree and are, particularly within the world of digitally driven design, thought to lead to the ultimate state of physical realization: a state perfect in its intention and perfect in its resolution. In this sense, precision is a pan-cultural aspiration that can be found even in worlds other than those that are technically governed, where intent for precision can be measured against a physical object. Novelists, mathematicians, poets, playwrights, film directors or painters all search for forms of precision in their respective fields. One imagines that the brush strokes in a Mark Rothko painting or the camera angles of a Hitchcock thriller are as precise as two sheets of aluminum coming together on a knife-edged corner. Whether with paint, words or lenses, people who make things practice their craft in relation to tools, techniques and systems, and it is the interrelationship with technology and materials where one articulates ideas that in themselves may be abstract or conceptual.

A BRIEF HISTORY SINCE 1995
—

When technology services an argument or an idea, meaning and content become materialized via an appropriate application of technology. Conversely, when technology itself is the argument, technique becomes content. This absorption of the conceptual into the technical is no doubt the most natural state of events when new tools or paradigms are introduced into specific cultures, and this state has come to define, however (in)accurately, the condition of architectural design that emerged fifteen years ago. Primarily through the use of software such as SoftImage and Alias Power Animator, packages that had already been introduced to the film industry, architects and their students were able to suspend architecture between the virtual and the material and at the same time begin the theorization process that comes along with all paradigm shifts. With tools used to model animated cartoon characters, it is no coincidence then, that the term "blob" flourished at the end of the 1990's, because the shape-making possibilities with NURBS software allowed new users to proliferate topological surfaces in unending measures, most of them generated out of excitement rather than discipline. Indeed, even a crudely sculpted digital model could be captivating, the equivalent of pouring random chemicals into a beaker in search of unknown reactions. While this excited many and possibly disturbed even more, such raw production of form was quickly disciplined by the likes of Greg Lynn and Jesse Reiser, both of whom invoked Gilles Deleuze's concept of the "anexact yet rigorous" topological body, or more accurately, a speculative form disciplined by precise derivation and modeling.[1] In fact, it could be argued that the longest-lasting

impressions left by the rise of digital culture were created at its very origin, when formal novelty immediately outstripped the modernist complexities of the Deconstructivist period of the late 1980's. A new regime of form-making had emerged, one that challenged all prevailing ideologies not through a different conceptual ideology but through a technical one. At this moment, the digital more decisively invoked a Kiesleresque freedom than a new machine-based precision. Although Frank Gehry and his team at the time were disciplining his more visually intuitive working method with the introduction of CATIA into the documentation (not design) process of his Bilbao Museum in the late 1990's, the computer was largely a medium of radical experimentation with 3D curvature, surfaces for which drawing or modeling by hand were nearly impossible to master.

With the advent of computerization in architecture, suddenly the "what could be done" agenda eclipsed the "what should be done" questions born out of conceptual thinking, creating friction not only among generations but also among those who imagined or experienced architecture as a slow accumulation of instincts and verifiable working processes. Indeed, this new technology challenged architecture perhaps by offering more and more freedom without the added discipline needed to effectively guide the new tools. By simply moving from pencils to mice, the act of making a drawing had shifted to the construction of a 3D digital model, altogether different in mood and feedback than either a handmade drawing or physical model. In the black ether of Cartesian coordinates, the digital world profoundly affected our senses, and further, our judgment. Only a massive paradigm shift such as this could sponsor such doubt, passion and rancor in a field that had always been defined by technological progress.

But what began as a wild frontier of formal experimentation with little expectation for construction, had by the 2000's transitioned into a scene that brought well-known architects with commissions into contact with technology that would ignite their curiosity for extreme architectural solutions. No longer fueled purely by the unconstrained freedom allowed by the machine, this work began to shape the identity of the digital world as we know it now: as an environment based on numerical precision and quantification. Projects such as Frank Gehry's Walt Disney Concert Hall (2004) and Herzog & de Meuron's Beijing Olympic Stadium (2008) typify the transition of spectacular forms of geometry into structure given life through technology. One is inclined to summarize this decade as a time of unfettered construction, quickly bringing to fruition the promise of exotic form-making and material experimentation set out by the young digital prospectors ten years before.

In this shift from a kind of art practice—the black screen as empty canvas—to one of information processing, ideas have returned in search of their disciplining agents, in theory at least. The arc of computerization is still clearly ascendant, but the initial, feverish conditions of its launch with seemingly endless design possibilities have given way to a culture that not only uses technology ubiquitously but also as a tool to leverage quantification into new forms of irrefutable logic. To a certain extent, decision-making has returned, and herein may lie the core of the new debate: has machine logic (data, the script, etc.) replaced human judgment as the most disciplined form of inquiry in architecture?

OPPORTUNITIES OF THE DIGITAL
—

Prior to the advent of robust computational power, architecture was to a certain extent governed, if not limited by the ability of the architect to manage and think through complex conditions with ordinary forms of representation (drawings, physical models, etc.). Being precise in this context involved a logic of form-making that related to industrial standards of construction. Modernism, for example, was a language of gridded, panelized construction systems derived directly from these standards. Customization, then, could be a laborious process. Today, precision is embedded in a design process that generates multiple unknown, less predictable and foreclosed design outputs via the manipulation of initial inputs (the parametric). This represents opportunity unhinged from the history of disciplinary forms of design control, as invoked for instance by typological or stylistic paradigms. Indeed, with the robust sets of tools now available in the design process, greater levels of complexity can be managed, allowing architects to operate with lesser-known, more provisional paradigms. Especially obvious in proprietary script and code-writing, architects are constructing, through processed means, outcomes that cannot be sketched out or illustrated in any *a priori* fashion. This, in turn, can lead to novel formal regimes that are driven by a productive relationship between theory (cultural query), logic (argument) and data

(requirements). Moreover, if modernism worked on the basis of clearly defined organizational devices such as the machine and philosophical mandates such as Form Follows Function, then a computationally charged environment takes input/output and causality to new levels in architecture. But whereas modernism sought to reduce forms to their most inflected, sober state of directness, new digital processes are defined by multivalent systems that can produce, given a particular agenda, forms that are entirely responsive to vast amounts of initial data. One thinks here for instance of biological models, concepts of cellular automata and time-based design processes that cannot in any essential fashion be explored outside of a digital environment, as they are far too complex to model otherwise.

In this context, two very dramatic conditions occur: 1) from an aesthetic point of view, new forms may emerge, giving architects who view form as an important and indeed necessary component of advanced design, a process of invention that relies less on sheer compositional skills and more on the directing of information, and 2) a clear belief that the machine precisely determines the forms and produces the highest level of performativity in them. When seen together, these conditions suggest that new forms are also innovative forms, capable of functioning across a variety of criteria, from basic program to atmospheric effects. Innovation, here, is defined as the renewal or improvement of existing models. In architecture, innovation rather than novelty is the precise term for incremental changes to prevailing types or paradigms. Through computation, forms that look different are also arguably capable of performing better, because criteria related to functionality can be simulated and inserted into a design methodology abetted by digital control.

Apart from implied or expressed interests in new genres of form, digital environments have also provided opportunities for greater levels of analysis and simulation across all aspects of design and construction. From versioning to optimization and beyond, architecture has become more fluidly experimental, creating a built-in R&D component to design that was previously reserved for rare projects with dedicated research budgets. Although progress is not always linear in such a fluid environment, new simulation tools employed directly by architects allow for more information through an iterative, comparison-based method. Often yielding matrices like information grids, multiple design schemes may be cross-referenced against one another, analyzed around issues such as affective behavior, assembly method, cost, time and sustainability. Machines, once the metaphorical model of Modernist architecture, are now the true servants to any architectural agenda that will rely less on the artisanal nature of craft and more on the mathematics of computation.

LIMITS OF THE DIGITAL
—

Has, therefore, the above-mentioned conflict surrounding idea as content versus technique as content entered into a new period of cessation, relieving the profession of the antagonisms of generational and ideological resistance to the computer? It is clear that craft, historically defined in relation to human skill acquired over years of experience, has been partially redefined through new forms of expertise with machines that remove the hand as the basic interface of both design and fabrication.

Whereas precision was formerly understood to be pre-invested in the work ethic of the architect (to think through an argument, then make a design which fits the logic), now precision can be supplied, at least partially, by machines. There are extremely heightened expectations of precision, based on the promise of digital analysis, simulation and fabrication; expectations that color the very thought processes involved in design. The innate passion for the rigorous practice of craft has passed into the hands of digitally controlled tools, allowing a variety of new contexts for precision to emerge. In one context, precision is understood to be ensured through the proper operation of software-controlled machines. In another, data themselves become precision. Indeed, data are one of the most prominent contemporary phenomena to be used in the construction of logical thinking. Thought to be definitive because of their mathematically derived accuracy, data present information and ideology as one and the same. As work becomes less defined by human-based processes, a new self-referential discourse has been conceived: if it was defined more by data and controlled by software and less by the impulses of intuition or judgment, then it must be rigorous, complete and ultimately, precise. Oddly enough then, as the digital realm offers the potential for new spatial and material experiences, it also sets standards and expectations perhaps no mania for accuracy can uphold, forming a sustained dissonance between that which can be designed and documented and that which can be built.

Prior to the point of material fabrication, the process of controlling data within design workflows has become routine, given the ubiquity of computing and the global standards (common platforms, software and file types) that are developing to facilitate data exchange. With simulation software such as finite element analysis and surface analytics applications for instance, it is possible today to thoroughly model the material behavior of structure and envelope under all conditions of temperature and stress to predetermine the viability of technical solutions. As part of the refinement process, the build-up of data prior to construction represents a kind of laboratory version of the building itself. Produced under complete digital control, the totality of this information is the sum total not only of the intelligence surrounding the design, but also of the faith in its error-free realization. Indeed, if numbers do not lie, then the outcome should be guaranteed. Although this sounds more like blind faith rather than a sober or realistic knowledge of construction, it is precisely this sense of trust in digital processes that has made even a well-constructed building cease to be the benchmark for architecture and in its place, a new mythology of perfection has evolved.

In industrial design, as a point of comparison, the development from the model (the unique thing or prototype) to the serial artifact (the mass-produced thing) assumes an escalation in precision (zero tolerance) and the production of maximum fitness, i.e. that it is fit to be produced and fully resolved within the dual ecologies of use-value and material production. But as a building, being more hand-made than machine-made, is always relegated to the model and realized only once because of its size, location and, most importantly, because of its construction systems, it cannot, in the terms applied to industrial design, reach the level of precision of the serial artifact. Yet the will to mastery over a model building, in the sense of a unique building, can of course be exercised in the design process, wherein different versions of the model can be developed, analyzed and updated in a sequential act of refinement. This iterative process then yields the ultimate state of digital description (or maximum fitness) before the building enters the realm of its one-off material realization.

However, with architecture being subjected to the forces of nature like few other media, this ultimate digital description becomes subject to the issues of tolerance, irregularity, approximation, human error and the unpredictability of materials, to name just a few of the many contingencies of building, making it impractical for the physical outcome to be literally measured against its digital precursor in a presumed search for the highest level of fidelity possible. In most material sciences related to engineering, the accuracy of a measurement system is the degree of closeness of a quantity to its actual value. Translated to architecture, accuracy is construed as the degree of closeness of the physical rendition of the building to its data set. While this has always been the case with architecture—that it is measured against a set of descriptive documents—the nature of contemporary digital processes has pushed the drive for precision from an obligation that characterizes the discipline of architecture to an expectation that presupposes a one-to-one translation from idea to realization. Surely a new discipline will arise out of these expectations, one in which numerical precision will no longer simply supply a convenient ideology for design. The power of digital toolsets will indeed engender or even proliferate conceptual processes that put machines in service of qualitative assertions and intellectual inquiry.

ENDNOTES
—

1. Deleuze, G.; Guattari, F. (1987) *A Thousand Plateaus*, University of Minnesota Press, 1987, p. 483.

HL23 AND THE MANIA OF ACCURACY
WORKFLOW CASE STUDY▶

In 2005, the Special West Chelsea District zoning plan was amended to accept development around the High Line, a new urban park on an elevated rail track that extends twenty blocks in New York City. As the High Line slices through mid-block, a new type of site emerges, yielding a hybrid building with an infill base and three-sided tower above. Typical to the area north of 23rd street, a 15ft easement was placed along the east and west sides of the elevated track, thus permitting an as-of-right tower width of only 25ft on the 40ft wide building site. The client requested a project with more than the allowable volume. The task was to design a non-conformist building that would resist the zoning envelope yet at the same time feel contextually responsive.

The project design was developed through a series of 3D models that from the very start closely considered the structural challenge of cantilevering over the High Line. A highly detailed model of all building components from structure to enclosure helped to develop a fabrication and construction sequence that would preserve the precision of the design. HL23 relies on the accuracy of shop-produced, prefabricated and coordinated components to attain its constructed level of fidelity to its digital precursor. The exterior cladding consists of large "mega-panels" that maximized shop-controlled fabrication procedures and simplified on-site assembly. Throughout construction and prior to installation, the structural steel frame was surveyed multiple times in an ongoing process to keep the fabricated panel frame well within allowable tolerances. Within an accurate frame, the shop-controlled megapanels were installed consistently with parallel joints and co-planarity panel-to-panel.

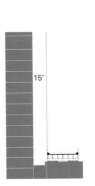
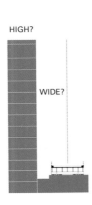
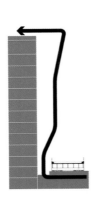

Workflow 1 (above left). A zoning variance allowed HL23 to cantilever beyond the 15' easement along the High Line.

Workflow 2 (above right). Rendering from design model looking north along the High Line.

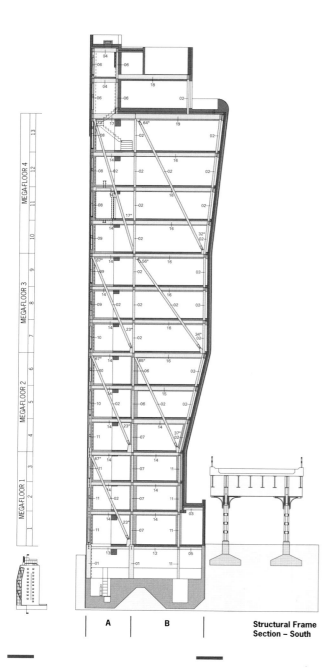

Structural Frame
Section – South

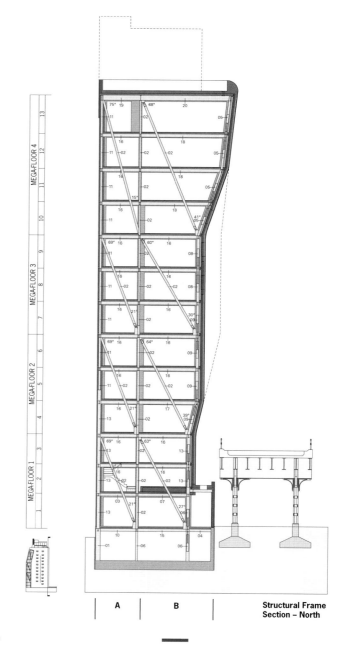

Structural Frame
Section – North

Workflow 3. The dimension of
the east-west section of HL23
expanded from 32' at floor 2
to 45' at floor 13. The building's geometric eccentricity
and small footprint presented
twisting and overturning
forces that were resolved
through perimeter diagonal
bracing. The north and south
façades were divided into two
bays: (A) a slim regular bay
equal to the width of the
stair/elevator core and (B) a
wider, more eccentric bay that
incorporates the changing
width of the building.

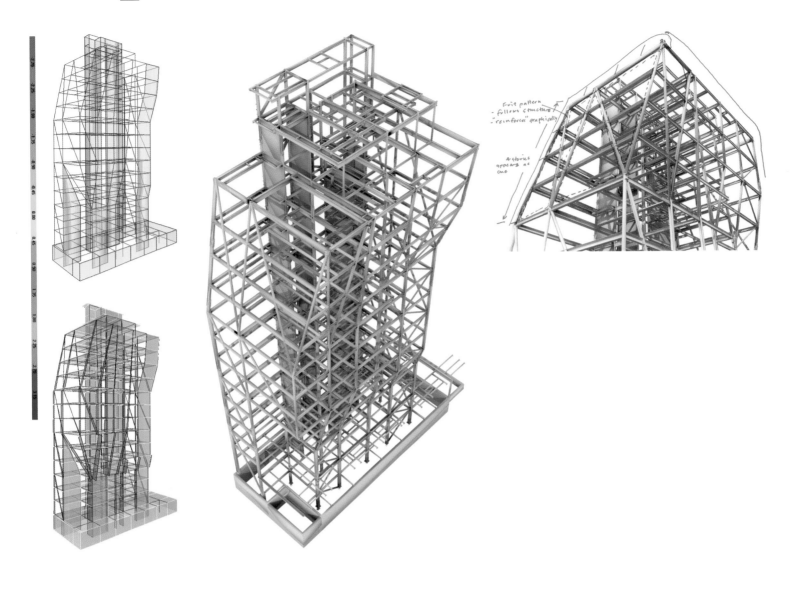

Workflow 4a (top left), 4b (bottom left). Early structural ideas, developed by NMDA prior to engagement with Desimone Consulting Engineers, indicated a braced frame at the perimeter of the building. Later, Desimone's finite element analysis revealed stresses in the proposed framing diagram, which in turn suggested how shear panels versus diagonals would be most efficiently used in the structure.

Workflow 5 (above middle). A working digital model of the structural steel frame was created by the steel fabricator Greton Steel of Montreal with information supplied by NMDA and Desimone Consulting Engineers. NMDA generated external envelope (surface) geometry and the desired location of column center-lines relative to the surface; Desimone determined steel shapes and dimensions.

Workflow 6 (above right). The structural model allowed NMDA to examine connection details, make adjustments to specific members and incorporate structural requirements into the design. This mark-up shows how the diagonal framing influenced the design of the frit pattern on the curtainwall.

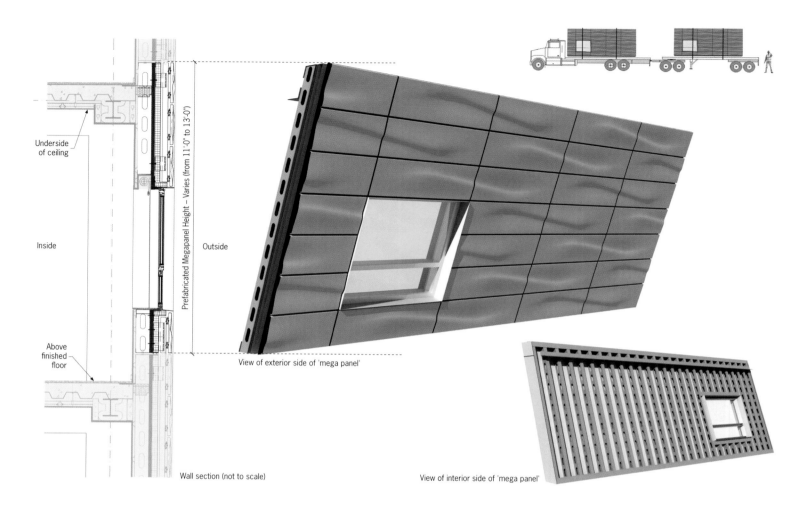

Underside
of ceiling

Inside

Prefabricated Megapanel Height – Varies (from 11'-0" to 13'-0")

Outside

Above
finished
floor

Wall section (not to scale)

View of exterior side of 'mega panel'

View of interior side of 'mega panel'

Workflow 7. The undulating
east facade consists of a
series of "megapanels" that
are hung from embeds in the
concrete decking. The exterior
face of the panels consists of
a tessellated grid of 11.5ft x
1.5ft stamped stainless steel
panels produced by TISI of
Buenos Aires. The production
of the back-up wall and the
final assembly of the megapanels was carried out at Island
Industries in Calverton, NY.

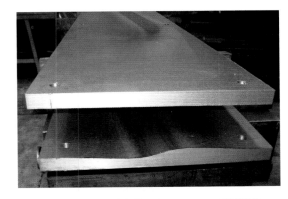

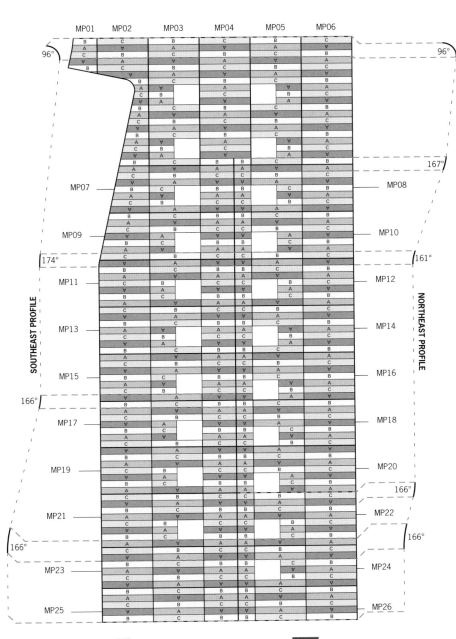

Workflow 8 (top left). View of milled steel dies for the stamped stainless-steel rainscreen panels for the east façade. Each die consisted of two pieces of milled steel bolted together, thus making four milled dies for each panel. Each half of the die took four days to mill. Handpolishing was required to rid the dies of the furrowed tool paths.

Workflow 9 (middle left). The overall pattern utilizes three unique panels, with one of these rotated to make a continuous field. The deformation runs across every other short end of the panel, but never across the pre-breakformed returns on the long edges. TISI dry-fit each megapanel in the factory, allowing for a close inspection of joint consistency and surface finish qualities.

Workflow 10 (bottom left). East façade stainless-steel megapanels ready for delivery to site.

Workflow 11 (above right). Atlas of stainless steel panels indicating individual panel types within each megapanel (MP).

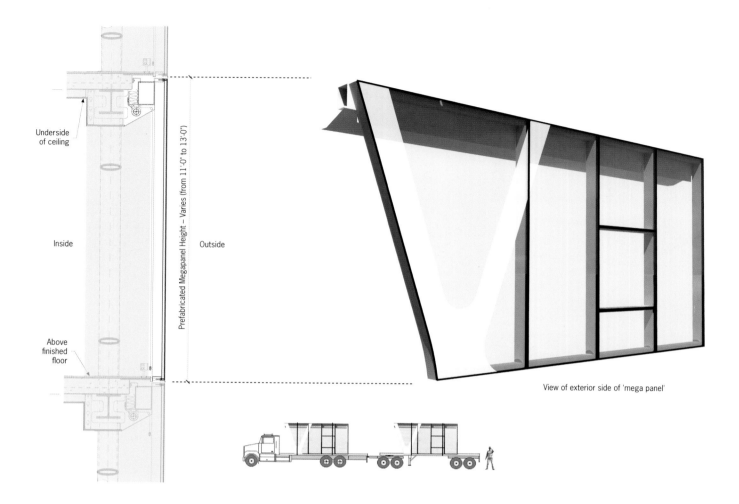

Underside
of ceiling

Inside

Outside

Above
finished
floor

Prefabricated Megapanel Height – Varies (from 11'-0" to 13'-0")

View of exterior side of 'mega panel'

Workflow 12. The north and south curtainwall megapanels were prefabricated by SGT Glass in Dongguan Province, China with oversized Insulated Glass Units (IGU's) that span from floor to floor placed into a welded steel frame. A hollow steel tube at the top (called a spreaderbeam) delivers stability across the entire megapanel.

Workflow 13 (top left). View of the SGT glass assembly factory with HL23 glass megapanels in the foreground. Steel frames are staged for the insertion of the custom IGU's with hand caulking applied afterwards.

Workflow 14 (bottom). View of the first completed curtain-wall megapanel at SGT. The steel frame inside is covered in a 1mm bead-blasted stainless sheet.

Workflow 15 (top right). View of the Lamborghini factory, c. 1969. Here, the Espada model is being produced, not on a rolling assembly line but rather on a fixed platform. While all cars are exactly the same, they are constructed individually like works of art, as much handmade as machine-made. The same could be said of HL23's glass megapanels.

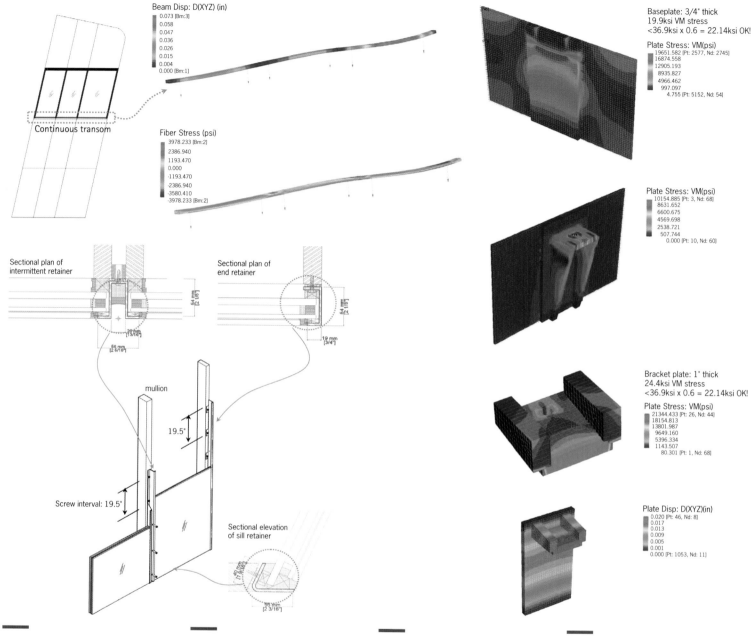

Beam Disp: D(XYZ) (in)

0.073 [Bm:3]
0.058
0.047
0.036
0.026
0.015
0.004
0.000 [Bm:1]

Continuous transom

Fiber Stress (psi)

3978.233 [Bm:2]
2386.940
1193.470
0.000
-1193.470
-2386.940
-3580.410
-3978.233 [Bm:2]

Baseplate: 3/4" thick
19.9ksi VM stress
<36.9ksi x 0.6 = 22.14ksi OK!

Plate Stress: VM(psi)

19651.582 [Pt: 2577, Nd: 2745]
16874.558
12905.193
8935.827
4966.462
997.097
4.755 [Pt: 5152, Nd: 54]

Plate Stress: VM(psi)

10154.885 [Pt: 3, Nd: 68]
8631.652
6600.675
4569.698
2538.721
507.744
0.000 [Pt: 10, Nd: 60]

Sectional plan of
intermittent retainer

Sectional plan of
end retainer

mullion

19.5"

Screw interval: 19.5"

Sectional elevation
of sill retainer

Bracket plate: 1" thick
24.4ksi VM stress
<36.9ksi x 0.6 = 22.14ksi OK!

Plate Stress: VM(psi)

21344.433 [Pt: 26, Nd: 44]
18154.813
13801.987
9649.160
5396.334
1143.507
80.301 [Pt: 1, Nd: 68]

Plate Disp: D(XYZ)(in)

0.020 [Pt: 46, Nd: 8]
0.017
0.013
0.009
0.005
0.001
0.000 [Pt: 1053, Nd: 11]

Workflow 16 (top left). In collaboration with Front Inc., the structural framing of each megapanel was analyzed and refined to accomplish the simple rectangular profiles and minimal sightlines desired by NMDA.

Workflow 17 (bottom left). L-profile aluminum cassettes with structural silicone secure the IGU's to the steel mullions. Since there is no racking between IGU's in the megapanel, a narrow 3/4in vertical joint is achieved.

Workflow 18 (right). Both the design and the installation of the megapanels relied on custom-engineered components. As part of the façade engineering, custom brackets were developed by Front to rig and hang the panels in place.

Workflow 19 (top left). Each megapanel was staged on a truck platform on the east side of the High Line before being lifted into place.

Workflow 20 (bottom left). For each bay, the attachment system demanded a bottom-to-top sequence. Here on the north façade, the sequence begins on the second floor terrace. Prior to installation, the steel frame was surveyed multiple times in an ongoing process to keep the frame well within allowable tolerances. With an accurate frame, the shop-controlled megapanels were installed with consistently parallel joints and co-planarity panel-to-panel.

Workflow 21 (top right). Spreaderbeam attachment to building frame embeds. Within 2m of the building, the megapanels are restrained by ratcheted chain connections, allowing for a slow and cautious adjustment of the panel position. Shims were inserted into the embeds for preliminary fine tuning of panel alignment.

Workflow 22 (bottom right). View from High Line of east façade megapanel installation. The top row of stainless-steel panels were left off, so that the megapanels could be caulked in the field. Later, all remaining panels were hand-set in the field. Like the north façade glazing, the rainsreen megapanels were sequenced from bottom to top.

Workflow 23 (top). Against the High Line, the diffused colors of the plant material reflect into the stainless steel. At this point the building reaches its most monumental effect: the respect for the High Line merges with the demand for non-conformity.

Workflow 24 (bottom). View looking west on West 23rd Street and 10th Avenue. The east façade facing the High Line is an accumulation of architectural events, a combination of folded and radial corners, 3D-stamped stainless-steel rainscreen panels and spandrel-free glazing with structural frit pattern.

Workflow 25 (right). The geometry and materiality of the east façade can be closely inspected by the passer-by on the High Line. Shifting perceptions of the form as well as shifting light conditions contribute to the animated and prismatic quality of the building.

CONTINGENCIES
—
EDITOR'S NOTES

There is a cautionary tone to Neil Denari's reflections on precision that reminds us that digital machines are driven by human decisions, and their output is subject to human interpretation. In relation to design, the operational precision of digital processes, from abstract formal generation via scripts to performance-based analysis and simulation, can confuse the difference between precise thought and precise execution. The ease with which seemingly definitive design results can be generated through user-friendly interfaces can cultivate a false sense of rigor that challenges architects to explore and understand the underlying logics of the tools they use.

These considerations become even more important as design processes move from explicit modeling, where a designer's input directly affects the resulting output much like hand drawing, to implicit parametric modeling, where design decisions are embedded in the logic of the program, creating layers of algorithmic separation between the designer's input and the resulting output. A younger generation of architects has perhaps come to this realization as they become increasingly interested in not only designing the input but also designing the algorithm. This engagement with algorithmic tools on a higher level, as part of a disciplined pursuit of design, much like Denari's obsessive hand drawings prior to the computer,[1] could be seen as a step towards what Denari describes as a new type of precise thought.

In the realm of actual building construction, the precision of Building Information Models can create expectations that confuse the difference between the virtual and the material. One of the implications of integrated design and fabrication workflows is that the long-standing gap between design intent and realization can be closed—that the models and drawings over which architects labor to reach a level of refinement and clarity no longer have to be interpreted by builders but rather can form a one-to-one link to tools of production. This ambition of zero tolerance seems to come within reach of architects who have always aspired to reduce dimensional contingencies in the material world to match their world of representation. Comparisons to the production efficiency of industrial objects, as Denari notes, makes the process of building seem antiquated and unresponsive to the benefits of new technology. Architects' long-standing fascination with prefabrication was the pre-digital attempt to gain more control over production by shifting from the myriad contingencies of the field to the controlled environment of the factory. "Field conditions" became the catch phrase for the inefficiencies of the site that could not be identified and planned for during the design phase. Denari's conclusion is that even with digitally integrated workflows between design and construction as well as the organizational shifts towards shared knowledge through all phases of a project, field conditions persist. The growing pressure to measure all aspects of design and construction in an act of precision is not only impractical, it is misguided. Unlike the industrial design model where precise is associated with standard through an iterative process of formal refinement, for Denari, precise is associated with unique: not just unique forms but also the unique thinking that develops from the rigorous and complex synthesis of new ideas with the constantly changing forces of nature and society. It is this synthesis—which can be enhanced by technology—that results in built form. This is Denari's version of designing design.

Along with the well-established benefits of exploring new combinations of geometry and managing complex design problems, several important questions are emerging with advanced parametric workflows in architecture. Do different inputs to an elaborate parametric design model result in truly unique outputs? As a discipline, should architecture attempt to quantify design methodologies that allow for a measurable cause-and-effect relationship between intent and result? Does the developing interest in custom parametric scripts shift design from a process, driven by the unique context of each project, to a product, with a predetermined range of possible solutions? Are the refined workflows that result in precise industrial design objects appropriate for architecture? Perhaps what needs to be acknowledged and defended by architects is that the one-off nature of buildings, even with their inefficiencies and contingencies, might be our most significant contribution to the quality of the built environment. The vibrant heterogeneity of cities is a measure of this phenomenon, as evidenced by Denari's HL23 project. The building's unique appearance along the High Line in New York City, after a formidable navigation of zoning regulations, development demands, financial constraints, not to mention construction challenges, is proof of the value of precise thought. Precise thought, in this sense, extends beyond technological capacities to enable social contingencies to be part of new workflows.

—

1. See McCarter, Robert (ed) (1987) *Pamplet Architecture No. 12: Building Machines*, Princeton Architectural Press.

WORKFLOW PATTERNS: A STRATEGY FOR DESIGNING DESIGN

ADAM MARCUS

Adam Marcus is an architect and Visiting Researcher at the University of Minnesota School of Architecture. He was a Senior Designer at Marble Fairbanks for five years.

Architecture's recent past has witnessed a remarkable amount of experimentation with ways of using digitally managed information—be it geometric, structural, programmatic, environmental, economic—to rethink how buildings are designed. Empowered by an opportune confluence of increased computing capacity, advanced 3D modeling software packages, a nascent interest in the mechanics of computer programming and new fabrication technologies, today's architects have been able to expand the discipline's limits, both in terms of form (what a building looks like) and performance (how a building functions). Yet while the range of these recent experiments has been remarkable, much of the new output ultimately falls into one of two domains. The first can be understood as an explicitly formal project in which complex geometry is generated by algorithmic rules, digital sculpting processes or other such computational tools. The second trajectory relies on computation and numerical processing to generate an architecture that can directly respond to or address specific performance criteria.

The challenge facing architects today is that these two divergent tendencies represent polarized and ultimately limited models for integrating digital information into the design process. On the one hand, a highly introspective design process inspired by genetic algorithms and scientific models risks total detachment from the everyday realities of architectural practice: scale, program, materiality,

construction contingencies, not to mention the need to address social, cultural or economic problems. Notable examples of this approach can be found in the work of Zaha Hadid or Greg Lynn, who have developed highly refined methods of using the computer to generate architecture of remarkable formal complexity. This sensibility also extends to younger designers like Mark Fornes, who engage in a process driven by mathematically derived rules and algorithms—an approach less sculptural, more rigorous, but nonetheless still as form-centric as those of Hadid and Lynn.

On the other hand, an empirical design process that prioritizes metrics and performance criteria—the quantitative ways in which a building can address specific functional goals—neglects architecture's more intangible and elemental aspects: spatial, symbolic and aesthetic qualities that distinguish architecture from building. The hyper-functional mindset prioritizes technical performance over everything else and commonly produces highly engineered building components that respond to very specific functional demands. Examples include high-performance façade systems designed for harsh climates by offices like Foster + Partners and Skidmore, Owings & Merrill, which are driven primarily by concerns of energy efficiency. This sensibility is also evident in much of the research conducted by academic programs such as the Center for Architecture Science and Ecology at Rensselaer Polytechnic Institute and the Product-Architecture Lab at the Stevens Institute of Technology. The mandate for sustainability is often the driving force behind this performance-driven model of design, but purely data-driven design—prioritizing technical performance above all else—runs the risk of fetishizing optimization at the expense of broader design goals.

Although the new digital tools in many ways emancipate architects from old models of practice, we find ourselves facing a choice between two poles of technological determinism: a detached formalism and a hyper-functionalism. And like the frustrating debate between form and function that preoccupied architecture for much of the last century, this one, too, is ultimately counterproductive and limiting. What is lacking is a more nuanced, synthetic understanding of how the management of digital information can be used to reconceive the architectural design process both quantitatively and qualitatively, both with a rich internal logic and an adaptive responsiveness to external inputs.

The fundamental question, it seems, is one of organization: how can the organization of information within the design process satisfy both quantitative and qualitative goals? As buildings become increasingly complex and as architects are required to satisfy ever more demanding programmatic and technical requirements, how can we enlist digital technology to address these competing demands such that technical challenges can be leveraged into architectural opportunity?

It is in this respect that the notion of pattern has re-emerged in architectural design, specifically as a critical tool for managing large quantities of information in the design process. Pattern's resurgence is most immediately evident in the richly articulated surfaces now ubiquitous throughout contemporary architecture, whether in the structural expression of buildings like OMA's CCTV Headquarters in Beijing [Figure 1], intricate façades such as Herzog & de Meuron's De Young Museum in San Francisco [Figure 2], or the provocative return of representational pattern in the work of FAT [Figure 3].[1] It is undeniable that pattern has visibly taken on a bold new presence in architecture, and although it is often associated with digital design techniques, there is a potentially deeper dialogue between pattern and digital technology that merits further investigation. If architects today are increasingly tasked with managing large and fluid quantities of information, then pattern can be understood as a design technique for organizing and taming these information flows. New computational technology provides the processing power to optimize design in new and unprecedented ways, but pattern gives us a way to visually assess the outputs of this digital computation. Optimization through pattern thus becomes an overlay of human and digital information processing, providing access to the power of computation through a qualitative filter of human intuition. Rethinking this age-old term—the word "pattern" is itself a kind of chameleon, appearing periodically in different guises throughout architectural history—in the context of information technology provides

Figure 1 (above left). OMA's CCTV Headquarters in Beijing.

Figure 2 (top right). Herzog & de Meuron's De Young Museum in San Francisco.

Figure 3 (bottom right). FAT's (Fashion Architecture Taste's) Sint Lucas Art Academy in Boxtel.

an opening for architects to move beyond the stalemate of technological determinism that has defined much of contemporary practice to date.

A look at two of the most notable proponents of pattern in architecture—William Morris and Christopher Alexander—provides some context as to how pattern can be understood as a tool for negotiating constraint and managing information. Morris, a nineteenth-century polymath famous for his deliriously recursive textile designs of stylized botanical forms, understood pattern as essentially an ornamental and optical domain. His was primarily a visual pursuit, focused on reconciling the dimensional and economic constraints of mass-produced wallpaper sheets with an obsessive desire to conceal the edge that inevitably is produced in any tiled system. Morris's goal was to produce a kind of field condition within the textile itself, an illusion of infinite continuity between and among tiles. His pattern designs are remarkable for imbuing the standardized, mass-produced tile with complexity to the point where the recursive behavior becomes discernible, but the limits of each tile are not. By bridging the demands of mechanical production at the height of the Industrial Revolution with the sensibility of the nascent British Arts and Crafts Movement (of which he is often credited as the main protagonist), Morris

offers us a model of pattern as a systematic tool to resolve competing pragmatic and aesthetic imperatives. [Figure 4]

The work of Christopher Alexander, in contrast to Morris's predominantly visual project, offers an alternate theory of pattern as an organizational system for architectural and urban design. One of the many fascinating, contradictory aspects of Alexander's career is that for an architect so rooted in the formative period of modern computer science (and whose writings are often credited for inspiring the development of object-oriented programming), much of his architectural impact has been in more conservative, neo-traditional realms. Although his system-driven theories have become gospel within movements of contextualism, regionalism and New Urbanism, they remain largely ignored by proponents of digitally generated form. In his seminal 1977 text *A Pattern Language: Towns, Buildings, Construction*,[2] Alexander codified a prescriptive methodology for designing buildings and cities, whereby the architect assembles predefined "patterns" (examples include "Light on two sides of every room" and "Private terrace on the street") according to specific rules of recombination. Although the fixed number of static patterns ultimately limits design agency (not to mention the fact that the 253 specified patterns reflect a specific set of social and cultural assumptions that may not universally apply to all contexts), Alexander's system was nonetheless revolutionary for suggesting that buildings and cities can be designed in a rule-based manner, using a kind of generative grammar of specific urban or architectural conditions that are interconnected by simple rules of compatibility. This represents a proto-algorithmic design process, in the sense that architectural form is not created in a top-down or gestural manner, but rather it evolves from basic building blocks that are assembled according to simple rules. These building blocks—what Alexander calls patterns—bear no resemblance to those of William Morris or to the visual façade patterns that proliferate today, but it is Alexander's understanding of design as a systematic process that continues to be relevant. Alexander was reacting against what he perceived to be the prevailing architectural sensibility at the time: a more intuitive, or arbitrary, top-down approach that he understood to be insensitive to functional concerns and exciting contexts. This breakthrough anticipated much of the contemporary interest in algorithmic form generation, both in the promise of using rule-based computation but also

Figure 4. William Morris's textile patterns sought to push the limits of industrial production to create infinitely-seeming works of art through a standardized means.

the potential pitfalls of an overly deterministic design process.

The precedents of Morris and Alexander—if radically different from each other—remind us that there is a long and diverse history of theorizing the role of pattern in architecture. But they also begin to suggest a more expanded definition of pattern as process, a way of designing with information itself as a raw material. Both examples—Morris's negotiation of material and economic constraints with his aesthetic goals and Alexander's system of elemental components bound by simple rules of recombination—can be understood as exercises in information management. And as architects today are tasked with addressing myriad forms of information in the design process—data as diverse as energy consumption benchmarks, material economies, structural efficiencies, programmatic idiosyncrasies—pattern offers a potential opening for architects to turn the management of large and variable quantities of information into a design opportunity.

A logical starting point for exploring how this expanded notion of pattern can be manifest architecturally is the design of façade and cladding systems, which typically are subdivided or modular in construction—and therefore patterned by default. In the context of new digital technologies that enable us to seamlessly integrate technical or performance-based logic into the design process, we can begin to identify several guiding principles for how a new approach to pattern can apply to architecture. Pattern is versatile: it is, by definition, repetitive and rhythmic but can also accommodate internal variation. [Figure 5] Pattern is decorative and structural yet irreducible to neither: the use of parametric modeling is able to produce a feedback loop between structure and effect—a mutually deterministic relationship between the structural logics of assembly and the decorative

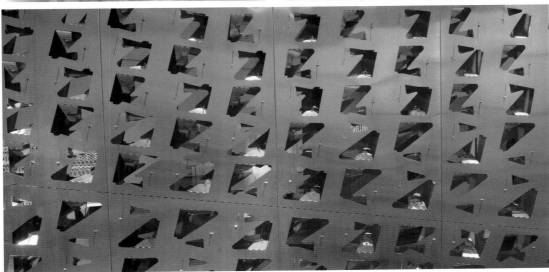

Figure 5 (top left). Acoustic ceiling of Marble Fairbank's Toni Stabile Student Center at Columbia University, New York. The ovals comprising the ceiling's perforation pattern are infinitely variable, which allows the pattern to adapt and respond to different acoustic conditions within the space.

Figure 6 (bottom). Flatform, Museum of Modern Art exhibition. Flatform is a panel system of stainless-steel sheets that are cut, scored and folded to form details of assembly without external fasteners.

Figure 7 (top right). Sunscreen ceiling of Toni Stabile Student Center. Parametric modeling was used to incorporate information from several different data streams into the perforation pattern of the metal sunscreen.

or ornamental effects of the resulting pattern. [Figure 6] Pattern can express, and respond to vast quantities and different kinds of information. [Figure 7] Pattern can be designed but can also be decoded or extracted from an existing environment, exposing conditions or relationships that otherwise may not have been evident. In all of these regards, pattern at once embodies both the pragmatic and the visionary; as with William Morris's textiles, pattern's need arises from constraints of material and economy, but its power lies in how those constraints are leveraged to yield a greater effect. It is in this sense that pattern can be understood to lie at the intersection of the technical and the aesthetic.

ENDNOTES
—

1. Pell, B. (2010) *The Articulate Surface*, Basel, Birkhäuser.
2. Alexander, C.; Ishikawa, S.; Silverstein, M. (1977) *A Pattern Language: Towns, Buildings, Construction*, Oxford, Oxford University Press. Much of the theoretical basis for *A Pattern Language* was developed in Alexander's Harvard doctoral thesis, which was subsequently published in 1964 as *Notes on the Synthesis of Form*. In this book, Alexander defined the act of design (creating form) as a strictly systematic exercise, an adaptive and incremental process structured by rules and parameters. His system-based approach was likely influenced by research Alexander conducted concurrently with his architectural studies, both at Harvard's Center for Cognitive Studies and at MIT's computer science department.

TONI STABILE STUDENT CENTER
WORKFLOW CASE STUDY ▶

In each of our projects at Marble Fairbanks, we seek ways of using information processing technology in the design process to engage in the dialogue between qualitative innovation and quantitative optimization, and pattern has become a crucial tool for accomplishing this. In designing the Toni Stabile Student Center for Columbia University's Graduate School of Journalism in New York, we developed a series of patterning strategies utilizing parametric modeling in the design of three highly engineered surfaces. Pattern is used as a technique for organizing technical data into a material response that engages in optical, spatial and communicative ways with the surrounding architecture. The patterns for the surfaces—two ceilings and a wall—were each generated through digital processes to address very specific technical or programmatic criteria, while also producing architectural or experiential qualities. Each surface employs a pattern strategy that quantifies the respective performance requirements, optimizes them and provides flexibility within these technical constraints to test iterative options that can be evaluated for their qualitative potential. Pattern thus becomes a technique for transforming the logic of optimization and performance into an aesthetic strategy.

The patterning strategies implemented in the Stabile Center also informed the overall workflow of the project, including the organization of the design team itself. A team of specialists was assembled to contribute relevant expertise to developing the specific performance criteria and digital modeling for each respective surface. The intent was to expand our network of allied consultants to maximize technical expertise while managing the flow of information and communication to guarantee that the architecture's qualitative effects remain linked to the overall design goals of the project. As a model for future design practice, this approach affords greater flexibility and agility for architects—many of whom may not have the in-house resources—to address increasingly complex technical challenges that require highly specialized knowledge. Importantly, the fabricators were included in design discussions from the start, allowing us to prototype full-scale mock-ups and test material performance, assembly techniques and different resolutions and densities for each pattern to evaluate the more spatial and qualitative effects of each surface. In this sense, the workflow itself can be understood as another type of pattern, in which the use of digital technology and parametric software facilitate a highly iterative, recursive process. Understanding workflow in this way enables us to address highly technical challenges of information management while also pursuing innovative design possibilities.

ZONE 1
ACOUSTIC PERFORMANCE

ZONE 2
GRAPHIC PERFORMANCE

ZONE 3
ENVIRONMENTAL PERFORMANCE

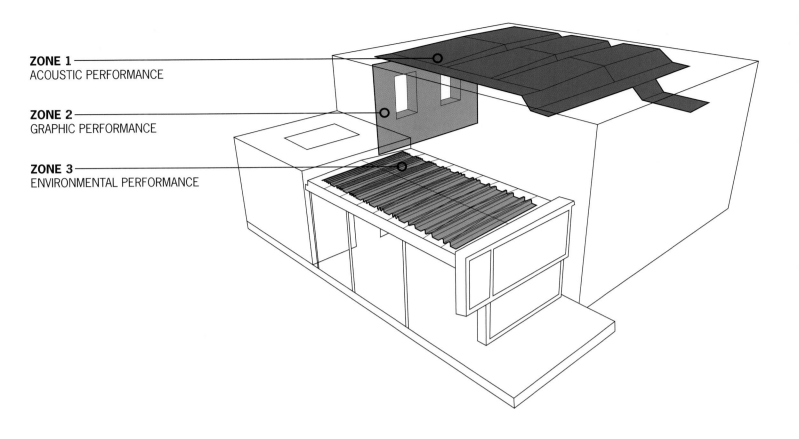

Workflow 1. Project Diagram.
The project is organized
around a central "social hub"
and includes spaces for the
Journalism Library, faculty
and administrative offices,
classroom space and a café.
Three zones within the
project were identified as
opportunities to develop pattern strategies for addressing
specific performance criteria
and enhance the experience of
each space.

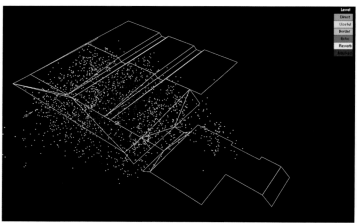
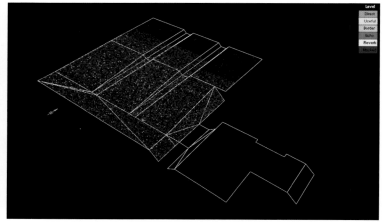

Workflow 2 (top). Zone #1:
Social Hub. The first zone,
the ceiling of the social
hub, is designed to provide
an acoustically absorptive
surface. The logic of the
perforation pattern was developed in two phases: first, an
acoustic model of the space
was developed to drive the
density of perforations, and
a second subsequent scripting
process integrated panel
geometry, lighting and sprinkler
layouts into the algorithm
and incorporated these elements into the pattern. The
digital model became the
repository for these technical

constraints but also provided
flexibility to test and refine
the more qualitative aspects
of the pattern. The final
perforation pattern satisfies
the acoustic demands of the
space while also providing a
dynamic index of its generative process.

Workflow 3 (bottom left and
right). Acoustic Simulations
& Zones of Intensity. Several
scenarios were generated
within the acoustical model
to identify the zones of
the ceiling that, through
increased acoustic transparency,
would reduce and eliminate
reverb and echo effects in
the space. These points then
became "zones of intensity" or
"attractors" for the pattern
generation script — areas
where the perforations would
become larger and provide
more acoustic absorption.

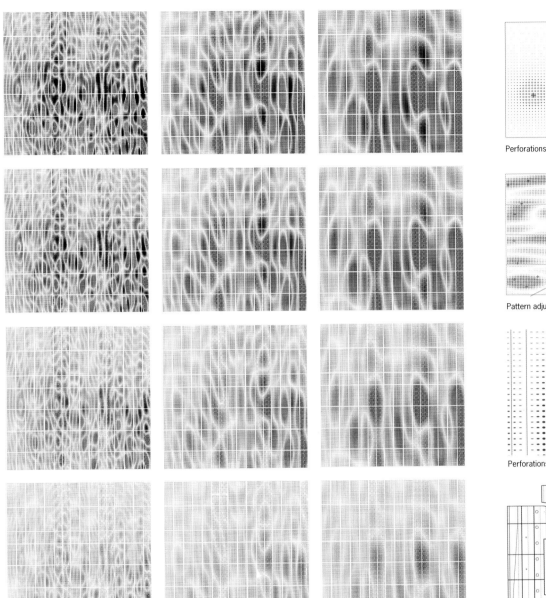

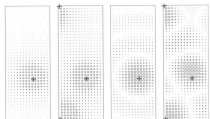

Perforations intensify at attractor locations

Pattern adjusts to panel joints and bend lines

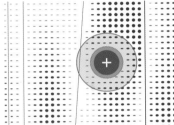

Perforations respond to light and sprinkler cut-outs

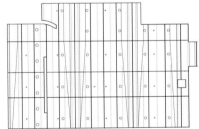

Panels and steel substructure grid

Workflow 4 (above left). Pattern Iterations. A custom script was designed to generate a series of unique iterations for the acoustic pattern, each of which relied on the attractor points while also satisfying the acoustic performance criteria for the space. The iterations were evaluated both for the density of perforations (which translated directly to fabrication time and cost) as well as overall qualitative effect.

Workflow 5 (above right). Refinement of Acoustic Pattern. The custom script was calibrated to respond to the existing building structure above the ceiling, as well as lights, sprinklers and AV equipment that would be integrated into the ceiling. The pattern generated from the acoustic analysis was modified by adding these rules to the parameters of the script:
1. All holes on 1-1/2in grid.
2. All holes can infinitely vary from 1in circles to 5/8in long ovals.
3. No holes within 1in of panel joint lines.

4. Any hole within 6in of panel joint lines must be less than 1/2in in diameter.
5. No holes within 1/2in of light/sprinkler cutouts.
6. Any hole within 6in of light/sprinkler cutouts must be less than 1/2in in diameter.
7. No holes within 1in of bend lines.

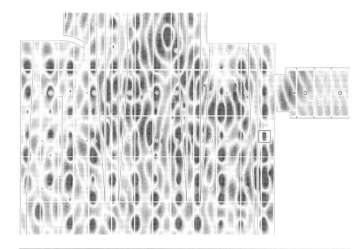

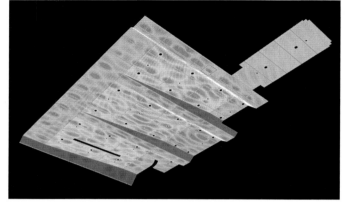

Workflow 6 (top left), 7 (bottom left), 8 (above right). The final pattern selected from the multiple options that satisfied the performance criteria was based on aesthetic preference.

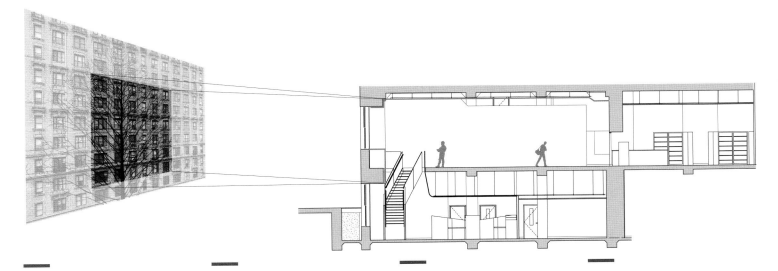

Workflow 9 (top). Zone #2: Broadway Wall. The second zone, the west wall of the social hub, was used to explore the graphic, experiential and spatial aspects of pattern. Image pixelation and resolution was manipulated to provide variable effects and perceptions from different locations and view angles. Generating the pattern became a question of balancing digital tools of image conversion with full-scale tests of the resultant legibility.

Workflow 10 (bottom). Pattern Generation: Inside/Outside. The pattern for this surface was developed by filtering a photograph of the view across Broadway just outside the wall through a digital process that converted it into perforations to be cut from metal panels. The intent was not only to project the image of the "outside" onto the "inside" of the wall, but to also allow for different perceptions and readings of the wall depending on the viewer's proximity.

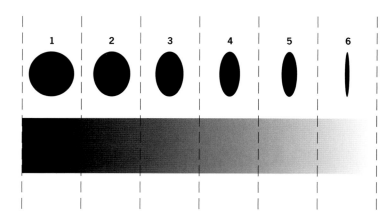

West wall, from 40'-0"

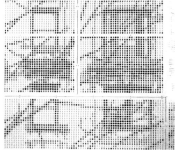

West wall, from 10'-0"

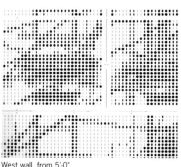

West wall, from 5'-0"

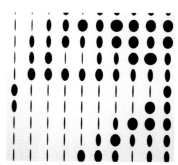

West wall, from 1'-0"

Workflow 11 (top left). Pixelation Logic. The pixelation scripting process used an alphabet of six discrete "characters", each corresponding to a specific range of tonal values within the black-to-white spectrum. Through a simple algorithm, the script converted the image into a perforation pattern by replacing the raster information with characters according to tonal value. The characters consist of a stepped gradient from zero ("0") to one ("1").

Workflow 12 (bottom left), 13 (above right). The pattern was calibrated to "snap" into focus at a specific distance of 40ft—the point at which one enters the space—and then dissolve into an abstract, field-like pattern of ovals as one moves closer.

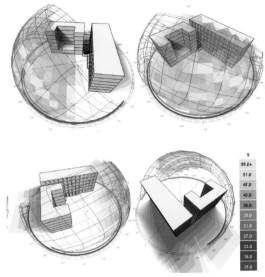

Workflow 14 (above left). Zone #3: Café Sunscreen. The third zone, a sunscreen ceiling hung below a new glass roof, was designed and engineered in conjunction with the glass enclosure to reduce the heat loads while also sculpting the quality of natural light. Through a process that integrated parametric modeling with environmental simulation software, two patterning techniques — corrugation and perforation — were developed in tandem to optimize the reduction of direct light and solar heat gain inside the space. The use of the model allowed for the technical performance criteria to be met, while also achieving a qualitative effect evocative of sunlight filtered through a tree canopy.

Workflow 15 (above right). Solar Studies. The peak cooling load, as the point at which the direct solar radiation absorbed by the roof is the greatest, was identified through a series of environmental simulations, and this load became the benchmark by which the solar shading system was designed.

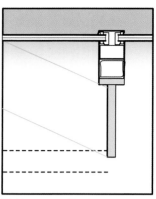

(A) Absorption. Find the one angle at which a corrugation receives the most direct solar radiation over the course of the year.

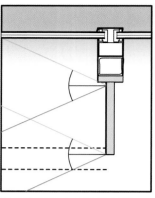

(B) Reflection. A vertical face (the roof structure) is used to bounce light into the space and absorb radiation. Angle of incidence equals angle of reflection.

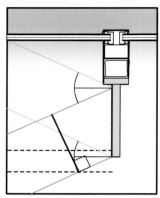

(C) Diffuse Light. Find a face perpendicular to the angle of reflection. This indirect face can be perforated to bring in the maximum diffuse light while minimizing heat gain.

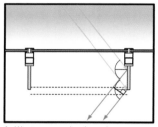

1. West corrugation (morning sun, coming from the east).

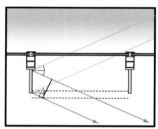

2. East corrugation (afternoon sun, coming from the west).

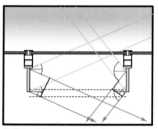

3. Establish east and west indirect faces.

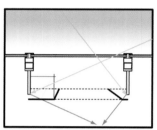

4. Adjust east face to provide horizontal surface for light fixtures and sprinkler heads.

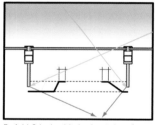

5. Add 3 inch wide horizontal surface at top of corrugations (minimum required for bending machinery).

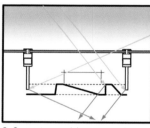

6. Generate remaining corrugation.

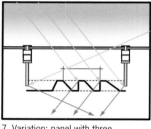

7. Variation: panel with three corrugations.

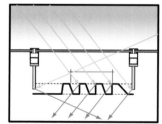

8. Variation: panel with four corrugations.

Workflow 16 (top). Algorithm Logic. The information from the solar analysis was in turn fed into a parametric model that used a simple algorithm to generate the bend profiles of the ceiling panels. The principles of the script involved using the corrugations to block direct sunlight, while letting indirect light bounce and filter down to the space below.

Workflow 17 (bottom). Typical Panel Generation. The algorithm used the principle of reflection (angle of incidence = angle of reflection) to generate the optimal corrugated shape to minimize direct light infiltration and maximize indirect light dispersal. The output geometry was constrained by several pragmatic aspects of the ceiling: adequate clearance for the light fixtures and sprinkler heads located above the ceiling, the material constraints of the CNC bending equipment used to break the steel panels, and the interface with the glass roof structure and mounting hardware.

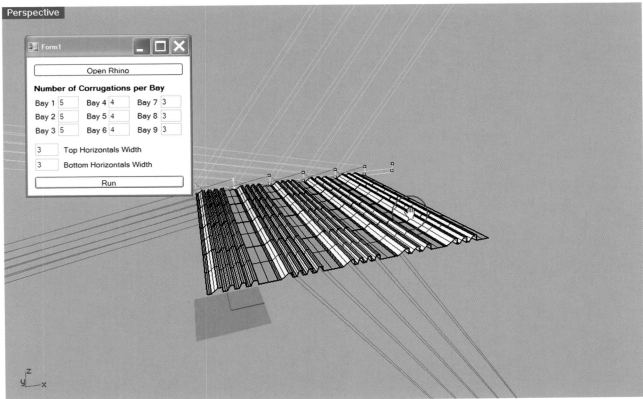

Workflow 18. The script was
also designed with a user
interface that allowed quick
adjustments to the number
of corrugations per panel
for testing the qualitative
effects of different depths
of the folding pattern.

Cloud pattern used to drive perforations

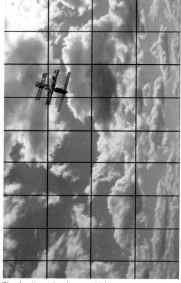

Cloud pattern showing panel joints

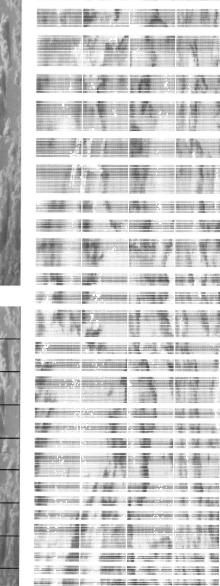

Final perforation pattern (unfolded view)

Detail of installed ceiling

Workflow 19 (above). Generation of Perforation Pattern. Once the corrugation pattern was determined, the resultant geometry was fed back into energy analysis software. Each face of the corrugated surface was then assigned a maximum allowable percentage of perforation that would satisfy the 80% solar heat reduction requirement established from the energy model. The quantitative rules for the perforation pattern determined only the percentage of open surface, while the logic for the pattern's variation was derived from an image of the sky as if one were looking straight up from the café through the roof. The size and geometry of the perforations were determined by balancing the need for a resolution that would allow the image to be legible with the cost of laser cutting the holes in the panels.

Workflow 20 (right). The light quality through the ceiling and the legibility of the perforated sky pattern change depending on the sun angle.

USE PATTERNS
—
EDITOR'S NOTES

In 2002, Arun Rimal of Arup's New York office was presenting some of the firm's proprietary digital software that included pioneering versions of environmental, structural and acoustic simulation tools similar to those used on the design of the Columbia University Stabile Student Center. Rimal concluded the presentation by demonstrating an early version of life-safety software that simulated the evacuation of workers in an office tower during a fire. Small dots were chaotically moving around a floor plan and then slowly organizing in lines at opposite ends of the plan, leading to the fire stairs and finally disappearing—everyone had escaped safely, the building had performed as planned. The architecture succeeded.

This new software marked a significant transition in the development of algorithms to simulate complex behavior in a building. The programmed subject was no longer an I-beam or the airflow through a room but a human being. Each dot was an algorithmic agent containing the complex decision-making process that people go through under life-threatening conditions, not one by one, but in relation to other agents under the same dire conditions. This was truly impressive. Behavior simulation of this type has become more common and is applied to numerous other human flow situations, such as city streets, theaters, airports and other places of large public assembly. These simulations are the descendants of, among others, the scientific management techniques of the modernist's "time and motion" studies to analyze worker productivity and the organizational diagrams of the Quickborner Team in the late 1950's; all sought a convergence between two types of patterns, the configuration of space and the activities of users.

Surface pattern as a new aesthetics of information both generated and decoded by computation is well established with many of the examples cited by Adam Marcus. Yet the exploration of use patterns as a new type of spatial generator is largely absent from current discourse and architectural experimentation. Any exploration of *use* patterns through computation exists either as analysis simulations, like the ones stated above for the purposes of testing emergency scenarios and increasing the efficiency of movement, or as compliance analysis with pre-established program adjacencies.[1] However, as one of the great strengths of computation is to generate and identify patterns within mounds of scattered data, these new techniques could also be utilized by designers to explore new use and program patterns in architecture.

How can the algorithmic processes of pattern recognition or pattern generation be used to explore program relationships that are based on simulating alternative and multiple uses within a single building? The formal theories and experiments of architects like Peter Eisenman and Frank Gehry have been taken to a new level with digitally generated form. How could the program theories and experiments of architects like Rem Koolhaas and Bernard Tschumi, in a similar vein, evolve through digitally generated patterns of use? The static diagrams that strive to identify complex interactions of users over time could be supplemented with dynamic patterns generated with multiple alternative logics through simple recombination scripts. For example, the normative behavior that serves as the basis for egress simulations to find a balance between building design and human activitiy—a digitally advanced version of the modernist's Form Follows Function—could be re-scripted with behaviors driven by multiple program objectives within the same building to explore a digitally advanced version of cross-programming. Such a development could revive and update the lively debates around the relationship between architectural form and program. Defining the design logics for this type of exploratory approach to the reconsideration of program could be the

next challenge for digital patterns
in architecture.

—

1. Working with the General Services
Administration, the federal agency responsible for procuring federal buildings in the
USA, Chuck Eastman has developed analysis software that assesses proposed design
layouts for courthouses in relationship to
established rules for program adjacencies.
Eastman, C. (2009) *Automated Assessment
of Early Concept Designs*, in Garber, R.
(ed) (2010) *Closing the Gap, Information
Models in Contemporary Design Practice.
Architectural Design* magazine.

INTENTION TO ARTIFACT

PHIL BERNSTEIN

Phil Bernstein is an architect, a Vice President at software provider Autodesk, and teaches Professional Practice at the Yale School of Architecture.

In 1599 the British architect, surveyor and mason Robert Smythson created a beautiful and exacting drawing of a twelve-light rose window for one of his projects. Shown in a recent exhibition exploring the role of mathematics in architecture,[1] the drawing explains the architectural configuration, construction sequence and installation, and stone fabrication of the window in a corresponding curving wall, and it is precisely this conflation of outcomes that makes this image so provocative. [Figure 1] Designer-builders of Smythson's generation saw little distinction between descriptions of design intent and the resulting built artifact, and divisions between the creators and consumers of design information were largely irrelevant in the long era of project delivery by the "Master Builder" approach.

Four hundred years later, the relationship between the processes of design and construction is much changed. The roles of designer and builder have diverged, are acknowledged as different professional disciplines, and are heavily elaborated into hierarchies of architects, engineers, specialty consultants, construction managers, subcontractors, suppliers, fabricators, erectors and others. Even a simple construction project today might involve hundreds of such people, and the means of transiting the gulf from "design intent" to "construction execution" is regularly unpredictable and often worse. The separation is exacerbated by the structure and approach of project delivery itself. Architects and engineers are responsible for creating the intent of the design but ignore, to a certain extent, the means and methods of construction. This state is manifest in "construction documents" that describe, in the abstract two-dimensional language of plan/section/elevation, the highly complex interaction of pieces that form a building. Builders, burdened

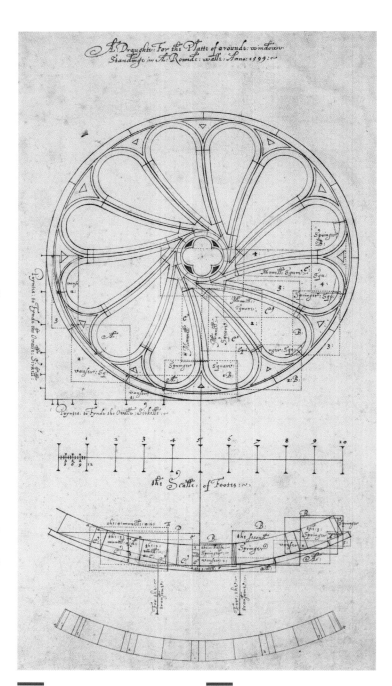

Figure 1. Drawing by Robert Smythson, circa 1599, "A Rounde Window Standinge in a Rounde Walle".

Other tolerance values considered and resulting number of types

 # Types: 9
Avg Deviation: 42.00
Max Deviation: 108.98

types and deviations:
type 0: max dev in type 74.69 : number of items of type 56
type 1: max dev in type 74.67 : number of items of type 147
type 2: max dev in type 75.08 : number of items of type 88
type 3: max dev in type 74.73 : number of items of type 62
type 4: max dev in type 75.35 : number of items of type 59
type 5: max dev in type 81.05 : number of items of type 22
type 6: max dev in type 70.73 : number of items of type 5
type 7: max dev in type 108.96 : number of items of type 1

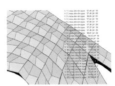

 # Types: 31
Avg Deviation: 8.88
Max Deviation: 22.38

types and deviations:
type 0: max dev in type 16.53 : number of items of type 11
type 1: max dev in type 17.40 : number of items of type 15
type 2: max dev in type 17.40 : number of items of type 65
type 3: max dev in type 16.65 : number of items of type 51
type 4: max dev in type 17.94 : number of items of type 18
type 5: max dev in type 17.55 : number of items of type 17
type 6: max dev in type 17.36 : number of items of type 29
type 7: max dev in type 17.27 : number of items of type 19
type 8: max dev in type 17.46 : number of items of type 25
type 9: max dev in type 16.67 : number of items of type 20
type 10: max dev in type 18.33 : number of items of type 18
type 11: max dev in type 18.09 : number of items of type 19
type 12: max dev in type 18.43 : number of items of type 20
type 13: max dev in type 18.09 : number of items of type 11
type 14: max dev in type 18.54 : number of items of type 10
type 15: max dev in type 17.64 : number of items of type 17
type 16: max dev in type 17.43 : number of items of type 11
type 17: max dev in type 18.03 : number of items of type 17
type 18: max dev in type 17.73 : number of items of type 12
type 19: max dev in type 17.61 : number of items of type 9
type 20: max dev in type 16.63 : number of items of type 4
type 21: max dev in type 16.53 : number of items of type 7
type 22: max dev in type 12.49 : number of items of type 3
type 23: max dev in type 22.13 : number of items of type 3
type 24: max dev in type 18.83 : number of items of type 1
type 25: max dev in type 22.39 : number of items of type 2

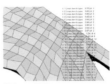

 # Types: 155
Avg Deviation: 1.36
Max Deviation: 4.2016

types and deviations:
type 0: max dev in type 1.74 : number of items of type 5
type 1: max dev in type 0.75 : number of items of type 1
type 2: max dev in type 3.03 : number of items of type 2
type 3: max dev in type 2.08 : number of items of type 3
type 4: max dev in type 0.43 : number of items of type 1
type 5: max dev in type 2.64 : number of items of type 2
type 6: max dev in type 2.80 : number of items of type 2
type 7: max dev in type 2.35 : number of items of type 1
type 8: max dev in type 2.64 : number of items of type 3
type 9: max dev in type 2.57 : number of items of type 3
type 10: max dev in type 1.24 : number of items of type 4
type 11: max dev in type 2.40 : number of items of type 5
type 12: max dev in type 2.42 : number of items of type 14
type 13: max dev in type 2.78 : number of items of type 7
type 14: max dev in type 3.05 : number of items of type 22
type 15: max dev in type 2.36 : number of items of type 10
type 16: max dev in type 2.26 : number of items of type 9
type 17: max dev in type 2.53 : number of items of type 11
type 18: max dev in type 2.80 : number of items of type 9
type 19: max dev in type 2.33 : number of items of type 7
type 20: max dev in type 2.59 : number of items of type 8
type 21: max dev in type 2.69 : number of items of type 4
type 22: max dev in type 2.97 : number of items of type 5
type 23: max dev in type 2.27 : number of items of type 1
type 24: max dev in type 2.29 : number of items of type 3
type 25: max dev in type 3.68 : number of items of type 2
type 26: max dev in type 3.59 : number of items of type 4
type 27: max dev in type 1.45 : number of items of type 2
type 28: max dev in type 2.73 : number of items of type 4
type 29: max dev in type 2.63 : number of items of type 2
type 30: max dev in type 2.68 : number of items of type 2

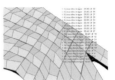

 # Types: 25
Avg Deviation: 11.30
Max Deviation: 43.97

types and deviations:
type 0: max dev in type 17.94 : number of items of type 12
type 1: max dev in type 22.65 : number of items of type 33
type 2: max dev in type 22.92 : number of items of type 88
type 3: max dev in type 23.32 : number of items of type 27
type 4: max dev in type 22.95 : number of items of type 25
type 5: max dev in type 22.55 : number of items of type 34
type 6: max dev in type 22.19 : number of items of type 30
type 7: max dev in type 22.48 : number of items of type 24
type 8: max dev in type 21.52 : number of items of type 22
type 9: max dev in type 22.42 : number of items of type 27
type 10: max dev in type 22.47 : number of items of type 18
type 11: max dev in type 23.04 : number of items of type 12
type 12: max dev in type 23.15 : number of items of type 21
type 13: max dev in type 23.92 : number of items of type 20
type 14: max dev in type 22.54 : number of items of type 15
type 15: max dev in type 23.25 : number of items of type 10
type 16: max dev in type 22.88 : number of items of type 7
type 17: max dev in type 23.59 : number of items of type 5
type 18: max dev in type 22.13 : number of items of type 3
type 19: max dev in type 18.83 : number of items of type 1
type 20: max dev in type 43.97 : number of items of type 2

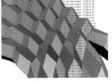

 # Types: 38
Avg Deviation: 9.06
Max Deviation: 29.99

types and deviations:
type 0: max dev in type 12.49 : number of items of type 5
type 1: max dev in type 17.45 : number of items of type 11
type 2: max dev in type 17.30 : number of items of type 15
type 3: max dev in type 16.84 : number of items of type 19
type 4: max dev in type 17.92 : number of items of type 19
type 5: max dev in type 17.55 : number of items of type 17
type 6: max dev in type 17.39 : number of items of type 20
type 7: max dev in type 17.40 : number of items of type 21
type 8: max dev in type 17.37 : number of items of type 13
type 9: max dev in type 17.12 : number of items of type 21
type 10: max dev in type 17.50 : number of items of type 16
type 11: max dev in type 17.36 : number of items of type 16
type 12: max dev in type 18.14 : number of items of type 16
type 13: max dev in type 17.20 : number of items of type 22
type 14: max dev in type 17.01 : number of items of type 16
type 16: max dev in type 17.89 : number of items of type 23
type 17: max dev in type 17.23 : number of items of type 14
type 18: max dev in type 17.77 : number of items of type 17
type 19: max dev in type 17.50 : number of items of type 15
type 20: max dev in type 16.97 : number of items of type 13
type 21: max dev in type 17.54 : number of items of type 15
type 22: max dev in type 17.52 : number of items of type 10
type 23: max dev in type 16.49 : number of items of type 6
type 24: max dev in type 17.62 : number of items of type 9
type 25: max dev in type 18.68 : number of items of type 8
type 26: max dev in type 19.04 : number of items of type 10
type 27: max dev in type 17.43 : number of items of type 8
type 28: max dev in type 17.46 : number of items of type 3
type 29: max dev in type 19.36 : number of items of type 2
type 30: max dev in type 19.00 : number of items of type 2

 # Types: 8
Avg Deviation: 54.34
Max Deviation: 114.835

types and deviations:
type 0: max dev in type 99.90 : number of items of type 114
type 1: max dev in type 100.00 : number of items of type 138
type 2: max dev in type 99.36 : number of items of type 95
type 3: max dev in type 99.82 : number of items of type 73
type 4: max dev in type 99.98 : number of items of type 19
type 5: max dev in type 114.83 : number of items of type 3

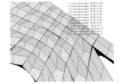

 # Types: 17
Avg Deviation: 17.57
Max Deviation: 56.122

types and deviations:
type 0: max dev in type 37.29 : number of items of type 18
type 1: max dev in type 37.08 : number of items of type 113
type 2: max dev in type 37.25 : number of items of type 45
type 3: max dev in type 37.72 : number of items of type 49
type 4: max dev in type 37.48 : number of items of type 48
type 5: max dev in type 37.29 : number of items of type 42
type 6: max dev in type 36.49 : number of items of type 29
type 7: max dev in type 37.13 : number of items of type 29
type 8: max dev in type 37.84 : number of items of type 31
type 9: max dev in type 38.22 : number of items of type 17
type 10: max dev in type 36.76 : number of items of type 10
type 11: max dev in type 36.70 : number of items of type 5
type 12: max dev in type 56.12 : number of items of type 3

Colors are relative to min-max of
current test – not absolute.

High   Deviation   Low

**Figure 2. Zaha Hadid Architects,
scripted parametric geometry
generation.**

with the frequently incompatible demands of aspirations of quality and short budgets and schedules, rarely find the insight in such drawings needed to complete the task at hand. Gaps, conceptual or otherwise, in these documents between design intent and completed artifact are manifold, and consequently the building industry is generally considered to face considerable challenges in terms of productivity and efficiency.[2]

DESIGN TO CONSTRUCTION IN THE AGE OF HIGH-RESOLUTION DESIGN REPRESENTATION
—

If Smythson were alive today he would likely be surprised (and disappointed) by the number of documents required to build his window. It would appear in large and small-scale plans, numerous elevations and wall sections, probably a detail or two, the window schedule and the specifications. Eventually a selected stone subcontractor/fabricator would prepare shop drawings. All these data would be created, collected, coordinated, evaluated and distributed before a single piece of stone was quarried in anticipation of eventual construction. The design-to-construction process would be overlaid with extensive correspondence and other documentation of its evolution, much of which is created in anticipation of possible failure and the inevitable claims that would result.

Yet elaborate documentation is not just a product of risk management strategy. Rather, it is a response to a series of factors affecting the axis of design intent to finished artifact. Buildings are of course much more complex today and performance expectations are high. Construction methodologies are more complicated, yet field crews less competent. The late twentieth-century translation of hand-drawing methods to computer-aided drafting made creating great swaths of detailed drawings first easy, then expected. But the transition from analog drawings to their digital counterparts did little to ease the flow of information from the designer to the builder. Could it be that drawings have reached the end of their unique usefulness?

By 2004 a new technology was pressing against the CAD tradition in architecture: in Building Information Modeling (BIM), drawings give way to three-dimensional, behaviorally correct digital models of a building from which drawings and other "meta-data" can be derived.

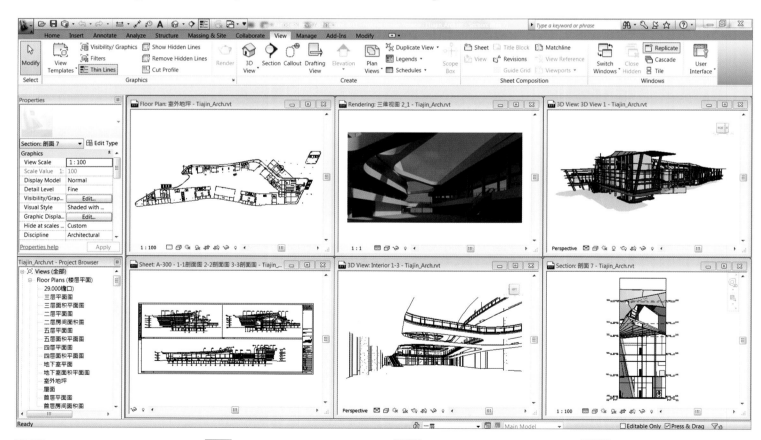

Figure 3. CCDI Group, multi-view Building Information Modeling display.

By 2009, a large number of designers and builders had adopted BIM approaches, and a majority of industry firms plan to adopt BIM by 2011.[3] BIM's popularity comes on the heels of widespread use of less sophisticated, but compelling 3D geometry modeling software. And in more computationally able shops, geometric modelers are driven by logic scripts that create results not from direct manipulation of drawings or models but from computer programs, expanding the design process to include both the algorithm and its result. Patrik Schumacher has suggested that such an approach be characterized as "Parametricism",[4] in a context where "versioning, iteration and mass customization" have been understood and prevalent, at least in the avant-garde, for some time. [Figure 2] This description posits parametric design as a process for the systematic generation of formal alternatives; a process in which the designer manipulates the computations, not the form itself. Mark Goulthorpe takes this concept to its logical extreme, suggesting that design is generated only through the "heuristic reasoning" of scripting; the creation of software instructions yields a result irrespective of formal outcome.[5] In both views, the design process includes strategies for both the formal end results and the procedural framework— manifest in rules, parameters, constraints and relationships—that achieves that end. Design intent and deliverables are thus bound up in both the abstract representation of the result and the underlying rules that created it.

Building on this combined interest in design and design logic, BIM offers new opportunities for designers to experiment on digital prototypes of buildings, and for builders to simulate construction virtually, before heading to the field. Designers and builders can share the underlying logic of the geometry of a model as well as its virtual materiality, extracting quantities, identifying clashes, even running analyses of energy usage or daylighting and shadows, all in the service of a more predictable result. The model includes both the tectonics of the design and some of its parametric characteristics: sizes and relationships of elements, combined with their geometry and material characteristics. [Figure 3] Conceptually, these data create a bridge between the design intention and the construction execution, using the model as a high-resolution digital prototype of the building. Almost in parallel, a new method of project organization has emerged, called Integrated Project Delivery, where the transparency of BIM offers deep collaboration between clients, designers and builders. With these two developments, the means of representation bridge the intent-to-execution gap.

Today designers and builders face a heady mix of representational technologies with BIM at the core, empowered by the enhanced processing potency of cloud computing, the ubiquity of connectivity and a panoply of display devices at various scales and resolutions, and the ability to rapidly capture existing conditions in three dimensions with laser scanning. [Figure 4] Every aspect of the design-to-build process is thus becoming virtualized and hence interconnected, integrated and interdependent. As the resolution, granularity and parametric characteristics of design models increase in quality, analytical insight provided by adjacent computing processes

Figure 4. U.S. General Services Administration, laser scan point cloud image.

will also advance, providing real-time feedback loops during the evolution of the design itself. Thirty years ago, and referring to a terminology coined by the German scientist and designer Horst Rittel,[6] Peter Rowe characterized problems related to the design process as "wicked", in the sense that its means and ends are difficult to define with precision, and advocated for "heuristic reasoning":

> "Architectural design problems can also be referred to as being 'wicked problems' in that they have no definitive formulation, no explicit 'stopping rule,' always more than one plausible explanation, a problem formulation that corresponds to a solution and visa versa, and that their solutions cannot be strictly correct or false. Tackling a problem of this type requires some initial insight, the exercise of some provisional set of rules, inference, or plausible strategy, in other words, the use of heuristic reasoning."[7]

Generation of the design scheme, once a product of reasoning, will more and more be informed by these analytical feedback loops from a dashboard of results running in parallel with form creation.

CHALLENGING THE LINEARITY OF DESIGN TO CONSTRUCTION
—

The once linear sequence of design-to-build—schematic design through construction administration—is simultaneously challenged. Where "design" was once the exclusive domain of the architect and engineer, and the constructor awaited the delivery of the "design intent documents" in the form of working drawings, today's integrated model-based processes are characterized by the massive parallel processing of design definition and construction execution. Where once the builder provided "constructability analysis", today he or she is just as likely to

have a parallel "construction discipline" model elaborated in high detail and to provide additional feedback to the design process itself during integrated delivery. [Figure 5] Any given subsystem like a curtainwall, defined generally in the architect's design model, will be connected to the subcontractor's fabrication model, and models will constantly change as one transmits its results to the other. A complex project's design might be born of a web of these digital data sets—models, scripts, analysis runs and scans.

Christopher Alexander suggested an understanding of design as an attempt to resolve an idea as "an intangible form in an indeterminate context".[8] That context becomes multi-dimensional when multiple disciplines contribute to the resolution of "design objectives". The heuristic approach, contemplated by Peter Rowe in the main before computers, has become both more determinant (in that it is now supported by streams of unambiguous information) and significantly more complex. Of course, the design process has always required the designer to manage the resolution of the overall idea at inconsistent levels of abstraction; examples include massing models, plan details, specification sections, even construction submittals. Those levels have become even more disparate in the age of digital design, where highly detailed modeling, parametrics and supporting analyses make the implications of design decisions much more evident. As each component of the evolving design, memorialized in interconnected models under the control of different disciplines, will be integrated, design resolution will in the future depend on managing flows of information and collaborative decision-making.

Design iteration—where an idea is defined, tested, edited and integrated—has become a much more subtle task and requires many more heuristics in this context. A given alternative can hardly anymore be evaluated without its immediate ramifications delivered directly to the originating designer. And yet ideas must be

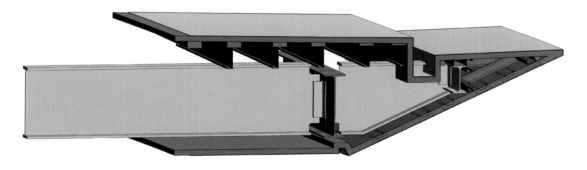

Figure 5. Tocci Building Group, construction model of building canopy.

given a chance to unfold without being immediately affected by computations that explain
every ramification of every decision. A well-
disciplined design process must be created, its
"wickedness" well honored and manipulated, lest
potential solutions collapse under a fusillade of
such information.

INTEGRATING META-DESIGN INTO DESIGN
—

Thus the new workflow processes contemplated
here suggest the creation of a new model for
design itself. While the objectives defined by
Alexander remain the same, the underlying strategies are profoundly different, in what might
best be described as the relationship between
"design" and "meta-design". The architect
remains obligated to resolve the intent of her
or his idea and to represent it to the builder
in a means sufficient for construction. But

Alexander's "indeterminate context" has
become much less so. Information provided
about existing conditions will come in the
form of high-resolution laser scans accurate
to 2mm. Design intent created by the design
disciplines involved will be digital, three-dimensional and behaviorally correct under BIM.
Some of those models will be self-generating,
created by a parametric overlay of scripts,
rules and constraints. Analytical dashboards
will provide instant feedback on key parameters including project costs, sustainability
and even code conformance. [Figure 6] As
delivery methods are increasingly integrated,
the constructor sits at the same table as the
traditional design players, and highly detailed
construction analysis and planning models
operate in parallel with evolving design models,
providing yet another stream of feedback. If
the architect remains responsible for both the

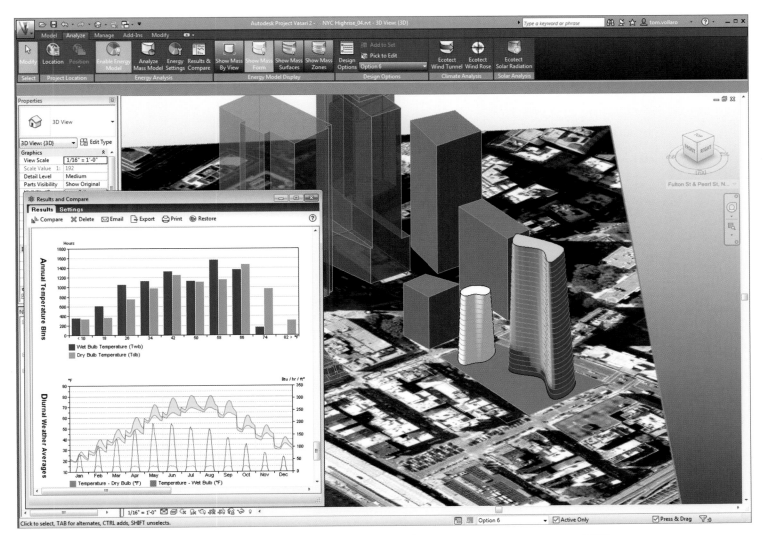

Figure 6. Autodesk Inc., energy dashboard and BIM analysis.

generation of the key design concepts and the proper integration of all of these streams of determinant information, he or she subsequently needs to become responsible for the processes by which they are executed.

While architects have always been responsible for the design of the design process ("meta-design"), those responsibilities have been traditionally classified as "project management" and often considered beneath the status of the architect as design leader. And in the age of construction managers, owners representatives, design-build and partnering— all maneuvers intended to address what Peggy Deamer has called the lingering dysfunctionality of the building industry[9]—architects have been perceived to have distanced themselves even further from these process obligations. There is little doubt that those aspects of current meta-design that are most proximate to creating form, including the use of advanced tools like BIM and parametrics, have become and will remain dear to architects. But there is a danger that the broader process problem, where design is either informed by or bombarded with streams of input from the expanding universe of digital sources, will be ignored to a certain extent in the name of protecting the "purity of the designer's prerogative". Meta-design in this sense is no less than the application of fundamental design principles to the process and organization of creation of intent ("the design") and execution (construction) that puts all the tools, data, expertise and insight available in the service of the final, designed outcome.

From now on, design sensibilities will need to be applied to a wide variety of issues traditionally classified as "Not Design". Data structures and model standards must be created that assure that each discipline involved can see and understand the work of others, and design decision-making must be explicitly structured with the same rationale. Analytical processes must be applied at the moment where they are most useful, rather than when they might prematurely destroy an emerging idea. If parametric models force designers to explicitly create rule sets, scripts and relationships, then it is also true that, unmanaged, these connections release a cascade of unintended consequences that are liable to become incomprehensible. Most important, design must emerge from a collaborative context where the expertise and insight manifest in models but created by humans, can best be organized around the design result. Each of these issues—and the interconnection of them

all into a coherent approach to design—requires a designed approach.

The ability to integrate meta-design into design is critical to the future of the practice of architecture and design itself. This integration must happen right at the intersection of intent and execution so beautifully articulated in Smythson's rose window drawing. At this moment, techniques like digital modeling, analysis and parametrics are artifacts of technological evolution. They shift the design toolkit available to architects and will continue to evolve into methods and techniques that are unknown today. What is clear today is that each, in different ways, has blurred the distinction between ideation of form and the means of producing that form in the final product, the building. Methods like BIM and Integrated Delivery, which operate at the heart of the intent-to-execution gap, have been developed not to support and encourage design but rather to address the well-known inefficiencies of the building industry. Architects must deploy these methods to further the larger objectives of design, by choosing to define design to include the concept of meta-design, or else leave those decisions—and the architectural results—to others far less interested in architecture.

ENDNOTES
—

1. Gerbino, A.; et al. (2009) *Compass and rule: architecture as mathematical practice in England, 1500-1750*, London, Oxford, New Haven, Conn., Yale University Press; in association with the Museum of the History of Science; in association with the Yale Center for British Art.
2. National Research Council (U.S.); Committee on Advancing the Productivity and Competitiveness of the U.S. Construction Industry; Board on Infrastructure and the Constructed Environment (2009) *Advancing the competitiveness and efficiency of the U.S. construction industry*, Washington, D.C., National Academies Press.
3. McGraw Hill Construction Analytics (ed) (2009) *The Business Value of Building Information Modeling*, New York, McGraw Hill.
4. Schumacher, P. (2008) *Parametricism as Style— Parametricist Manifesto*, lecture presented and discussed at the Dark Side Club, 11th Architecture Biennale, Venice 2008, http://www.patrikschumacher.com/Texts/Parametricism%20as%20Style.htm
5. Goulthorpe, M. (2009) Parametric Profligacy, Radical Economy, in Bernstein, P.G.; Deamer, P. (eds) (2010) *Building (In) The Future: Recasting Labor in Architecture*, New Haven, Yale School of Architecture, and New York, Princeton Architectural Press, pp. 44-59.

6. For more information on Horst Rittel see Gänshirt, C.
(2007) *Tools for Ideas. An Introduction to Architectural
Design*, Basel, Birkhäuser, p. 51.
7. Rowe, P. G. (1982) A Priori Knowledge and Heuristic
Reasoning In Architectural Design. *Journal of
Architectural Education*, 36 (1), pp. 18-23.
8. Alexander, C. (1964) *Notes on the synthesis of form*,
Cambridge, Mass.: Harvard University Press.
9. Bernstein, P.G.; Deamer, P. (eds) (2010) *Building (In)
The Future: Recasting Labor in Architecture*, New Haven,
Yale School of Architecture, and New York, Princeton
Architectural Press.

BIM 2.0
—
EDITOR'S NOTES

Phil Bernstein has been one of the most prolific and persuasive advocates for the potential of Building Information Modeling (BIM) and Integrated Project Delivery (IPD), in an attempt to address the divisive organizational structure of the AEC industry. The obvious benefit this provides his firm should not overshadow his deep commitment to progress in industry and the advantages and opportunities this provides for architects. While BIM and IPD, as emerging industry standard workflows, show promise to address procedural problems, Bernstein is encouraging architects to capitalize and expand on this development to address design concerns. Meta-design, for Bernstein, lays out a framework for this to happen with a clear acknowledgement of the various concerns and motivations of architects, builders and owners.

With the growing integration of design, production and project management into a single digital workflow, the distinction between designing the design

and designing the design process becomes less evident. The same digital models used to develop and document the architectural design are full of potential to also design the process of production and management. As one possible version of meta-design presented elsewhere in this book, Marty Doscher describes the workflows developed by Morphosis for their building envelopes, in which the architect's design models, often supplemented with custom scripts, can influence the work of manufacturers and contractors in the interest of design. Doscher refers to this approach as "an execution framework—an organizational logic for building sequences and the primitives for proceeding directly into fabrication and construction".[1] This example demonstrates several important lessons: such an approach need not be comprehensive across an entire project, it may or may not implement standard BIM software, and it can be driven by incentives other than pure efficiency.

The separation that has evolved between design and building execution has created two offsetting conditions for architects: first, it has created a mythology of insight that preserves the status of the architect as an executive-level arbiter among a large and diverse team of collaborators in an often chaotic process. Second, it has removed this insight so far from the knowledge base of building that architectural design risks becoming optional rather than necessary. As design information becomes more virtual and the exchange between insight and knowledge becomes more intertwined with the means of execution and production, it becomes more difficult for architecture to remain separated from building and simultaneously preserve its own status. The source of this mythology of insight might partly lie in the elusive aspects of architectural design in relation to the definitive nature of buildings. Even with the expansive sets of analytical data and simulation processes available today,

which as Bernstein notes, make design decisions more evident, arbitrary choices are still part of the process. Buildings are never entirely the result of unambiguous and rational decisions. And while integrated digital workflows undoubtedly facilitate more systematic decision-making, they need not be a reductive constraint to what is fundamentally an open, creative process.

To cite one example, Reiser Umemoto rely heavily on the representational capabilities of digital tools yet have a healthy skepticism with regard to scripting or performance optimization as tools to generate design. In fact, they go to great lengths to set up conditions for maximum expressive freedom in an attempt to avoid the aesthetics of a one-to-one correlation with computational techniques. They do this, interestingly enough, by engaging in the quantitative phases of the design workflow in order to assure design flexibility to pursue qualitative effects.[2] In their

014 project, they worked with the structural engineer to design the exterior shell not to be structurally optimized, but rather to be slightly "over-engineered" so as to allow for design flexibility without affecting the integrity of the structure. While the tendency of a purely efficient workflow would have led to a structurally optimized design, the specific input of the architect redirected the workflow. One could argue that they applied a "design sensibility," as Bernstein puts it, to the development of the project constraints, in the interest of qualitative design options outside of the design space defined by pure efficiency.

This relationship between the systemization associated with digitally integrated workflows on the one hand and architects' desire for flexiblity in design processes on the other is just one of the challenges in the design of a "meta-design". Does a digitally integrated meta-design in architecture tend towards technologically determined results? For instance,

BIM has the ability to create highly integrated building descriptions that are part of a very thoughtful *process design*, but the resulting *building design* might be generic and uninspired. Bernstein acknowledges that BIM and IPD were not developed to encourage innovative design, but rather to address procedural inefficiencies. The ambition to use them to form a comprehensive integrated workflow puts architectural design in a new relationship to industry that can be a threat or an opportunity. How this turns out will depend on how design workflows are integrated with industry workflows—this is Bernstein's challenge to architects.

—

1. See "Disposable Code; Persistent Design" by Marty Doscher in this volume.
2. See "The Scent of the System" by Jesse Reiser and Nanako Umemoto in this volume.

DIAGRAMS, DESIGN MODELS AND MOTHER MODELS

BEN VAN BERKEL

Ben van Berkel is a Founding Partner of UNStudio and is Professor of Conceptual Design and Head of the Architecture Department at the Stäedelschule in Frankfurt am Main.

Ben van Berkel was interviewed by Scott Marble.

Scott Marble: The work of UNStudio holds a unique position in the evolution of digital processes in architecture from the early 1990's, when you were exploring how topological diagrams could drive complex program and formal relationships through early software programs, to your most recent work that now incorporates the most advanced techniques of optimization to realize large urban projects. While it is almost passé to focus so much on digital processes today, it is undeniable that these processes are deeply embedded in how architects work, so how has your thinking evolved regarding computation in architecture?

Ben van Berkel: A few years ago, Caroline [Bos] and I produced a book called *Design Models*[2] that looked critically at the advantages and disadvantages of the digital as it related to the production of architecture. In this book, we emphasized the importance of guiding the digital—of working with prototypes and other driving ideas to be able to filter the information provided by digital processes. After working with parametric and other computational techniques for many years and through the many teaching positions that I have had, I have discovered that it is still necessary, even essential, to maintain a critical mind towards what the computer can do. It is a powerful tool that has

created questionable trends. Like other trends within a discipline that become very fashionable—like the use of silkscreens in art during the 1950's and 1960's for example—you have to be careful not to lose the real advantages of what a tool can do. In the case of Pop Art, silkscreens as a tool generated the possibility to produce art works at great speed, as we know from the works of Warhol, Rauschenberg and Hamilton. Suddenly a series of portraits could be produced in just a few hours. So this new technique generated new insight into how one could produce art, and art with new effects. The same can be said of the computer; it similarly generates new advantages, but we need to remain mindful of what these advantages are. I have always been very supportive of digital design techniques and the virtual, even to the point that in the 1990's I suggested that the invention of the computer in architecture was almost as important as the invention of concrete in architecture had been. But I didn't go further than that.

SM: Scripting and other generative approaches using computation for design output are becoming increasingly common, at least in the more progressive offices this seems to be the case. When broad design intent is quantified into a process of inputs and outputs, is this always a reductive process or can it be used as an exploratory model? In other words, is "digitizing" design intent always reductive?

BvB: I don't believe that the principles you work with when you design design necessarily reduce information. Our office utilizes programming for many projects and this includes creating new kinds of scripts to combine multiple programs. We have always worked with multiple programs, but now we have skilled people in the office, including programmers with links to Google, who are far more advanced in combining programs, so we are not limited to working with single programs like Grasshopper or other stand-alone applications. So in this respect, designing design refers more to expanding intent rather than reducing intent. What is also interesting about new computational techniques like scripting and parametric modeling is the potential to more holistically explore the relational and inclusive aspects of architectural design. Vast amounts of interrelated information become far more manageable, so while it might be seen as reducing information, the more fascinating aspect for me is that it can adapt large amounts of complex questions into unexpected relational answers, which is more of a design exploration. However, you still might find that the output from a model is as complex and unresolved as the input given to the computer—you might incorporate information

about the site, the infrastructure, the programmatic issues or the construction factors, and then discover that your model is not producing useful results. This brings me back to my point that, despite all of the technical dexterity and expertise, you still have to introduce a design model—you have to give direction to the design system. You need to have a theoretical framework to guide and direct the information. You might not necessarily use all of the information but what is interesting about the concept of designing design is that you can combine and hybridize information as part of a design process. [Figure 1]

Imagine a modernist process diagram before computers: on the left hand side is the aesthetic quality of architecture, including aspects of psychological behavior and visual impact, and on the right hand side is the functionality or utility of architecture and both are connected by a line. Today, that diagram can be stretched so far that the two ends of the line can become a circle, making it very difficult to see where the aesthetic and utility aspects of a project begin and end. And if you

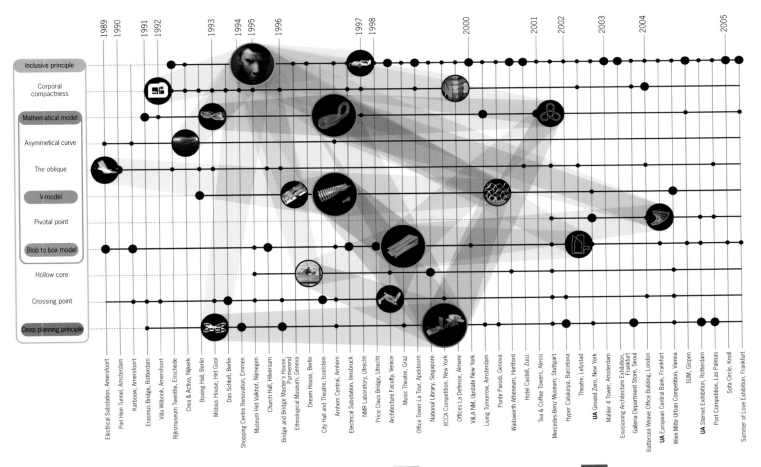

Figure 1. Overview of UNStudio design processes and evolution of the different design models, showing when and on what projects they were used. Although often derived from mathematical concepts, design models are interpreted through the conditions of a specific project and give theoretical direction to the more technical design systems.

give a twist to that circle, like the diagram of the Möbius House [Figures 2, 3], you can develop a design model, which I have discovered can guide design information much further than the modernist mechanical linear model that we worked with previously. By combining a theoretical framework through a design model with the processing capability of the computer, you can filter information in a particular way that is far more relational.

SM: How would you position design models in the context of your earlier work on the diagram—are design models the new diagram or is this a completely different concept? You described the condition today, where information has to be managed and set up in relational structure in order to act on it, but then you

made it clear that this in itself is not enough. You have to have something to drive the information. In most of your work, both past and recent, the power of the diagram is still very present: the Mercedes-Benz Museum is arguably your most complex interpretation of a design model into architecture. What is your current thinking on the diagram and its role in this context of massive amounts of information that influence design today? Can the diagram still drive design information in the same way that it did ten or fifteen years ago?

BvB: No. That is clear. In our earlier work like the Möbius House, we instrumentalized the diagram in a far more primitive manner. We did not literally translate the Möbius diagram into the Möbius House but rather employed it

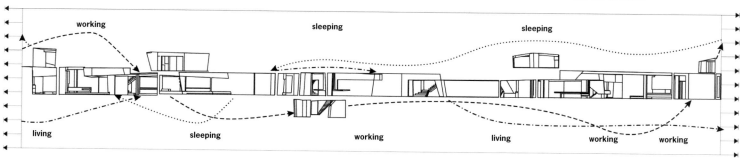

Figure 2 (top). UNStudio's Möbius House in Amsterdam. This project was a precursor to the use of computation to filter and manage relational design information.

Figure 3 (bottom). Möbius House. The unfolded drawing describes how the Möbius strip is interpreted as a diagram that organizes light, space, materials, time, movement and patterns of living into the geometry of the house. The generation and use of

diagrams anticipated many of the computational ideas found in later work.

in a particular way with a lot of architectural imagination. For example, the concept of the Möbius House was driven by three geometric angles, seven, nine, and eleven degrees, which were then repeated, much like a mathematical model, in a serial manner throughout the house to transform the diagram into spaces for living. [Figure 4] Although it was far more primitive in this earlier work, the generation of diagrams anticipated a lot of computational ideas found in our more recent work. The diagram notions of repetition, translation, rotation, etc. evolved naturally into computational processes and encompassed particular kinds of experiences of directionality and complexity that have matured in our more recent work.

Later, we discovered that in higher-level, more abstract processing of complex information, you could no longer use the diagram in such a simple way, which is when the diagram was extended to the idea of the design model. The design model could still operate like a diagram, but as a model, its particular geometric and organizational principles could be utilized across many projects and at several different scales of a project.

"Design models are well known in the fields of computer programming and engineering, where their meanings consists of a document containing a set of requirements and goals, formulated with the aim of reducing the range of options for implementation. Architects often begin with a concept sketch and work in a linear fashion with frequent interruptions, as design often goes in repeating cycles. These interruptions are experienced as setbacks and there is no way to value the alternations of the repetitive design process because the designer has not articulated pre-formed objectives, and only has the original concept sketch to fall back on. So we have to ask ourselves, how can the potential danger or benefit of any proposed changes be evaluated on the basis of this vision? We see design models as packages of organizational or compositional principles, supplemented by constructional parameters, which act as a more sustainable and reusable guide to architectural projects. The design model does not include site-specific information but rather exists at a more abstract level and may be implemented in various situations and projects. It is formulated in such a way that it becomes an internal point of reference that can be used for the duration of the process to help check if the design is progressing according to your principles and purposes."[3]

BvB: With design models, it became possible to identify and work with the proper scale of the project by combining and proportioning information that is relevant to the scale at which the information applies. Currently, I am

Figure 4. UNStudio's Graz Music Theater. Rethinking the disciplines of geometry, building processes and other realities of construction through a renewed design imagination has to drive digital processes.

very interested in the idea of how to proportion information to guide design. Where before we proportioned "mass", we now proportion "information" in the architecture, but we have to know where, what and how much value to give to the information, based on the parameters we are working with. In a way it is strange to call it proportioning of information because we used to proportion geometry and forms, but these can be combined with information. Indeed, information can now inform the geometry, it can inform the form.

SM: Imagination has been part of your work for a very long time. What do you see as the relationship between imagination and computation? While they could be seen as opposites in that one is qualitative and the other quantitative, it is also true that for developments at high levels of computation through fields like artificial intelligence, the brain has regularly been used as a model. There is a very interesting reciprocal

relationship between human imagination and rational computation. What are your thoughts on this relationship relative to the design process?

BvB: I often have long discussions with my friend, Robert van Lier, from the Donders Institute for Brain, Cognition and Behaviour in Nijmegen on this topic. What I have discovered in these conversations in relation to our design process is that all of my intuitions related to the development of the Möbius House—repetition, the ways you could start to play with double images, the suggestiveness of the figurative versus the abstract—were not learned through the use of the computer but rather by trying to intuitively articulate new forms of spatial aesthetics. And that is only possible by using your imagination and experience to formulate a vision of something and always be ahead of the computer. If digital techniques become more important than the thinking process, a bizarre condition develops where just because

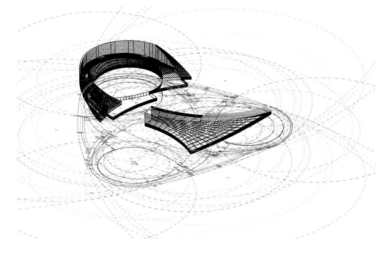

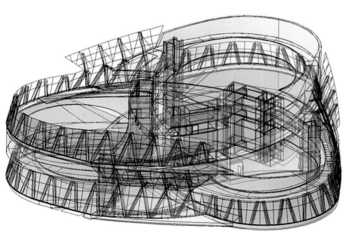

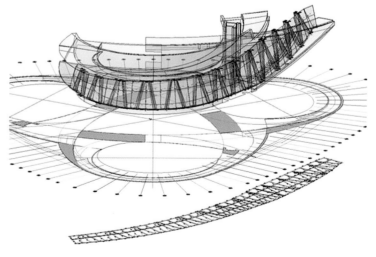

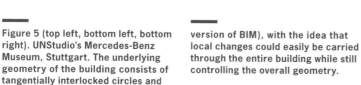

Figure 5 (top left, bottom left, bottom right). UNStudio's Mercedes-Benz Museum, Stuttgart. The underlying geometry of the building consists of tangentially interlocked circles and arcs. This system was programmed into the mother model (an early version of BIM), with the idea that local changes could easily be carried through the entire building while still controlling the overall geometry.

Figure 6 (top right). Model showing a section of the Mercedes-Benz Museum. Regularly stepping out of a digital workflow serves as a reminder to distinguish between information used to design and information used to manage.

something can be modeled on the computer, it can get built, which is what is now happening around the world. While we know that it is possible to attain highly diverse architecture with computational design, we have lost sight of how important it is to keep thinking. We need to stimulate our imagination and renew architecture through the rethinking of the disciplines of geometry, building, how you work with infrastructure and other realities of construction. [Figure 4]

SM: This is a perfect segue into the relationship between "Designing Design" and "Designing Industry", because the design model for you seems to serve the purpose of bridging the gap between more abstract thinking and more concrete realities. You also speak of "mother model", primarily in reference to the construction of the Mercedes-Benz Museum. Is the design model and the mother model the same? Or is the mother model a more specific version

of a design model? How do you see those two models relating?

BvB: The mother model is a further extension of the design model. The design model encompasses the theoretical or mathematical principles of a project, and then the mother model is the actual 3D model that is constantly in flux and being changed as the project develops. It is adaptable and linked to all of the consultants and team members working on the project. We have discovered over the last few years that the mother model can control quick digital exchange and better manage and integrate all of the information of the design team. In one day, you can exchange information with dozens of specialty consultants and have updated information back the next day in the same model. This was a very new process in 2004 when we were working on the Mercedes-Benz Museum and brought the first programmers into our office. We didn't even have BIM software at that

Figure 7. Mercedes-Benz Museum.
Sixteen months into construction.

time, so we had to set up these early mother models ourselves and only later started to use BIM. This initiated our interest in the possibility that today, the architect can actually develop new concepts of control through techniques that originated with the mother model. [Figures 5, 6, 7]

We are also still fascinated with how the diagram can play a role today. When we wrote *Move*[4] we described three phases of design, starting with *imagination*—without the imagination you are nowhere. Then there are *techniques* that guide you through the information related to a project. Now we are more in the third phase where we are testing out the *effects* that a building can generate. I am more fascinated with making a building that can actually have four or five different readings and how computation can play a role. It is almost like reverse engineering—we reverse-engineer much more than we project-engineer. Reverse engineering is how one can learn from building techniques back towards design. From the history of cultural production we have learned that knowledge is generated through the mind's eye. Therefore, the more you produce in architecture, the more knowledge you gain from it and you can enrich and refine that knowledge and apply it back to design. I think there are many aspects in the production of buildings that can inform the intellectual ambitions of architecture.

SM: The use of Building Information Modeling is becoming increasingly popular right now and likely will become the new industry standard workflow. With this in mind, an important question is whether BIM is simply a management tool or if it has the potential to be a design tool? The way in which you described the mother model is partly as a control mechanism that allows you to manage the complexities of materials, schedules, budgets and other project constraints in the context of a construction site, not in the context of a design process. Can BIM, currently understood as a tool to manage information, be creative enough to sustain an architect's interest?

BvB: Yes and no. The aesthetic-functionalist model that we described before, where the concerns of quality are distinct from the concerns of utility in modernism yet intertwined in the contemporary digital context, can also be used to describe how architects have to think today. The architect has to know when to switch on and off the values related to either the aesthetic or to the efficiency of a project. One needs to develop new forms of concepts of control when working with contemporary building and design techniques, because we need to know where to stop when a design technique is becoming either too pragmatic or not pragmatic enough. I believe that when one talks about design in the future it will be much more integrated with all phases of a building project and you will have

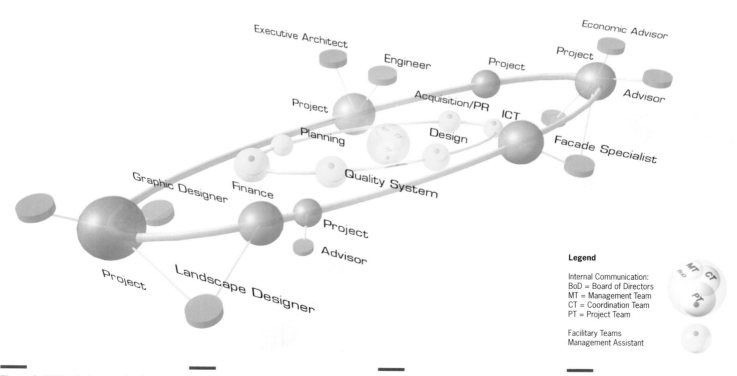

Legend

Internal Communication:
BoD = Board of Directors
MT = Management Team
CT = Coordination Team
PT = Project Team

Facilitary Teams
Management Assistant

Figure 8. UNStudio is organized as a network practice wtih several teams and specialist platforms.

to know and distinguish between managing design and designing design. This condition is complicated and not well defined today because anything seems possible with regard to digital processes from both the design and construction side, and the results can be so seductive that it needs discipline to know how and when to separate information used to design from information used to manage. For that reason, it is very important to regularly step out of the digital workflow and work with physical models, sketches and other kinds of analog techniques. We must not lose touch with those aspects of design that cannot be formulated into a digital workflow. The management of information is something else, which has to do with the way you network, distribute and then bring information back together.

SM: But is the management of information a design issue?

BvB: It is. But I'm trying to argue that design can no longer be defined as a linear process, even though this is still common today, but instead, has to be understood as a much more complex process. Let me describe another diagram: if you draw a line from the left to the right that represents your design process, you can draw a lot of arrows that go backwards and forwards on that line, sometimes with a big loop and sometimes with a small loop. You can even

bend the line into a circle again and have the line overlap back and forth within the circle. This diagram can start to represent the amount and type of information that goes into designing a project, but it also shows the organization and relationship of that information. Therefore, it is not so easy to describe where management is design and where design is design. I think young architects will have to learn how to deal with this and not conflate the two. I think addressing this in a very direct way will need to become part of the future of architectural education; issues like managing design, managing information and programming are not very popular in design schools today. However, as an architect you can bring a hierarchy to the distribution of the finances and the business model of a project that includes design. It is important to talk about business design and what is attainable for architects in this context. It is only by understanding the underlying financial issues supporting a project, issues which might not directly relate to the architectural design, that you can begin to design the conditions of a project to achieve creative and magnificent results. [Figure 8]

SM: Do you think that new digital tools have a role to play in this ability for architects to better understand and impact the business structure of a project? With the lessons learned from the Mercedes-Benz project, where you introduced

Figure 9 (above left). The façade of UNStudio's Star Place in Kaohsiung was generated by the step-by-step rotation of the vertical fins. This was tested digitally through several iterations.

Figure 10 (above right). Graz Music Theater. Modeling of all geometry made it possible to control the design digitally in addition to providing precise data for concrete formwork and other construction processes.

an integrated mother model that required buy-in by all parties involved with the project, do you now begin new projects by taking the lead on how to organize the team and the workflow?

BvB: Yes. This is a question that nobody ever asks me, but it is exactly what I mean about business design, and is related to what you are calling designing industry. When we begin a project with a new client, I will request responsibility for some of the management tasks and explain how we can do this, in a far more advanced manner, through digital exchange. These tasks include selecting the team of specialists with the client and then controlling the distribution of information to all of these specialists (which normally is what management offices do). We will request part of the management fee and then add four or five people to the team, who are only doing the digital exchange between all of these different specialists. When a project moves to construction, we are also able to play a more central role. Because we have so much 3D information in the model, contractors will often come to us and request detailed production drawings. They often ask us to produce the fabrication drawings from our 3D model, for which we get an additional fee. We have now developed this capability that gives us more control to maintain the design throughout the construction process. There is no additional liability because after the contractor takes the 3D model, they confirm that all of the drawings produced from the model are correct and then assume responsibility. This is a very new way of working and although there are many obstacles at the moment, architects have to take a more

proactive position to overcome these—it's a matter of how you handle the process.

After the Mercedes-Benz Museum was completed, we applied similar processes to those utilized on that project to several others including the Star Place in Kaohsiung, Taiwan [Figure 9], the Music Theater in Graz, Austria [Figure 10] and Arnhem Central Station in the Netherlands. But the most advanced and developed process for us to date is on the Raffles City project in Hangzhou, China. This is a 400,000sqm mixed-use development with retail, offices, serviced apartments and hotel facilities, and it is so complex and moving so fast that we have an in-house team of over twenty people, including many programmers, working to design and manage the process. We are incorporating more sophisticated digital design techniques, including geometry optimization, to integrate the design goals of the design model with the constructability goals of the mother model, which is continuing to raise the bar for architecture.

ENDNOTES
—

1. Interview of June 2, 2010.
2. van Berkel, B.; Bos, C. (2006) *UNStudio: Design Models—Architecture, Urbanism, Infrastructure*, New York, Rizzoli.
3. Ibid. pp. 17-19.
4. van Berkel, B. (1999) *Move*, Amsterdam, Goose Press.

RAFFLES CITY
WORKFLOW CASE STUDY ▶

UNStudio's mixed-use Raffles City development is located near the Qiantang River in Hangzhou, the capital of Zhejiang province, located 180km southwest of Shanghai. The project incorporates retail, offices, housing and hotel facilities and marks the site of a cultural landscape within the Quianjiang New Town Area. The twisted geometry of the towers is derived from a design concept to integrate the mixed-use program with the urban and landscape conditions of the site. This formal gesture introduces a complex geometry on the façade that gets resolved through custom scripts that negotiate the unique requirements of each program type with environmentally responsive building components, efficient use of materials, manufacturing constraints and overall constructability. This is latest of several UNStudio projects that use parametric transformational design techniques to integrate formal, programmatic and performance design concepts.

Views

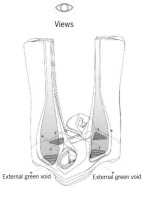

External green void   External green void

✕

Green connection

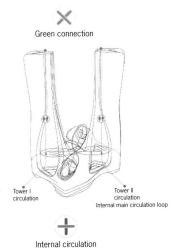

Tower I circulation   Tower II circulation
Internal main circulation loop

✚

Internal circulation

Workflow 1 (above left).
Initial design rendering.

Workflow 2 (above right).
Design principles for the orientation of the towers, based
on views, green connection
and internal circulation.

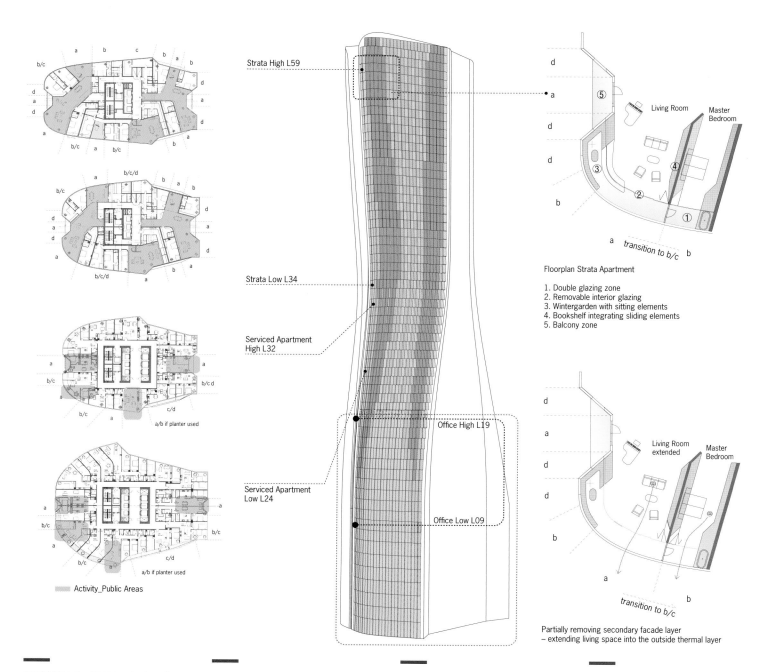

Strata High L59

d

⑤

Living Room   Master
              Bedroom

d

③

④

b   ②

              ①

a   transition to b/c   b

Floorplan Strata Apartment

1. Double glazing zone
2. Removable interior glazing
3. Wintergarden with sitting elements
4. Bookshelf integrating sliding elements
5. Balcony zone

Strata Low L34

Serviced Apartment
High L32

Office High L19

Serviced Apartment
Low L24

Office Low L09

d

a

d

d

Living Room
extended   Master
           Bedroom

b

a   b

transition to b/c

Partially removing secondary facade layer
– extending living space into the outside thermal layer

Activity_Public Areas

a/b if planter used

a/b if planter used

Workflow 3. Early study of
double façade system for strata
apartments throughout the
various levels of the tower.

[A] ■ **Urban Facade**
[B] ░ **Landscape Facade**

Facade total surface: ~ 39,600 SqM [100%]
Urban facade surface: ~ 28, 200 SqM [71%]
Landscape facade surf: ~ 11,400 SqM [29%]

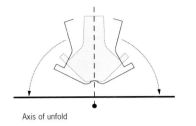

Axis of unfold

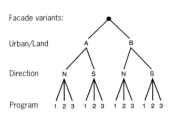

Facade variants:

Urban/Land

Direction

Program

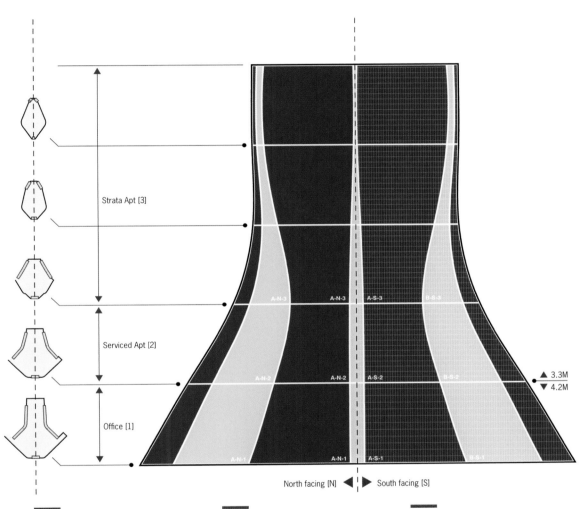

Strata Apt [3]

Serviced Apt [2]

Office [1]

▲ 3.3M
▼ 4.2M

North facing [N] ◀ ▶ South facing [S]

Workflow 4. Initial study of
shading components related to
program.

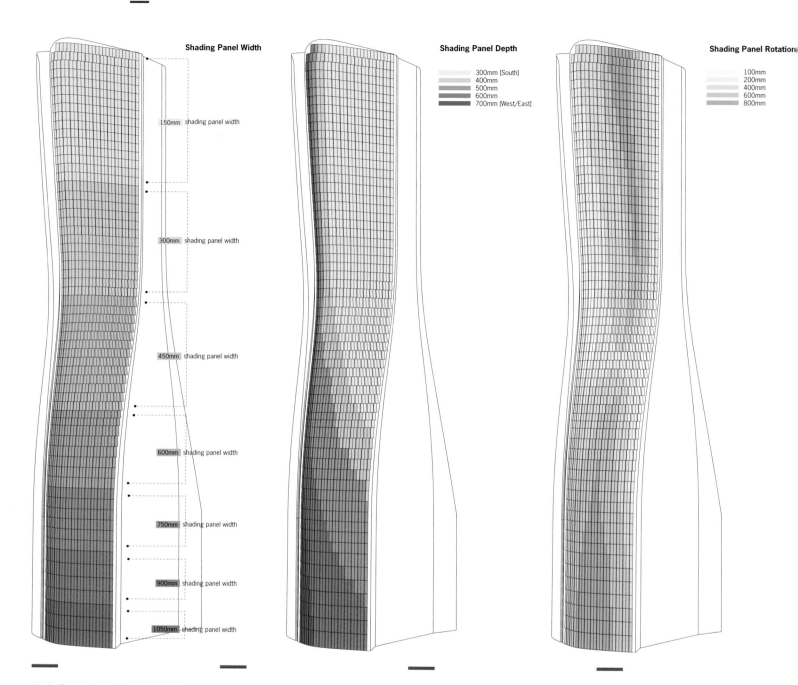

Shading Panel Width

150mm shading panel width

300mm shading panel width

450mm shading panel width

600mm shading panel width

750mm shading panel width

900mm shading panel width

1050mm shading panel width

Shading Panel Depth

300mm [South]
400mm
500mm
600mm
700mm [West/East]

Shading Panel Rotation

100mm
200mm
400mm
600mm
800mm

Workflow 5. The optimization
of differently sized glass
panes and shading panels was
based on varying width, depth
and rotation.

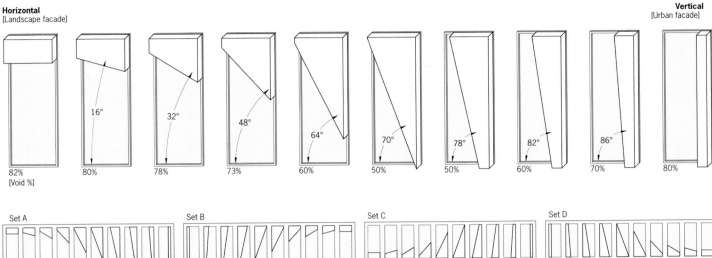

Horizontal
[Landscape facade]

Vertical
[Urban facade]

16°   32°   48°   64°   70°   78°   82°   86°

82%   80%   78%   73%   60%   50%   50%   60%   70%   80%
[Void %]

Set A   Set B   Set C   Set D

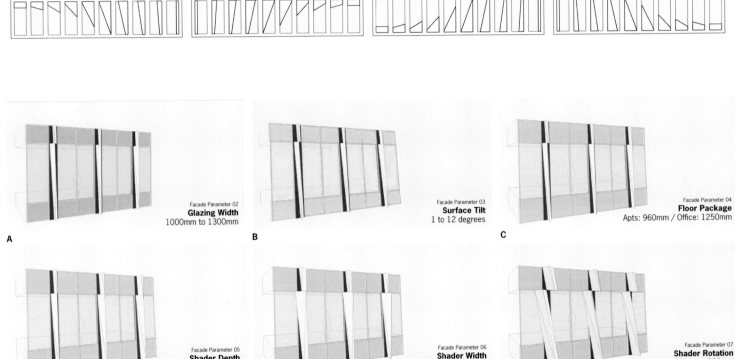

A

Facade Parameter 02
Glazing Width
1000mm to 1300mm

B

Facade Parameter 03
Surface Tilt
1 to 12 degrees

C

Facade Parameter 04
Floor Package
Apts: 960mm / Office: 1250mm

D

Facade Parameter 05
Shader Depth
300mm to 600mm

E

Facade Parameter 06
Shader Width
200mm to 500mm

F

Facade Parameter 07
Shader Rotation
-200mm to 600mm

Workflow 6 (top). Initial study of shading components related to program.

Workflow 7 (bottom). The overall parameters, influencing the façade design along with the minimum and maximum range of adjustability. Working together within a single system, these parameters could satisfy all of the geometric conditions of the façade design and also provide output information for fabrication.

A. Parameters: Glazing Width. This allowed the panels to change width within a range from 1000mm to 1300mm.

B. Parameters: Surface Tilt. This allowed the panels to tilt off the vertical axis within the range from 1° to 12°.

C. Parameters: Floor Package Height. This allowed the panels to be assigned a floor depth based on the program of apartments or offices.

D. Parameters: Shader Depth. This allowed the depth of the shading component to adjust within the range from 300mm to 600mm.

E. Parameters: Shader Width. This allowed the width of the shading component to adjust within the range from 200mm to 500mm.

F. Parameters: Shader Rotation. This allowed the shading components to rotate within the range from 200mm to 600mm.

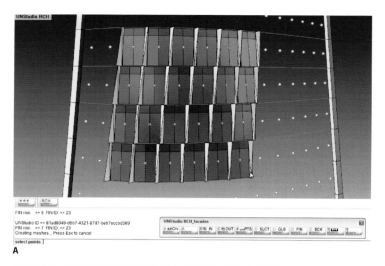

A

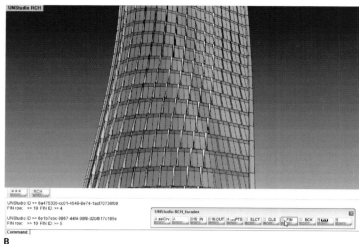

B

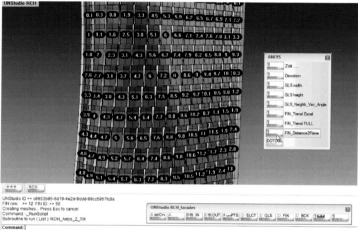

C

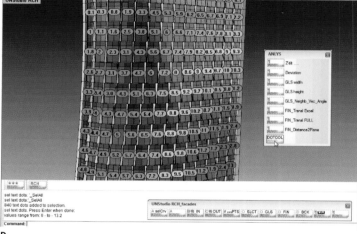

D

Workflow 8a (top left). Custom tools generate insert points along control lines that define the building geometry. These points are linked to an Excel file containing the parametric definition of the façade parts. In the script, different heights, widths and angles are optimized to minimize the number of different glass panels while maintaining the overall design geometry.

Workflow 8b (top right). These façade parts can then be arrayed along this line, adjusting to the curvature of the controlling geometry.

Workflow 8c (bottom left). Once arrayed, the façade parts can provide output data describing the geometry of each part for production, amount of material and other information as defined in the script.

Workflow 8d (bottom right). The script also contains an evaluation tool that identifies when the parts extend beyond the allowable range of variation that has been defined in the parameter setup (those shown in red). This allows the design team to adjust the driving geometry

until all parts fall into allowable ranges.

Workflow 9 (right). Elevation rendering of design model.

邻近地标
最大高度 300 米
Neighbouring landmark
max height 300 m

250 m

250 m

51 m

31 m
裙房 plinth

0.0 m
地面 ground

NETWORK STRATEGIES
—
EDITOR'S NOTES

Since it began as a small firm in 1988, UNStudio has positioned itself as a network practice committed to new forms of collaboration with diverse project teams, quietly evolving into a multi-disciplinary global network. They have aggressively expanded their services by leveraging the value of design to address a broad range of problems related to standard industry practices. Much of this expertise has been built up by exploring new design processes and project delivery approaches. They approach the organization of each project as a design issue and digital workflows have been instrumental in this effort.

UNStudio has been an innovator in the evolution of digital design in architecture and over the course of their career have developed a unique workflow through the use of diagrams, design models and mother models that has progressively expanded in its capacity to respond to the demands of their larger and more complex work. Their breakthrough project,

the Mercedes-Benz Museum in Stuttgart, stands as a benchmark in the use of a digital workflow. Bringing together the generative design potential of the diagram with a parametric design system, the digital workflow serves to elaborate complex formal and programmatic relationships in 3D with a mother model (their version of BIM) to manage site and construction logistics. The appeal of the diagram as a design technique, used in many of UNStudio's early projects, has been its ability to simultaneously guide design choices and remain open to interpretation—to be specific in its formal logic but flexible in its application.[1] The trefoil used for the Mercedes-Benz Museum served as the transition from a pre-digital use of the diagram, where it was initially used as an organization concept to quickly explore spatial and programmatic iterations, to its later use for defining specific geometric rules for a parametric model.

This work occurred prior to the common use of BIM software in architecture offices, and the level of sophistication required led to one of their many collaborations with specialty consultants. Arnold Walz, an expert in parametric modeling, developed custom scripts based on the geometric rules of the trefoil, capturing the interdependent 3D relationships of the design of the building element in a model.[2] This developed into the mother model, which was used not only to refine the design but also to maintain the intricate formal relationships during construction: the geometry of downstream work was parametrically adjusted to site conditions. Some of the more complex geometry that resulted from this model was extracted as the basis for CNC manufacturing of double-curved concrete formwork. This allowed the concrete to be poured with a high level of precision that was required for surface continuity at the critical zones where floors transition to walls. Without this level of control on a building of this complexity,

the cumulative effect of slight dimensional variations would have resulted in misalignments and critical compromises to the design.

The ongoing refinement of these workflows has given UNStudio the knowledge base to redefine their role in subsequent projects. The information embedded in the prototype mother model for the Mercedes-Benz Museum became the seed for new levels of organizational development for their practice. In-house research platforms support this effort: the Architectural Sustainability Platform, the Innovative Organizations Platform, the Smart Parameter Platform and the Inventive Materials Platform. The Smart Parameters Platform is focused specifically on the integration of computational tools into design processes and the development of workflows to streamline the exchange of digital information between all research platforms and the overall studio operation, also including outside design and fabrication specialists.

Designing industry depends on proactive strategies of this kind. Architects are in a unique position to leverage the digital information that they developed as designers of buildings in order to also become designers of building processes. As van Berkel notes, much of the information needed for fabrication and construction processes are already in the models. One of the future challenges for architects is developing the workflows to access this information.

—

1. See van Berkel, B.; Bos, C. (1998) Diagrams—Interactive Instruments in Operation, in *Any 23, Diagram Work: Data Mechanics for a Topological Age*, New York, Anyone Corporation.
2. Interestingly, this work was done entirely in Mechanical Desktop, a software developed primarily for mechanical engineers but with an open API that allowed sufficient programming flexibility. Walz later formed designtoproduction with Fabian Scheurer and also collaborated to generate fabrication files for the formwork for the double-curved concrete surfaces.

DESIGNING
ASSEMBLY

DESIGNING ASSEMBLY: HOW TOOLS SHAPE MATERIALS THAT CONSTITUTE SPACE

FRANK BARKOW & REGINE LEIBINGER

Frank Barkow and Regine Leibinger are Partners at Barkow Leibinger Architects.

The phrase "Revolutions of Choice" signifies architectural opportunity as driven by the rise of digital capabilities and competences, but it also means something more essential: an architect's longing for the agility, authority and ability to predict and control the very nature of architectural making that is arising from our imagination. How can we better mediate between the tools we use and how might they inform an architectural outcome? Perhaps symptomatic of our restless generation is an oscillation between practice, research and the academic studio. In doing so an experimental thread unites these areas of endeavor, further mediating between the speculative and practical, emphasizing discovery that can be measured, judged and eventually made useful. Starting with critical resistance to the status quo of the building cultures we find ourselves in, the following case studies speak more accurately to the profundity of ideation and handling of materials as one mutually intertwined activity.

Design follows technology. Identifying and harnessing new technologies, coupled with curiosity and imagination, reinvigorates a process of making and invention. This orientation empowers architects to become our own best experts in assessing technology and developing innovative applications to achieve design goals. It also challenges the standard approach of relying on manufacturer's products from building catalogs and, instead, establishes a process where architectural elements can be developed within the practice. This is an inclusive and comprehensive expertise, which intersects

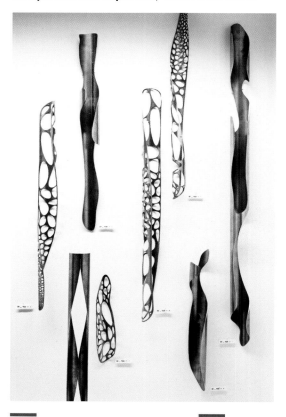

Figure 1. An inventory of design techniques (off-cuts) is derived from exploring the capability of a CNC tooling action to manipulate specific materials. These examples were produced from a revolving laser cutter.

design with sustainability, economics, materiality and time-management, in a way that we are
in a position for best determining an outcome.

Our practice has been transformed significantly in the last fifteen years. Digital and
analog processes have been integrated through
all project phases, from initial speculative
experimental research to conclusive building
projects. Designing assembly, as a material
issue, is the most characteristic aspect of this
shift. Developing an understanding of how tools
shape materials that constitute surfaces, form
and space marks a production path and workflow that reverses how we previously worked
at the outset of our practice. Our competence
in digital technology has evolved from being
initially and exclusively limited to its use as a
drawing tool, to its now expanded role where the
digital is a guidance system for tooling materials.
Locating an expansive network of fabrication
partners, tools and testing sites has been
essential to supporting this research. Much of
our recent work has been supported by access
to emerging technologies outside of traditional
architectural boundaries, such as the automobile and machine tool industries, to cite two
current examples.

Three focus areas locate how the workflow,
that links initial research to final realization of
a building, develops and evolves in a research-
based practice.

OFF-CUTS
—

We start by setting up a research area of
experimental prototyping that is specific to a
material and a digitally controlled tooling technique. This initial step tests materials against a

machine to develop a range of possibilities for
transforming the material independent from a
particular utility, purpose or economic constraint. This produces a body of work or archive
that is architecturally latent, scale-less (other
than its own physical size) and open-ended as to
how it might be applied. [Figure 1] The archive
is constantly being added to or edited if a better
method is discovered along the way. Material is
tectonically transformed by a tooling action
(bending, cutting, stacking, casting, etc.) and
typically involves a serial logic of repetition
and differentiation, allowing individual material
components to aggregate and join to form
larger and more complex assemblies. Tools are
understood and explored precisely in terms of
their capabilities and limitations to transform a
material. [Figures 2a, 2b]

Often this work begins with student interns
who are asked to investigate a particular CNC
or digital machine and learn its capacities,
including what type of action it is capable of
and on what materials, the speed of production
and economic consequences. After gaining this
knowledge, we begin to speculate and design
work-pieces or *off-cuts* that test the limits of the
machine. In other words, there is a quest for an
architectural prototype that emerges from the
control and the constraints of a technical system. These *off-cuts* are cataloged in inter-office
manuals, our website and more formal catalogs
such as the *Atlas of Fabrication*,[1] available to all
designers throughout the practice.

Scripting tools offer another degree of digital exploration and control. Initially applied to
generate abstract patterns incorporating both
repetition and differentiation, these are now
used to solve complex geometric construction

Figure 2a (above left). In the off-cuts,
materials are tested against machining abilities and limits to explore the
consequences of the digital techniques and processes, such as speed
of production, economic feasibility
and material durability.

Figure 2b (above right). By working
directly with the machine manufacturers and operators, a thorough
understanding of production logics
allows us to design beyond the limits
of standard building components.

problems. This knowledge, often brought to the practice by student interns, flattens an inter-practice hierarchy where student architects take lead roles on project development that in the past they would merely support. This is an essential part of the academic studios that we teach within the context of the practice. These internships, with accessibility to technology and professional consulting, make for compelling supplements to traditional academic training, where academic work (far removed from practice and industry) is complemented by architectural apprenticeships. Now the realities of ideation and production can exist as simultaneous and overlapping activities.

The identification of fabrication partners offers direct access to a range of industrial machines to conduct research. [Figure 3] One of our initial partners, Trumpf GmbH is a leading machine-tool manufacturer in Stuttgart, Germany, who introduced lasers to the cutting of sheet metal in the 1970's. Their large and expanding line of machines helped set up our initial archive of off-cuts. While architectural applications of Trumpf machines is a minor portion of their market, the possibilities are enormous and this relatively new initiative is well under way. Another significant partner is Holzbau Amann, a fabricator more directly involved in construction, who has the capacity to digitally cut laminated structural timber and assemble these components on site, a process which was utilized for our Cantina project (see workflow case study at end of article).

In order to maintain this research area as a vital source for architectural applications,

it requires an initial autonomy within the practice. This autonomy enables an experimental approach where success (or failure) is independent from ongoing project deadlines, budgets, codes or other forms of restraint that would hinder a more inquisitive approach. This autonomy is especially critical in the context of highly regulated and controlled building cultures, as is the case in Germany. The autonomy is achieved, in our practice, by a rotating team of student interns and architects, designated to work on research projects as they develop. Research also takes place in an academic setting when a fabrication partner and/or technique is introduced to explore design in relationship to a specific technology. At the Harvard University Graduate School of Design, we teamed with Chris Bangle of BMW and used his concept car GINA (a kinetic/elastic concept for a car body and interior) as a way to rethink American suburban housing with an emphasis on sustainability and production. At the Ecole Polytechnique Fédérale in Lausanne we teamed with structural engineer Mike Schlaich to explore infra-light concrete as a sustainable, self-insulating concrete that can now be poured with digitally produced formwork, which in turn can be mass-customized.

When a building project begins, the appropriate research work is activated from the archive, or a new line of research is developed specifically to address the new project. A single building project might employ one or more research areas to be applied as built-ins, cladding, façades or even primary structural systems. At this stage, experimental research is more thoroughly tested to better understand its appropriateness and adjustability to the application of a building systems. Modeling here occurs at scales of 1:50 up to 1:1. At this stage, we determine if we can use the same fabrication partner from the research phase for construction or if we need to change. This stage of research is still developmental and inconclusive.

ONE-TO-ONE
—

Construction mock-ups, historically used to pre-determine a building's appearance, scale or color, have evolved to be used where aesthetic effect is understood more comprehensively in direct relationship to physical performance (weather, structural robustness, sustainability and tectonic physicality), economic viability and time-managed buildability through digital means. Digital mock-ups facilitate slight changes, allowing a more

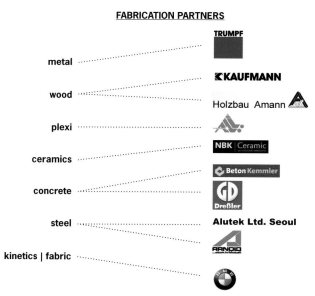

FABRICATION PARTNERS

metal · · · · · · · · · TRUMPF

wood · · · · · · · · · KKAUFMANN

Holzbau Amann

plexi · · · · · · · · ·

ceramics · · · · · · · · · NBK Ceramic

concrete · · · · · · · · · Beton Kemmler

GD Dreßler

steel · · · · · · · · · Alutek Ltd. Seoul

ARNOLD

kinetics | fabric · · · · · · · · ·

BMW

Figure 3. Working relationships with industry-specific partners on both research projects and building projects provide greater control over the production of projects.

refined evaluation of comparable choices prior to a physical mock-up.

The *one-to-one* is a physical prototype that can be used both as a mock-up for client approval and also for architectural installations and exhibitions. Depicting nothing more than itself, the *one-to-one* architectural installation offers an intermediate test between experimental research and final building. The installation, as a format, offers a public forum that helps direct internal experimental speculation: materials and tooling techniques can be tested both technically and experientially, as viewers engage and occupy the installation physically and spatially. In contrast to a fragment of an incomplete whole (a mock-up), the *one-to-one* installation offers a complete autonomous architectural proposition in full effect. [Figure 4]

The *one-to-one* installation and the mock-up are also instrumental in offering an alternative to the enduring and troubling gap between representation (historically drawings and models) and building. With digital software acting as a guidance system for tools rather than merely producing visual representations, we use *one-to-one* constructs to extend the current limits of the architect's imagination and engagement with the building process. We refute the tendency towards representing architecture virtually or digitally, conceived as

a superior alternative to the physical prototype. We maintain a commitment that the experience of material, effect and haptic workability cannot be adequately simulated. A material's atmospheric effect as situated on site is unpredictable. Light, weather and movement are just some of the many conditions that no digital simulation can perfectly predict as a physical architectural outcome. Therefore, the *one-to-one* is an instrument that we front-load into the design process so that it can be more effective as a design tool within the whole process, rather than remain exclusively as a final check before construction. [Figure 5]

The digitally fabricated *one-to-one* also sets up new solutions for off-site assembly processes with all of the advantages of prefabrication and its ability to accelerate building schedules, reduce waste and improve quality, accuracy and precision. Digitally fabricated building components can be assembled off-site as larger but still transportable building parts that can then be assembled on site and "just-in-time" with other systems, speeding up construction and requiring a much smaller on-site staging area. Digitally coordinated assembly processes can manage the aggregation of complex prefabricated components arriving on site to couple with other large components, thereby eliminating the necessity of tooling

Figure 4. The *one-to-one* physical prototypes build a bridge between research experiment and full-scale building component.

materials on site sequentially, one at a time, to construct a building.

TRICKLING DOWN/BUILDING UP: ARCHITECTURE FOR EVERYDAY
—
The third aspect of this process is to conclusively make evident the value of fabrication research by folding it into ongoing building projects. This has evolved from initially "accessorizing" buildings with digitally fabricated components to now seeing primary structural and cladding systems digitally fabricated and assembled. [Figures 6a, 6b] This is an opportunistic approach to exploit technology in a comprehensive way. At the same time, we find ourselves interfacing and integrating digitally conceived and fabricated components with those that are analog or conventionally constructed.

Different building cultures around the world offer different opportunities and limitations, so that the degree of adjustment, emphasis on the digital, or materiality shifts not only between project types but also project locations.

When these advanced technologies become applicable for everyday building types (offices, factories, housing), complexity can coincide with economy, speed of construction

Figure 5 (bottom). With the Gate House for the Trumpf Machine Tool Factory, physical mock-ups were produced early in the design process and used as design tools to look at atmospheric conditions that are harder to model and represent digitally.

Figures 6a (top left), 6b (top right). The roof for the Gate House involved intricate laser cutting of plate-steel parts with bolt holes and connection angles that were assembled into a box-beam structure. The roof was factory-prefabricated in strips that

were bolted together on site and then lifted into place.

and prefabrication. This evolution would add a middle scale of work, located between more radical academic work typically at an installation scale, high-end small "boutique" work and large-scale projects with high budgets. Digital processes can re-instate a new culture of craft, materiality and tectonics, a culture that can support and coincide with the urgency of sustainable practices, improved time-management during construction and the economic limits of everyday architecture.

Technology is a trigger that drives our work in directions that imagination alone cannot do. This, combined with the things we make and do, offers new possibilities for invention, complexity and the ultimate possibility for authenticity. [Figure 7]

ENDNOTES
—

1. Barkow, F.; Leibinger, R. (2009) *Barkow Leibinger: An Atlas of Fabrication*, London, Architectural Association Publications.

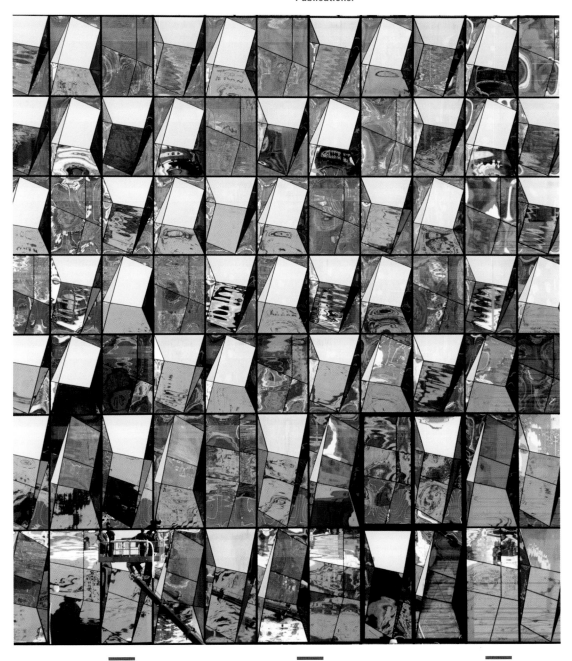

Figure 7. For the Trutec Office and Showroom in Seoul we laser-cut standard aluminum extruded components at multiple angles and joined them with custom-made brackets to create a 3D façade system with a high degree of variation. When installed, the frame and glazing assemblies created a kaleidoscopic effect by reflecting traffic, pedestrians, advertising signage and other urban conditions surrounding the building.

CAMPUS CANTINA
WORKFLOW CASE STUDY ▶

Located just outside Stuttgart, this cantina provides café and event space for workers at the campus of Trumpf, an international power tools, laser fabrication and metal manufacturing company. The glass-enclosed building is covered by a cantilevered, complex roof structure of steel beams and wood cells, developed with engineer Werner Sobek. The project utilized a digital workflow incorporating structrual, environmental and fabrication feedback, refining the process developed for the previously completed Gate House project a few hundred meters away.

Workflow 1. For the design of a Campus Cantina for Trumpf, we activated research previously done on cellular and voranoi ordering systems for large-span structures. This research utilized parametric modeling to develop an adaptable geometry that could respond to differences in structural loading, lighting, acoustics and geometry in relation to a particular material. This led to studies in sheet steel, wood, tube-framing and concrete, now focusing specifically on a large-span roof.

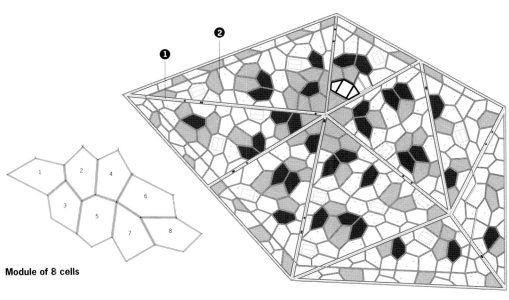

Module of 8 cells

Roof Structure
❶ Primary structure
Steelbeams h: 60-150 cm, w: 30 cm

❷ Secondary structure
Wooden cells [glulam BS 14]

Skylights
Wooden cells with artifical lighting
Wooden cells with perforated acoustic surface
(interior)

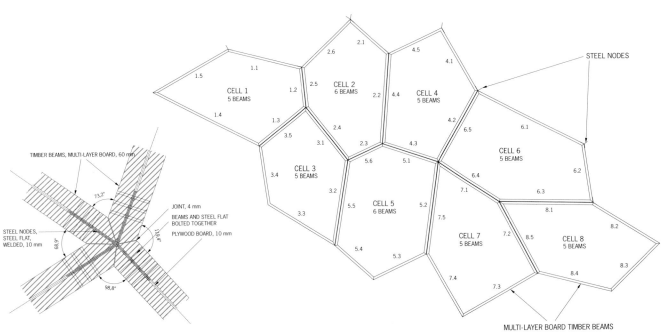

Workflow 2 (top). Several geometric iterations were studied, each considering a particular material, then evaluated with structural engineer Werner Sobek for performance and architectural effect. In later versions, a steel-and-wood hybrid structure was developed, consisting of primary steel framing and columns (strong and capable of long span) and a secondary infill of glu-lam wood cells (sustainable and easily workable). Through environmental optimization processes with Transsolar, our energy/sustainability consultant, and

Bartenbach, our lighting consultant, each cell was assigned a performative role either as an acoustic panel (perforated wood), a skylight for daylighting (initially ETFE membrane, then triple-insulated glass) or a source for artificial lighting (aluminum honeycomb deflector) for evening use.

Workflow 3 (bottom). Selected for its ability to span and address environmental concerns, the cellular glu-lam infill was computationally optimized to save material weight, find an ideal cell size and organization and maximize effective daylighting.

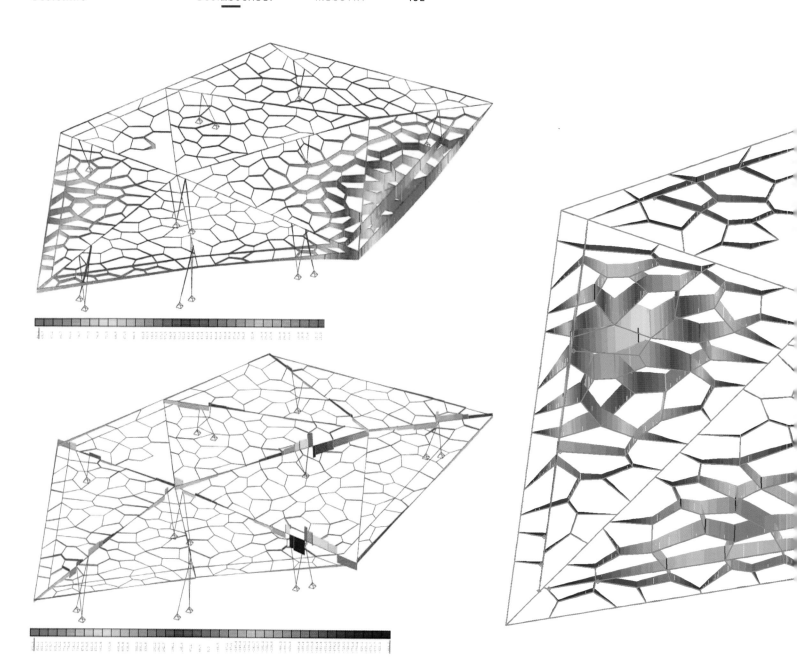

Workflow 4a (top left), 4b
(bottom left), 4c (above
right). The placement of
cells, with depths of 90cm,
120cm and 150cm, was adjusted
through structural optimization in response to structural
loading requirements, which
led to deeper cells in the
middle of a span and shal-
lower cells on the perimeter.
Another optimization strategy
determined the range of cell
types and sizes that would
act in unison as a structural
diaphragm.

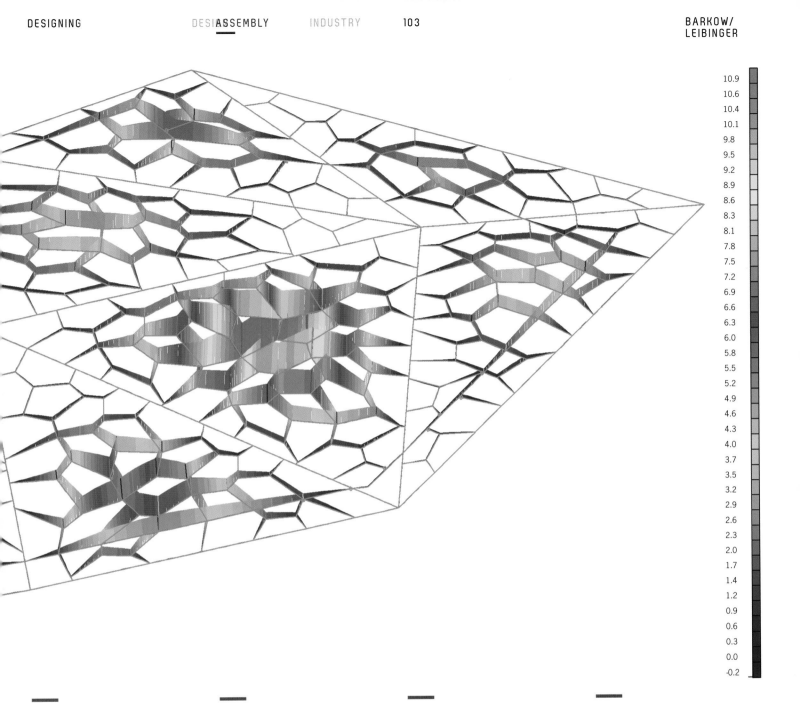

  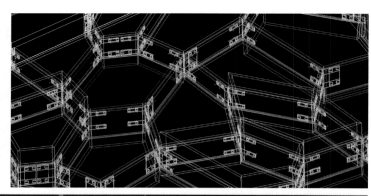

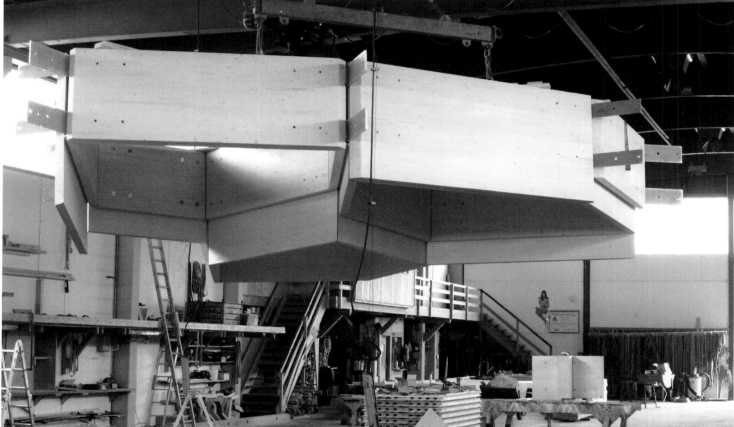

Workflow 5 (top left), 6 (top middle), 7 (top right). After they had been selected as the wood fabricator, the engineers of Holzbau Amann began producing the roof mock-up on the basis of our digital model, working closely with Sobek to optimize cell sizes, numbers and depths and then develop structural connection brackets and fasteners.

Workflow 8 (bottom). The physical mock-up verified the decisions made through the digital optimization process and demonstrated the buildability, costs, speed of prefabrication and on site assembly, finish and ability to control daylight. The mock-up, as approved, set full production into motion.

Workflow 9. Temporary shor-
ing was used to support the
wood cells until they were all
connected and could act as an
integrated structural system.

Workflow 10 (above). In addition to fabrication, Holzbau Amann took responsibility for seeing their prefabricated wood cell assemblies installed on site.

Workflow 11 (right). Completed project.

TOOLING FORM
—
EDITOR'S NOTES

It is easy to be critical of the first generation of digital design, in which the euphoria of formal exploration seemed to drift far away from the logics of materials, assemblies and production methods. A common process from this period was a sequence of linear steps, in which the architect would generate a formally complex design that would subsequently go through various stages of translation, rationalization and optimization by engineers, fabricators and other digital specialists in order to be realized as a building. Ironically, one of the by-products of this period was a rapid growth in advanced fabrication and assembly techniques, largely driven by the challenge to build these designs—here it was form that drove technical innovation.

The impact that this work had on the development in industry has become the foundation for new design approaches that are more responsive to, and even inspired by, the possibilities of digital fabrication techniques. The split

between design and production that limited the previous period has transitioned to integrated workflows in which information from any phase of a project can drive initial concepts. The work of Barkow Leibinger exemplifies this approach. In their non-linear workflow, design ideas develop through an exploration of machining techniques—where fabrication and assembly logics originate—and then work back to encompass site and program concerns while also projecting forward to consider inhabitation and the experience of the user.

"Our practice is positioned at the determining rather than the receiving end of emerging technologies. This is an incredibly dynamic and challenging time, where the vectors of sustainability, economics, desire, digital means and aesthetics coincide, driving new forms and architectural possibilities."[1]

An Atlas of Fabrication, Barkow Leibinger's catalog of experimental *off-cuts*, full-scale *one-to-one*

constructions and completed buildings describes behind-the-scenes steps of how they proactively engage with industrial manufacturing for both speculative design explorations and project-specific fabrication of building components. The unique relationship that they have with Trumpf, the world's largest manufacturer of laser cutting machines, as both a client and source of technical expertise, has allowed the numerous projects they have completed on the Trumpf campus to become a testing ground for specific techniques and workflows used on other projects. Their close alliances with fabricators provide them access not only to industrial machines, but also to the expertise of the people who design and operate these machines. Fabricators become an extension of the design team. In this regard, direct file-to-fabrication workflows have recast the dialogue between architects and fabricators both technically and culturally. Technically, design and fabrication have merged into the common language of digital

code, forming an unambiguous communication link between what architects do (make drawings) and what fabricators do (process material). Yet this link is not just the transfer of a file, but also an opportunity for an intricate exchange of knowledge that conditions how architects design and how fabricators use machines.[2] Technology can serve as a common language to synthesize diverse knowledge and expertise and subsequently encourage a shift in the culture of industry.

If designing assembly is the process of linking material production to design tools through a rigorous digital exchange of information, the work of Barkow Leibinger, and in particular their concept of *off-cuts*, comes as close as any author in this book to exemplifying this new workflow. Following the tradition of architects like Walter Gropius, Konrad Wachsmann, Jean Prouvé and Charles and Ray Eames, Barkow Leibinger tie design innovation to manufacturing processes and use the precision of tooling techniques and logics of assembly to explore form and geometry. In a refreshing reversal of more autonomous digital design processes—where form was generated as an abstract visual index of an algorithmic logic, with little or no acknowledgement of the creative potential of the constraints associated with building—the work of Barkow Leibinger originates at the point where these constraints are the greatest.

Their practice serves as a working model for a younger generation of architects who have embraced fabrication as the foundation for both design exploration and new types of design practice. This younger generation has found a renewed source of inspiration in the materialization of design and an empowerment in the ability to design, model and fabricate within a continuous digital workflow.[3] While much of this work exists at a small scale in a controlled setting, projects like the Trumpf Campus Cantina serve to assure that the ambitions of this younger generation of architects are both attainable and essential to the future transformation of industry.

—

1. Barkow, F.; Leibinger, R. (2009) *Barkow Leibinger: An Atlas of Fabrication*, London, Architectural Association Publications.
2. See "Digital Craftsmanship: From Thinking to Modeling to Building" by Fabian Scheurer in this volume.
3. For excellent examples of this type of work, see Iwamoto, L. (2009) *Digital Fabrications, Architectural and Material Techniques*, New York, Princeton Architectural Press.

DIGITAL CRAFTSMANSHIP: FROM THINKING TO MODELING TO BUILDING

FABIAN SCHEURER

Fabian Scheurer is a computer scientist and Co-Founder of designtoproduction.

How are digital tools changing the process of architecture and building? From the perspective of a computer scientist, this discussion has a potentially surprising starting point: contrary to sculptors, for example, architects very rarely work out a design on site, on a one-to-one scale with their hands dirty from manipulating an actual building material. The clay in architectural design processes is usually replaced by immaterial means, starting with a pattern of neuronal activity in the designer's brain (an idea) and then gradually being externalized, refined and materialized as spoken or written language,

drawings, plans, scale models and so on. The result, at least ideally, is an unambiguous set of instructions for the builders, who then actually get their hands dirty in a separate phase of the process. In short, architectural design is a process of developing, describing and communicating ideas and of generating, transforming and exchanging information—over different media and between numerous involved parties.

Once we look at the design process from this point of view, it becomes clear as to why the current development in digital design and fabrication tools has fostered a great deal of expectations. Computers are tools to store and manipulate information, and their connection via the internet has formed the most powerful

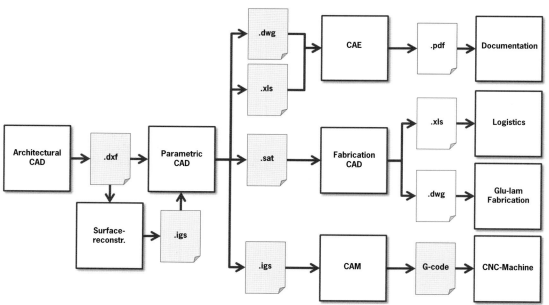

Figure 1. Diagram showing the flow of information between the various software programs used for planning and fabricating the timber roof structure of the Centre Pompidou-Metz by Shigeru Ban and Jean de Gastines.

platform for information-interchange ever. The idea of integrating computer-aided methods from design (CAD) through engineering (CAE) to manufacturing (CAM) and seamlessly transporting the information from the designer's idea to the materialized result is indeed captivating. In reality, however, it is still a huge challenge to form such a continuous "digital workflow". Why is this so difficult?

THE LANGUAGE OF ARCHITECTURE
—

One very common complaint concerning the integration of digital workflows is the insufficient state of software and hardware technology and its multitude of incompatible standards. This is not at all restricted to architecture but seems to be a universal problem in all domains that try to map their analog processes into the digital realm. Why is it not possible to finally come up with one universal standard file-format for the building industry—one that can be used by architects, engineers, builders and all other involved parties to store knowledge about a building and the process of its realization in one integrated model, which then delivers unambiguous, consistent information to everyone in the project? [Figure 1]

In former, analog times, changes on one document had to be retraced in all associated documents of all other involved parties, which rarely ever worked and thus led to inconsistencies. Moreover, architects and engineers used different standards for drawing and describing things. And even within a single domain, one line on a plan or one number on a spreadsheet could have a multitude of different meanings, depending on interpretation. Like any other (natural) language, the language of architecture was ambiguous. But as those who read and understood this information were more or less successful at performing plausibility tests all the time—depending on their knowledge and experience—they were able to interpret the given data more or less adequately.

Computer languages, on the other hand, are unambiguous, formal languages. Anybody who ever tried to program a computer came to a point where a single missing semicolon somewhere in the code prevented the whole program from running, or even worse—led to unexpected and wrong results. What holds true for a computer program is equally valid for all data to be processed by a computer.[1] In order for an algorithm to make sense of the given information, both have to be unambiguously encoded in a formal language, correct to the last semicolon.

Therefore, a digital model of a building that has to be automatically processed by a computer program needs to be unambiguous in order to obtain correct results. An algorithm does not "guess" the correct interpretation of some data based on experience and intuition like a human expert would do. It interprets the information based solely on its built-in rules. Wherever it detects ambiguities or contradictions it stops with an error message. However, in order to be able to detect these uncertainties, programmers must have anticipated the problem and implemented the necessary checks within the program. Otherwise, as is often the case, the algorithm will not even note the problem and just carry on with some interpretation that is utterly incorrect.

In order to come up with a unified data format for all building purposes, including descriptions of shape, material and the building process itself, we would first have to develop a unified, formal, machine-readable language for unambiguously describing all these aspects of architecture. Although there has been an ongoing attempt since 1995 with the "Industry Foundation Classes" (IFC), an open standard for so-called "Building Information Modeling" (BIM), there have been long delays between releases of new versions.[2] This timeframe between releases poses an interesting dilemma: while new versions of software packages with new functionality appear on the market every year, a four-year innovation cycle for the underlying data format seems rather unhurried. Can the IFC standard keep up with the development?

STANDARD VS. NON-STANDARD
—

Standards are defined to make life easier. They ensure that different CAD programs read the same information from the same data and that the quality of service is comparable among bidders in a tender. But standards do not only make life easier, they also make life simpler. Standards reduce the infinite possibilities of the real world to the least common denominator of all involved parties. In the case of the IFC, for example, a building cannot have any curved free-form shapes. They simply cannot be described within an IFC model, because the definition of such shapes is not (yet) part of the IFC standard. A precise mathematical theory of those shapes (called NURBS[3]) has been available since the 1950's, and many of today's CAD packages provide the necessary functionality to model them. But obviously, when IFC2x3 was defined and approved only a few years ago, the precise modeling of curved shapes was regarded as low priority compared to other features. When you look at architecture magazines today, you might think that that was a downright wrong decision by the developing association IAI.

On the other hand, putting the curved buildings that made it to the pages of the architecture magazines in relation to the total volume of buildings erected during the last four years, the decision seems more reasonable. Why inflate a nice and lean standard with a feature that is needed for less than one percent of all buildings in the world? All AEC software would have to correctly interpret the NURBS definition just in order to be compliant to the IFC standard, regardless of the fact that in hardly any project this feature will ever be used. What a waste of software engineering resources! Since most of the IAI members are software vendors and draw their decisions on the basis of economic considerations, they consequently decided not to waste scarce resources to address less than one percent of the building industry. Apart from that, even the least-standard buildings contain a lot of standard nuts and bolts. And although the next version, IFC2x4, will contain NURBS there will always be non-standard objects that can be neither described in standard terms (or languages or file-formats) nor built with standard tools from standard materials. No matter how many new functionalities are added, a standard tool will always only work for standard designs. And creative designers will always try to escape or overcome the standard. So, how do we deal with non-standard architecture?

UNIVERSAL MACHINES
—

Where no standard solution for a problem is readily available, a custom solution has to be found. And here is the real advantage of digital tools: they are "universal machines". The functionality of a computer is not inscribed in its hardware but is defined by the software loaded into its memory. If the needed function is not available in one version of the software, an extended version can be programmed and run on the same hardware without changing the computer. This functionality has become so common in design practice that it does not make us think anymore. But going one step further into fabrication, the same principle still applies—and often surprises designers who have been educated to use industrialized, mass-produced components: a computer-controlled (CNC) fabrication machine does not care whether it is producing a thousand similar or a thousand different work-pieces. If the needed

Figure 2. CNC milling allows fabrication of complex non-standard components that can fit together into an intricate structural assembly.

components are not readily available, a CNC tool can custom-produce them for almost the same price as industrial standard components, while the machine itself stays unchanged. [Figure 2]

These developments have changed the prospects of non-standard architecture quite drastically. When standard software can be extended to precisely fit the needs of the designer, and individual components can be custom-made instead of arraying standardized, industrially fabricated pieces, then a new world of possibilities opens up. Yet at the same time, any ad-hoc extension of a standard tool will lead to incompatibilities in the workflow. If something outside the IFC standard is modeled in a CAD software by means of a custom extension, the extended information can no longer be passed on to an IFC-compatible standard CAM software.[4] The chain of information breaks and to close the communication link again, both the exchange format and all dependent tools have

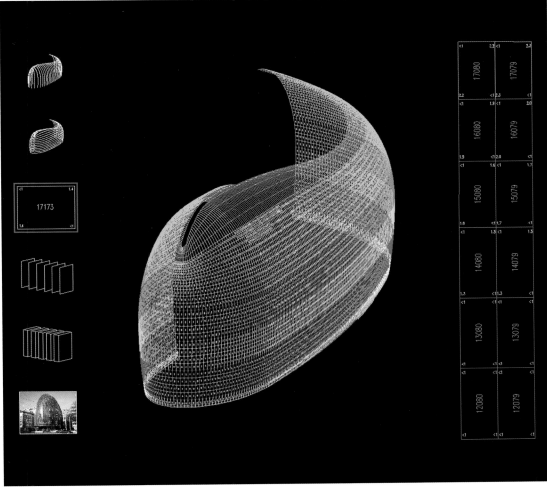

Figures 3a (bottom), 3b (top). Planar glass panels on the façade of Renzo Piano's Peek & Cloppenburg department store in Cologne.

to be extended appropriately. And besides data exchange, other challenges arise.

LOGICS OF MASS CUSTOMIZATION
—

Architecture's departure from repetitive, industrialized, orthogonal designs can quickly become a labor-intensive nightmare. For example, when façade panels are to be curved, new workflows have to be developed, because standard building materials come in either straight sticks or flat sheets. To avoid the problems of bending, curved shapes can be approximated with small planar facets, but that requires meticulous optimization of the panel sizes in order to achieve both visually appealing and economically balanced results. And no matter whether the components are curved or straight, every component and every joint has a slightly different geometry due to their non-regular shape. The convenient set of standard detail drawings is replaced by hundreds and thousands of individual workshop drawings or thousands of individual programs for a CNC machine. [Figures 3a, 3b]

Today, drawing can be automated. Many CAD systems can take the defining properties of a component or joint as input and deliver a perfect drawing (or model) as output. Instead of drawing a line by pointing and clicking with the mouse, the user writes a custom program, or "script", that generates the line in the model based on a set of rules and parameters. Some CAD systems even allow the construction of such "parametric models" by graphically connecting "algorithm building blocks" without writing a single line of program code.[5] Hence, the functionality of standard CAD software can be extended with custom tools to allow innovative and curious professionals, who lack a degree in software engineering, to build their own digital tools. The designer becomes a toolmaker. But no matter how such a parametric model is built, it adds another layer of abstraction to the modeling problem. Instead of producing a description of an object by building a digital model, first a program has to be written, which then generates the description of the object. Obviously, this additional effort only pays off when something more complex than a line has to be drawn more often than just once. If the same script could generate drawings for all the different joints of a non-standard façade, it would make sense to invest a couple of weeks into programming.

This requires that instead of finding one well-formed, unambiguous description for one single component, a common abstract description has to be found that satisfies the needs of all individual components. And in order to eventually materialize the components, a complete production chain has to be implemented, including planning, material procurement, (digital) fabrication, quality management, logistics and assembly of individual one-off components.

In the consumer goods industry this is known as "mass customization". The client defines the measurements of his new shirt or the configuration of her new car, and some days or weeks later the product arrives, custom-built to the

Figure 4. The curved wooden wall of the Kilden Performing Arts Centre in Kristiansand, designed by ALA architects. Its 3,500sqm are assembled from 125 prefabricated wall elements, containing 250 straight and 1,250 individually curved timber girders as well as 12,500 individually tapered oak cladding boards. All those components were defined in a parametric CAD model and CNC-fabricated.

given specifications. In architecture, mass customization is often associated with pre-fabricated houses. Economists would call that a business-to-consumer (B2C) model, and it requires finding a sufficient number of clients, each one paying for one "customized" house, in order to remunerate the initial investment of the fabricator. However, with large architectural projects mass customization also works on a business-to-business (B2B) model. The façade of an office building, a museum or a concert house easily comprises many thousand components, and they may all be ordered by just one client. Implementing an integrated planning and production process for those components can easily pay off within a single project. A project-specific standard is created: a complete mass-customization solution, starting with a digital planning tool that parametrically defines the shapes of all necessary components and resulting in digitally fabricated parts delivered to the construction site. After the project is finished the whole process usually gets discarded, because no designer would want to build the same idea twice. Apart from that, large projects usually go on for a couple of months or even years and involve many people from diverse

Figure 5. All 4,000 joints in the timber roof structure of the Centre Pompidou-Metz have a different geometry, but they follow the same simple rules.

disciplines. For future projects the team members and the available technology will likely be different, requiring a new process.

SYSTEMATICS AND COMPLEXITY
—

It has become clear that a parametric approach has its biggest advantage where complex solutions are achieved by simple systems. A successful parametric model is as simple as possible, while still covering the extreme cases. When the tightest curved panels and the most skewed joints define the parameter range of the solution, all other cases can be easily addressed and the whole façade or roof can be constructed from only a few types of parametric components. This approach to simplicity is too often confused with solving the simple cases first and then adding a few special cases wherever the simple solution fails. On orthogonal standard buildings, this works reasonably well, but on non-standard buildings with complex shapes, things are different.

Complexity can be defined as a measure for the amount of interdependencies in a system. When complex systems are not designed with great care, the high level of interdependencies is liable to lead to a solution tree that branches to the point where all cases are special and every single one has to be solved individually. By Kolmogorov's definition,[6] this is the most complex state possible: 100% exceptions, with every single case described separately. In order to reduce this complexity and design, a good parametric system, a common rule on the basis of all those special cases has to be found. This can then be encoded in a lean parametric model, and by changing the parameter values a couple of thousand customized data sets for automatically fabricating individual components are easily generated.

But if the changes result in violating the parametric border conditions of just one single component—maybe a glass panel of a façade gets a notch too big to be cut from a standard size—the whole system stops working. Either the façade has to be changed again until all parameters are within their range, or a special case has to be introduced to the system to solve this exception.

Unfortunately, all this is not a question of buying the right software tool. Computers are good at storing information and crunching numbers, but it takes human thinking to find a good solution and describe it concisely. It takes a team of specialists knowledgeable of all stages of the planning and fabrication process, who define a common model just complex enough to describe the solution.

MINIMAL MODELS
—

The purpose of a model is to condense the complexity of the real world down to a level where certain things can be communicated or simulated without having to build the real thing first. Contrary to current belief, a perfect model does not contain as much information as possible, but as little as necessary. The art of modeling is based on the ability to sort out, to leave out everything that is not relevant for the given purpose, while including everything that makes a difference. The quality of a model is therefore closely related to its purpose. What might be a good model for a structural engineer, because it contains a structural wall panel that spans continuously from the ground to the top floor, is likely to be less useful for an interior designer, who needs to get the inner wall areas

between floor and ceiling painted in every story. To make the same model useful for both parties, either the same wall has to be described twice—which adds redundant information and leads to inconsistency—or rules have to be defined that translate the engineer's definition of the wall into the definition needed by the interior designer—which adds complexity to the interpretation algorithms. Multiplied across an entire building, these increased definitions for single components inescapably lead to models that are "fatter" than necessary for either purpose. And when we naively continue to integrate all necessary information for all involved parties from design to facility management, our models will quickly become clumsy, slow and not useful for anyone. This is why on reasonably large architectural projects, there will always be a multitude of models serving a multitude of different needs.

If a model is to be used as the input for computer-controlled fabrication equipment, it

Figure 6. Each of the 32 roof modules for the Heasley Nine Bridges Golf Resort in South Korea, designed by Shigeru Ban, has a footprint of 81sqm. It is assembled from some 150 individual timber components, CNC-cut-to-fit within half a millimeter.

A tolerance gap of only 2mm between the modules was sufficient to hoist the elements into place.

has to be very precise. Even large-scale CNC tools are able to work within tolerances smaller than a millimeter, allowing the prefabrication of meter-long components that click into place like Lego bricks. [Figure 6]

But lacking any sense of quality, the machine also reproduces flawed input data with the same unforgiving precision—if there is a kink in the CAD model, there will be a kink in the final product. Taking into account the numerical errors occurring during the modeling and calculation processes,[7] the precision of the model has to be even a degree higher than that required for fabrication. Usually the CAD models produced in architectural or engineering offices do not even come close to these requirements, because their purpose is to generate renderings or drawings. Only when it comes to fabrication, does the description of geometry have to be absolutely precise and contain every single bolt hole that has to be pre-drilled before the components are shipped to site. To precisely position those details the mathematics, so comfortably hidden behind the CAD software's buttons, suddenly have to be dealt with in the form of normal vectors, curvature measures and coordinate transformations—a field of expertise that is often tolerantly skipped during the education of architects and engineers. What initially could have been described in a sleek, elegant mathematical formula now has to be dealt with in the form of a clumsy point cloud and long tables of coordinates, because somewhere along the process a lot of fix points were defined just a tiny little bit off the mathematical surface—what was easier to model early in the process results in difficulties later down the line.

To produce a roof the size of the Centre Pompidou-Metz, a CNC machine of a size that needs its own factory hall runs for six months, twenty-four hours, seven days a week. Neither the raw material, which has to be custom-made and ordered weeks in advance, nor the finished components can be stored in one place, so both procurement and production have to run just-in-time synchronized with the assembly schedule.

Fabrication and building sites are far apart, so the components have to be transported and need to fit onto standard trucks and containers, which adds dimensional and weight constraints as well as a few extra joints on large pieces. All connections have to be precisely positioned and joined on site, which sounds much easier than it is on a curved puzzle with 2000 pieces, each the length of a bus. It would be unrealistic to expect all this being already defined in an architectural model. The knowledge that needs to be embedded in this process is distributed over at least half a dozen domains. In order to integrate this know-how, they all have to work together, understand each other's needs and sort out all interdependencies. And as the project is non-standard, there is no standard procedure to follow.

This is the main difference to industrialized production: mass production is based on standardized processes with standardized interfaces. The input and output of every process step is clearly defined. As long as the interfaces between them stay unchanged, every section of the process can be optimized locally and individually without considering the other sections. In other words: all the specialists can comfortably stay within their domain, their borders clearly defined by agreed standards.

CRAFTSMANSHIP
—

Setting up the process for a non-standard project means first and foremost defining those interfaces. All the interdependencies have to be untangled carefully while constantly being concerned about both the final result and an efficient process to get there. Again, this needs experience and expert knowledge, deeply rooted in practice. But even more, it needs the ability to look beyond one's own domain, to consider the consequences of every decision and—since the necessary know-how will not be embedded in the brain of one single expert—the willingness to team up and collaborate. It needs a group of specialists each being extremely experienced in his/her field, open enough to discuss with others and committed to quality. In short, it needs craftsmanship, as defined by Richard Sennett: a sort of craftsmanship that is not identified by the fact of actually getting one's hands dirty in a workshop, but by intrinsic motivation—an "enduring, basic human impulse, the desire to do a job well for its own sake",[8] a combination of "material consciousness" with the experience of years of practice,[9] a strategic acceptance of pragmatic

Figure 7. designtoproduction works as an interface to bring non-standard architectural intent into the real world through optimization, simplification and organization of input material and processes.

ambiguity, rather than an obsessive perfection-ism, and a never ebbing desire to learn. In this context, modeling experts, computer programmers, engineers and architects can all be good craftsmen. Their skills are never going to be replaced, but can be dramatically enhanced by digital tools.

ENDNOTES
—

1. Computers following the so-called "Von Neumann Architecture"—and that means almost all contemporary computers—do not even differentiate between program code and data and store both in the same memory.
2. IFC was developed by an association of firms named the "International Alliance for Interoperability" (IAI). Many software packages for the building sector are already able to read and write IFC data and by many the IFC are seen as the future of digital workflows in building. Currently, IFC2x3 as of February 2006 is the latest approved version, a release candidate for the next version IFC2x4 was presented in May 2010. Detailed information on the IFC can be found online at the IAI website at www.buildingsmart.com. For an overview on BIM, see Eastman, C.; Teicholz, P.; Sacks, R.; Liston, K. (2008) *BIM Handbook*, New Jersey, John Wiley & Sons.
3. Non-Uniform Rational B-Spline Surfaces (NURBS), as a mathematical theory to precisely define curved surfaces, were developed in the French car industry in the 1950's.
4. It might be able to pass on the data, but the CAM software has no valid interpretation rules to make any sense of it.
5. E.g. "GenerativeComponents" for Bentley's Microstation or the "Grasshopper" plugin for McNeel's Rhinoceros software.

6. In algorithmic information theory, the Kolmogorov Complexity of an object is defined by the shortest description of the object in a given language.
7. Due to the encoding of real numbers into strings of zeros and ones, computers make tiny rounding errors in every calculation. Apart from that, many geometrical operations cannot deliver mathematically precise results but only approximations in order to keep processing time within reasonable bounds. If those errors add up the result can be completely flawed—which for example is a common reason for failing operations in Boolean geometry.
8. Sennett, R. (2008) *The Craftsman*. New Haven & London: Yale University Press.
9. A common estimate of the time required to master a craft is ten thousand hours.

CENTRE POMPIDOU-METZ
WORKFLOW CASE STUDY▶

Shigeru Ban, Jean de Gastines and Philip Gumuchdjian won an international competition to create an extension to the landmark Centre Pompidou in Paris. Their design for the new building, located in the eastern French city of Metz, included several suspended, rectilinear galleries under a curved roof that was inspired by a Chinese hat made of woven straws. As the project developed, these straws evolved into 18,000m of timber beams with a cross-section of 14 x 44cm to form the roof structure. These beams had to be individually CNC-fabricated, with intricately designed joints to maintain the design intent, preserve the structural integrity and allow efficient on site assembly. As part of the construction team, designtoproduction created reference geometry for the roof and provided the timber construction company with the necessary CAD-tools to efficiently define, detail and produce nearly 1,800 double-curved wooden glu-lam segments.

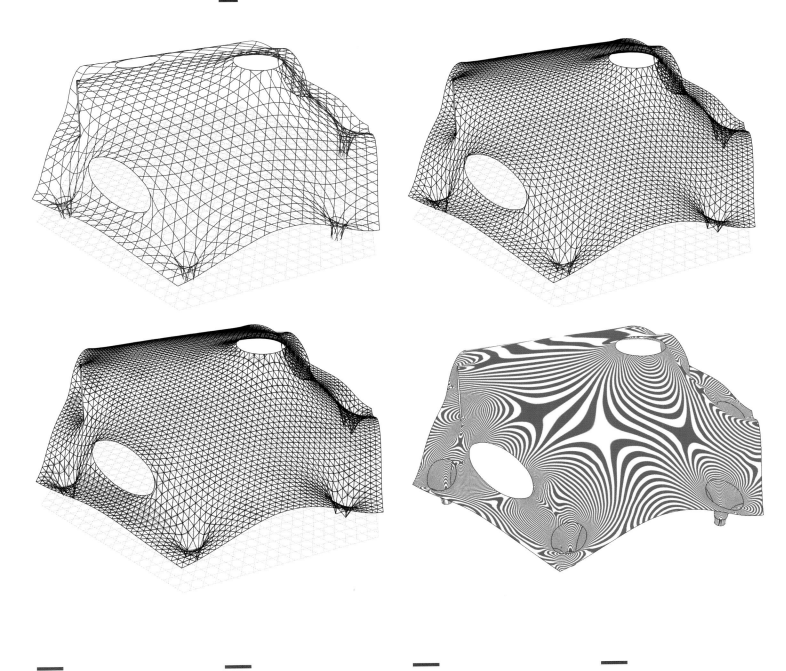

Workflow 1. The mesh for the
roof structure of the Centre
Pompidou-Metz as originally
provided by the architects
was more free-form in design
and could not be built in an
economic manner. designtoproduction helped rationalize
the form into a triangulated
mesh, based on a system of
rules that could be calculated
and constructed. A wireframe
model was developed from this
refined geometry.

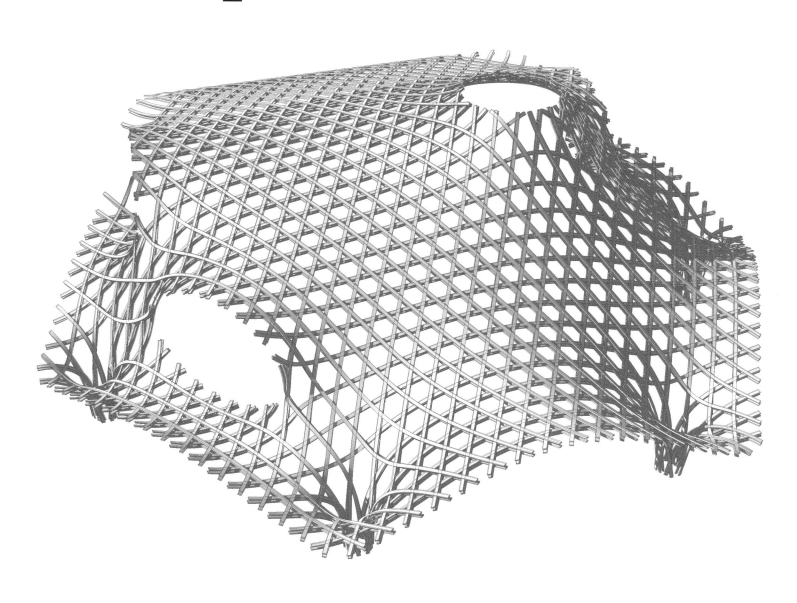

Workflow 2. From the wireframe, a structure could be
designed that would conform
to the underlying geometry.
In this case, wooden glu-lams
were used to create the complex, curving structure.

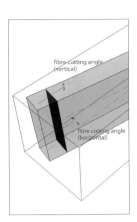

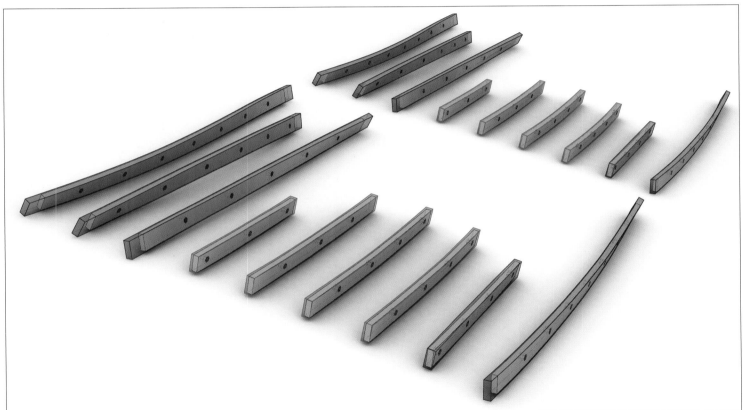

Workflow 3 (top left). Because no two connections were the same, specific joinery had to be created at each intersection, resulting in a complex schedule of assembly details.

Workflow 4 (top right). It was important that the material properties of the wood, such as how it would behave when cut at a certain angle, be programmed into the system early on in the process, so that the wireframe could parametrically adapt to these rules.

Workflow 5 (bottom). designtoproduction was able to provide the timber fabrication company with the necessary files to define and detail all 1,800 double-curved wooden glu-lam segments. Each curved timber piece was first made up into the approximate geometry, indicated by the outlined shaded surfaces. The precise geometry used to mill the finished member is shown by the inner solid surface.

Workflow 6 (top left). CNC machining tools would mill the final precise geometry derived from the model. The machines could perform quickly and operate on each piece of structure at the same rate, regardless of differences in design.

Workflow 7 (bottom left). Each piece was coded to fit together on site like a kit-of-parts. The plugs at the connection points allowed precise alignment for site assembly.

Workflow 8 (above middle). Roof structure being assembled on site.

Workflow 9 (above right). Completed project.

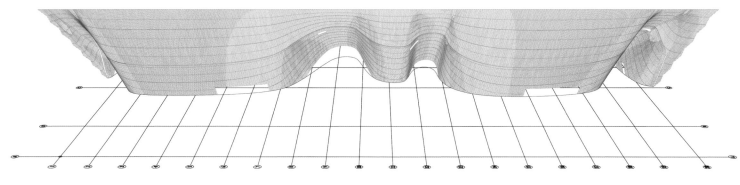

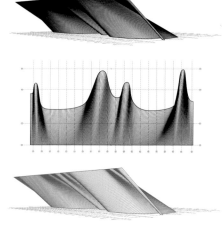

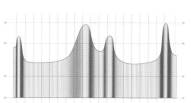

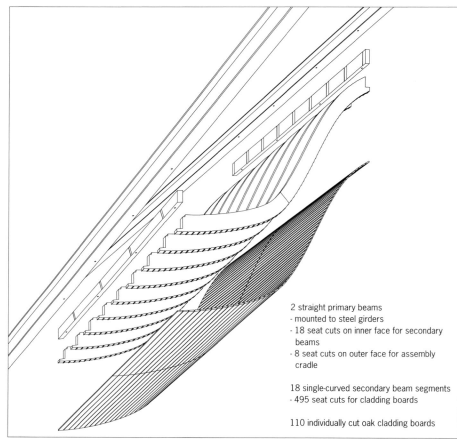

2 straight primary beams
- mounted to steel girders
- 18 seat cuts on inner face for secondary
  beams
- 8 seat cuts on outer face for assembly
  cradle

18 single-curved secondary beam segments
- 495 seat cuts for cladding boards

110 individually cut oak cladding boards

KILDEN PERFORMING ARTS CENTRE
WORKFLOW CASE STUDY ▶

Working in close collaboration with the architect, engineer and timber specialists, designtoproduction developed a fabrication and assembly concept for the curved wooden façade of the Kilden Performing Arts Centre in Kristiansand. The workflow consisted of refining the design geometry from the architect in response to fabrication and assembly logics and then developing a parametric 3D model. The model contained data for 14,309 glue-laminated girders and locally sourced oak cladding that were then output from this model and delivered to the timber fabricator for CNC fabrication. This was one of several timber projects realized through a refined workflow, where the structural engineering of complex timber structures, provided by SJB Kempter Fitze, and the craft and digital timber fabrication skills of Lehmann Timber Construction were integrated through the parametric modeling of designtoproduction.

Workflow 1 (top). The initial model provided by the architects for the Kilden Performing Arts Centre seemed to be a simple ruled surface. However, varying undulations in the surface created unresolved geometry that was impossible to detail, fabricate and construct.

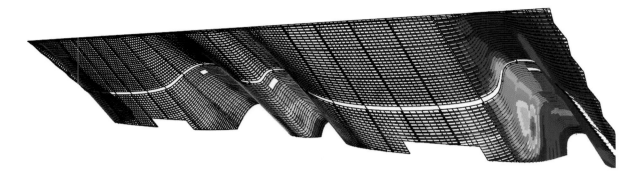

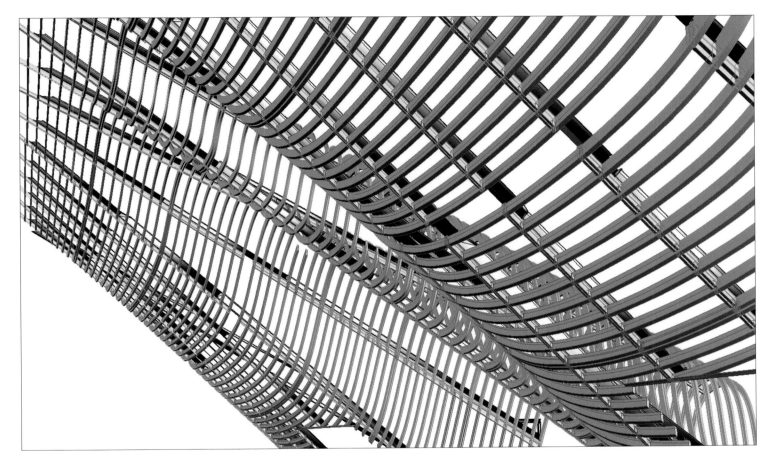

Workflow 2 (facing page, left). designtoproduction rationalized the surface so that it used similar-sized planks and reduced the gaps and pinching of the original mesh.

Workflow 3 (facing page, right). The design goal was to create an underlayment system of ribs onto which the finished oak cladding boards would be fixed. The model included "seat cuts" that were CNC milled into the underlying ribs to make installation both easier and faster.

Workflow 4 (bottom), 5 (top). Developing the model parametrically allowed the designers to push and pull certain areas of the façade and get updates on the constructability of the system in real time.

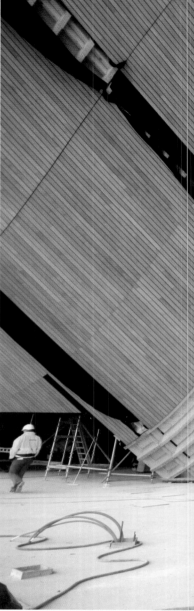

Workflow 6 (above left). The
parametric model contained
information to CNC fabricate
14,309 glu-lam members and
finished oak boards. Assembly
logics were embedded in the
joint details of each individual member.

Workflow 7 (above right). The
substructure of glu-lam beams
were secured to primary steel
girders. The glu-lams were CNC-
milled to accommodate these
beams.

Workflow 8 (above left). The curved wood surface not only creates a dramatic façade at the waterfront but also provides beneficial acoustic properties to the theater inside.

Workflow 9 (right). By working directly with the fabricators and the architects, designtoproduction was able to straddle the line between design concept and buildable solution, simultaneously reducing complexity and increasing efficiency.

WIREFRAME ALGORITHMS
—
EDITOR'S NOTES

One of the natural assumptions about Building Information Modeling is that the ultimate BIM model contains as much information as possible. Information gaps, which are a by-product of trying to describe a complex 3D object with 2D drawings, are supposedly eliminated by a comprehensive virtual model, creating an expectation that the design will be built exactly as planned. This assumption is partially a consequence of the AEC industry continually referencing the design and production workflows in the aerospace and automobile industry as a model, where detailed modeling of each part and high-level geometry resolution between all systems is a requirement for design and manufacturing. This comparison has played an important role in highlighting workflow inefficiencies in the AEC industry. Versions of highly integrated workflows have been explored on some of the more ambitious architectural projects in recent years. It is likely, however, that a more flexible model is needed for the particular conditions that define

the difference between the two industries. Aerospace contracts are almost always design-built, which establishes standards and an industry-wide alignment of motivations and incentives that differ greatly from the AEC industry.[1] Additionally, the one-off design of most buildings makes it a very different procedural problem from the mass production of a jet or car, where the time and effort required to create a comprehensive digital model can be justified through its repeated use.[2]

The approach proposed by Fabian Scheurer is based on multiple minimal models—the art of good modeling where one is able to include as *little* information as possible to accomplish the goal at hand. This approach is especially relevant for the work of designtoproduction, as they specialize in solving highly specific, information-intensive problems related to fabrication, assembly and construction execution. As Scheurer notes, manufacturing tasks usually require digital

modeling at higher levels of resolution and tolerance than design tasks. Minimal models address this difference but raise the question of how to maintain continuity of design information from one minimal model to another without rebuilding anew each time. This will require another evolution of digital workflows, where the base design geometry of a building will be created as a wireframe that functions as a digital armature capable of receiving additional information as it develops during the design process or as it is needed during the manufacturing and construction process.

designtoproduction is a workflow consultant. They produce targeted workflows between the formal innovations of architects and the manufacturing potential of CNC technology, filling some of those gaps in the design-to-production process. They are not experts in manufacturing, or the processes of construction, but through careful collaboration with experienced fabricators who

have an intimate understanding of materials, and builders who know the logistics of site conditions, they are able to transfer this knowledge into code that manages the relationship between design geometry, material characteristics and assembly parameters. For the Centre Pompidou-Metz, for instance, they worked closely with Holzbau Amann, an established timber construction company in Germany with decades of experience in structural timber projects. By combining designtoproduction's programming skills with their knowledge of craft, Holzbau Amann were able to extend their conventional manufacturing capabilities to produce the double-curved glu-lam members that define the roof structure.

Much has been written about how the direct link between design and production through digital fabrication brings the engagement with materiality, detail and craft back into focus for architects. However, this is a very different type of engagement compared to modern times. Detailing is no longer defined by the negotiation of tolerances between pre-manufactured building components but rather, by the design of customized assembly logics with embedded material intelligence. Design-to-production workflows communicate that intelligence and drive the manufacturing process. This is what designtoproduction does. Positioned between the detailing done by architects and the means and methods of contractors, they are typically hired by building contractors to solve logistical issues related to fabrication but arguably, they serve architects even more so by preserving the integrity of their designs.

This raises the question of when and where the renewed focus on materiality, detail and craft is really occurring. The future promise of encoding the knowledge of craft into algorithms lies in these algorithms being available to architects in the early stages of design. The time and effort to post-rationalize geometry could

be repositioned to become part of its formation process. Production workflows could parallel design workflows.

—

1. Integrated Project Delivery (IPD) is the AEC industry's current response to the potential of this business model, and while it addresses many of the legal obstacles to integrated workflows, it remains to be seen how it will impact design innovation.

2. See Neil Denari's discussion of precision in "Precise Form for an Imprecise World" in this volume.

ALGORITHMIC WORKFLOWS IN ASSOCIATIVE MODELING

SHANE M. BURGER

Shane M. Burger was Director of the Computational Design Unit and Associate at Grimshaw Architects from 2003-2011. He is currently Director of Design Technology at Woods Bagot and Director of the Smartgeometry Group.

NATURAL AND INTUITIVE
—

In mid-2008, I spent a stimulated series of days working with the founder and chairman of our firm, Sir Nicholas Grimshaw, developing a mixed-use tower in Manhattan. During the previous weekend, I made the decision to transfer a number of our design decisions for the tower into a computational model in GenerativeComponents. The reasons ranged from the methodological to the practical: by working with the model dynamically within an associative geometry environment, we could embed a range of site requirements and design decisions into a well-defined design space for creative exploration. Significantly decreasing the feedback loop in this way resulted in increasing design iterations for the team. This well-defined design space afforded us the

confidence that all iterations would satisfy the requirements posed by the site and program challenges, and we could turn our attention to the possible geometric variations that best exemplified the building's intended character.

The design geometry was rigorous; from years of working on projects with complex geometries, we knew that any reduction to the manual re-modeling of rigorous geometric systems simply due to parameter changes was an immediate time-saver. When Nick sat down at my desk to review the design, I spent a minute explaining what he was seeing on my screens. On the left monitor was a basic geometric model showing the visual results of each parameter and how it affected the building's geometric profile. On the right monitor was a collection of control sliders (geometric control and program distributions), input parameters (zoning requirement, right-to-light rules), and a dynamically updated spreadsheet estimating per-floor and per-program square footages and potential building costs. Having spent fourteen years honing my digital design skills, with the previous five focused on advancing algorithmic

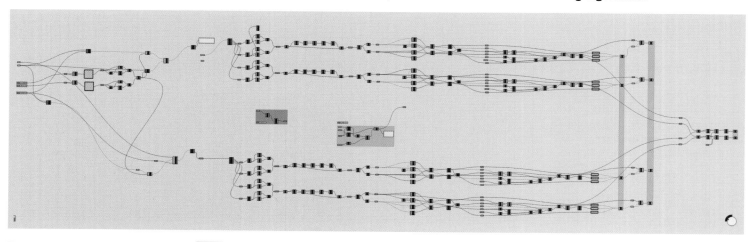

Figure 1. Symbolic diagram of design relationships.

techniques, it was a welcome surprise to experience an entirely unimpressed Nick while I manipulated this range of parameters in a geometric control jig. With symbolic diagrams, data and shaded viewports spread across two large screens, the discussion centered entirely on design explorations—not on the technology on the screen. [Figure 1] For Nick, this usage of associative geometry was a direct manifestation of the design methodology Grimshaw Architects was founded upon, simply in digital form. It was natural and intuitive. All I had done was embed our design process, through diagrams and formal relationships, into a digital model available to us for iterative design.

This story exemplifies the concept behind how our firm, and specifically those who are part of our Computational Design Unit (CDU), works as digital tool builders and developers of design spaces in the pursuit of architecture. The creation of rule systems through algorithms grounded in the realities of site, program, material and construction is rooted in Grimshaw's past history of designing formal geometric systems influenced by industrial design fabrication. These rule systems are manifested through 3D associative modeling, where digital objects in the scene are embedded with properties and rules through complex relationships to other objects. The advent of this entire technique, often called computational design, developed as a tool that allows us to embed design intelligence rooted in the office's design methodology, as it has existed for almost thirty years.

FIRST PRINCIPLES DESIGN METHODS
—

The International Terminal at London's Waterloo Station laid the groundwork for Grimshaw's use of associative geometric systems. Sir Nicholas's earliest work demonstrated the tenets of First Principles design methods as expressed within the "British High-Tech" architectural movement: expression of material properties and structural forces, and performance-driven design through a pervasive examination of energy and environmental effect. Through a love of the archetypal "industrial shed", numerous early projects were developed as a kit-of-parts: bespoke industrial design objects systematized to create space. The desire at Waterloo was to create a logical system for spanning multiple train tracks in an open-air station within the constraints of an eccentric site. Taking its cues from Brunel's train sheds, yet reflecting the construction methods and materials of the modern day, Waterloo's kit-of-parts system was not developed based on explicit measurements, but instead on a collection of implicit rules and relationships between parts.

The template was simple: two bowstring trusses spanning over the tracks, following the changing site boundary from one end to the other. [Figure 2] While making the truss arcs tangential for the entire length of the changing site boundaries resulted in unique trusses at each junction, the implicit-rule-based system made the instructions for developing each truss clear. This system was further developed using early CAD technology through the assistance of engineer YRM Anthony Hunt Associates. The result is complex without being complicated.

Figure 2 (above left). The Waterloo International Terminal in London by Grimshaw Architects. The geometry for the parametric roof model was developed from tangential arcs with shifting radii to follow the changing width of the site from one end to the other.

Figure 3 (above right). The geometry of each structural arch adjusts slightly to conform to site boundaries.

The Waterloo International Terminal is a collection of rigorous structural and geometric rules, overlapping to create a visually unique structure. [Figure 3]

Waterloo's influence over the development of design systems went beyond Grimshaw. Years later, the same group of individuals at YRM who developed the structural CAD models resulting in Waterloo's geometric rules, formed the Smartgeometry Group. The founding directors of the Smartgeometry Group, Hugh Whitehead (Foster + Partners), J. Parrish (Arup Sport), Lars Hesselgren (PLP) and Robert Aish (then of Bentley Systems, now Autodesk), sought to re-invigorate the usage of algorithmic design techniques explored at Waterloo within the architectural and engineering professions through the development of CAD associative modeling tools. The Smartgeometry Group, working with Bentley System's R&D, helped to develop the pioneering computational design software GenerativeComponents, for which Waterloo Station provided an early testing prototype. [Figure 4] Now, through a yearly international workshop and conference, the Smartgeometry Group continues this development with the next generation of computational designers.

ITERATIVE DESIGN MODELS: FROM DIRECT MODELING TO ASSOCIATIVE MODELING
—

Computational tools, including both direct modeling for design exploration and visualization, and algorithmic modeling for complex systems, have become increasingly commonplace at Grimshaw over the past five years. Direct modeling, the process of 3D modeling each geometric object based on explicit coordinates, had been the standard design tool in this office for many years. Despite regular use of formal geometric systems to develop building forms following Waterloo, these rule systems were unable to be embedded in the digital model due to software limitations. Grimshaw suffered from the typical problems associated with direct 3D modeling: rules and algorithms, documented external to the 3D model through diagrams in sketchbooks, were implemented at each design iteration, resulting in hours or sometimes days of manual re-modeling as conditions or design intent changed. Each parameter change essentially required the designer to hit the delete key and start from scratch, following each rule down the line again to completion, only to have more parameters change the next day. With a constant need to visualize the ever-changing design

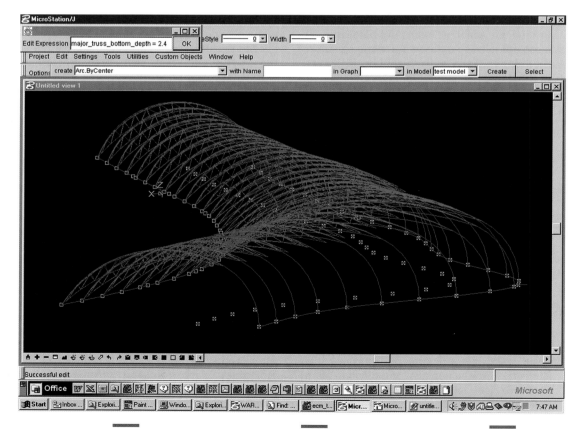

Figure 4. Tests of an associative geometry model in an early version of GenerativeComponents.

as it progressed, this time-consuming process was a necessary evil.

As opposed to modeling the solution directly, associative modeling enables the designer to set up relationships and restrictions from which the design will result. In essence, you are embedding the designers' thinking into an active model—the creation of a design space in which every result satisfies the requirements of the design upfront, freeing one to explore solutions playfully.

Early testing and development of associative modeling systems occurred between the New York and London offices in 2003, beginning with the roof design of the Eden Project's Education Resource Centre. Based on the phyllotaxis pattern of sunflowers, the roof geometry and

panelization was developed with an early alpha version of GenerativeComponents, as a collaboration between a junior staff member and our structural engineer at the first Smartgeometry Workshop. [Figures 5, 6] In New York, the early development of the dome in the Fulton Street Transit Center implemented additional layers of control in the computational design process via natural light analysis and fabrication output. [Figure 7] For the Transit Center, seemingly banal elements such as the inclusion of OSHA

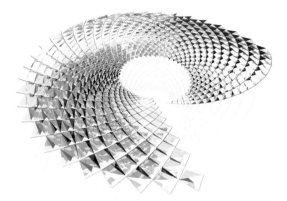

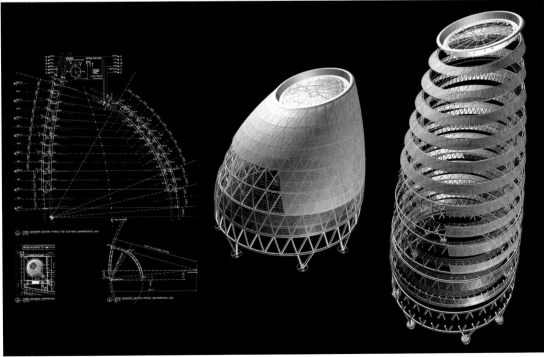

Figure 5 (top left). The Eden Project Education Resource Centre, Cornwall, by Grimshaw Architects. Roof structure and panelization developed from the phylotaxis pattern found in sunflowers.

Figure 6 (top right). Final completed roof made from standing seam copper and photovoltaic panels.

Figure 7 (bottom). Fulton Street Transit Center by Grimshaw Architects. The dome geometry is based upon a pair of arcs and an array of offset circles. The associative model generated structural frame centerlines and fabrication

drawings for both the glass and perforated metal skins.

regulations as an input parameter for a maintenance access ramp demonstrated the power of the system to aid in solving a wide range of design problems.

During subsequent projects, the use of associative modeling tools began to yield a different model for iterative design, both in how teams interacted with our engineers who were focused on analysis, but also within the team structure inside Grimshaw. I was consulted on a regular basis to create a digital tool to be used by the team in developing their design much in the same way a woodworker will develop a control jig to limit aspects of the fabrication process. After the creation of a well-developed jig and clear control system, the team would take complete ownership over further iterations within this design space, confident that all iterations would meet the requirements of the design as embedded in the jig.

On the Museo del Acero (Museum of Steel) in Monterrey, Mexico, associative modeling systems were used to develop two elements in the design: a steel-plate folded-roof structure and an exterior louver cladding system. For the roof, a simple set of geometric rules based upon a circular array of points projected on inclined planes set out the initial geometry (see Workflow Case Study at end of article). From there, flat panels connecting the point arrays

were constructed, and a slider and variable-based control panel was created, allowing the team a wide range of adjustability within the system. Sliders, akin to volume controls on a recording-studio mixing board, are very common among associative-modeling tools as a way to iterate across a range of input numbers, viewing their impact on the model dynamically. When the team developed a tight feedback loop with their structural engineer, Werner Sobek, and received the results from the finite element analysis suggesting adjustments in plate arrangements and fold depths, changes would be made dynamically in the model, and a new model would be exported within minutes for another round of analysis. The final design was flattened using simple unfolding algorithms, handed to the contractor for fabrication, and a set of assembly drawings was created by deriving angles and coordinates from the digital model.

The louver system for the exterior of the "cast hall" was an opportunity to develop a more sophisticated and expressive control system for geometry. Surpassing the limitations of a one-dimensional control provided by sliders, a more tactile system was used to manipulate louver rotation by way of a 3D control surface. Using the inherent smoothing properties of a NURBS surface, a number of points on a control surface

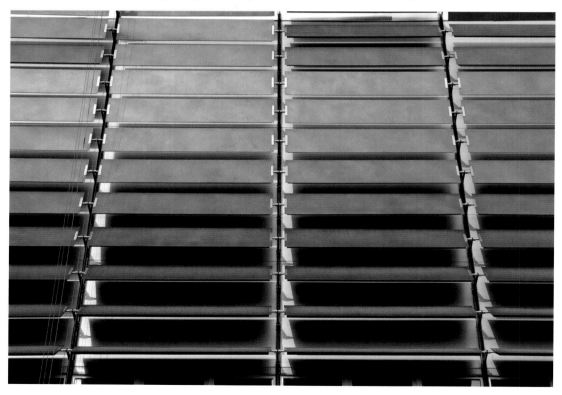

Figure 8. Museo del Acero. Louver rotation was generated by a three-dimensional control surface linked directly to each panel.

were mapped directly to the panels. Any change in Z-depth for the control surface resulted in a rotated panel within certain constraints. With the project architect in front of the screen, we willfully manipulated the control surface to create a sequence of blended louver openings aligned with windows and view axis. This model was then live-linked with the final construction output, a simple spreadsheet listing each louver's alpha-numeric code and its corresponding rotation value. Within two days, the subcontractor was on site with a printed version of the spreadsheet, rotating the louvers into place. [Figure 8]

ON THE WAY TO SHARED ASSOCIATIVE MODELS FOR FABRICATION

—

For a number of years, computational design tasks at Grimshaw were completed by myself and eventually a small group of dedicated staff. This resulted in the founding of a more formal group called the Computation Design Unit (CDU). An applied research and development group created to structure work with new digital design tools, the CDU's scope includes advanced geometric and associative modeling, early environmental analysis, fabrication and visualization. This arrangement, common in a number of larger architecture and engineering firms, persisted for two years. Recognizing that the landscape of computational design was changing, a new model for the CDU was necessary. As algorithmic workflows began to become part of the standard academic curriculum in universities around the world, we began to find that junior staff were quicker to engage such processes on a regular basis.

In order to manage algorithmic workflows as embedded in associative modeling tools, the CDU moved to a distributed model with project-embedded designers. Staff of Grimshaw who are members of the CDU play two roles: they act as computational designers for their projects, working directly within the team, and they also engage in general R&D, covering the topic of "Project Technology". While we have not implemented the Google "20 percent time" model[1] for personal projects or R&D, we have engaged in topic-related group development of techniques.

Recent general group development has yielded a number of repeat-use systems focused on patterning and panelization. In many cases, these systems are developed initially as bespoke tools for a competition or project design study, but are subsequently generalized for reuse through the cleaning-up of code and descriptive annotations within the symbolic diagrams. Another team is able to take this new generalized tool and reuse it on their own projects to achieve similar effects.

Supported by tools like 3D printers and laser cutters, junior architects who are experienced with computational design tools encounter fabrication issues early on. Model-making has served as an educational tool, providing direct contact with material properties. As restrictions against shearing, common in sheet and some

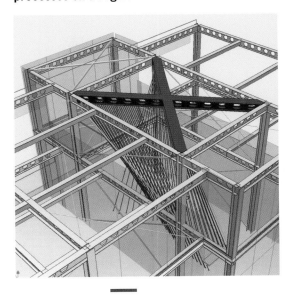

Figure 9 (above left). In this project by Grimshaw Architects for AMG headquarters in New York, the glass and steel stair was modeled with full material and structural constraints built into the design system from the beginning.

Figure 10 (above right). Rendering of the final design showing steel cables and glass treads.

model materials, limit the ability of some materials to take on double curvature, design teams encounter patterns as a method of subdividing surfaces to flat panels. Embedding material and assembly constraints into the design model is beginning to become regular practice on projects where a direct link between Grimshaw and the fabricator is possible. For example, our New York Industrial Design team received material and structural properties for the design of a glass tread and steel cable stair for the headquarters of AMG, a stair fabricator, and used this information as constraints in setting up a parametric solid-modeling tool. This level of direct interaction with the fabricators yielded a more informed design space. [Figures 9, 10]

Using elements of modern digital manufacturing processes as part of computational models still faces barriers with some of our most common project types: transit and infrastructure. On these projects, we often cannot have a direct tie to fabrication, due to the separation between the architect and the construction process (both its means and its methods) that is mandated by large-scale infrastructure and government work. While this does not affect internal usage of computational tools to develop the design, it does restrict the output to traditional 2D drawings. The issue of how to

express more complex elements of the design is addressed by developing "geometric method statements": drawings outlining the rules we used to generate our 3D systems. These drawings enable any fabricator to reconstruct Grimshaw's system in the computational design software of their choice (with the added benefit of excluding any fabricators without sufficient computational design skills from applying for the work).

Our hope is to move beyond this practice by engaging all fabricators in the development of a shared associative model as early as possible in the design process. In recognizing the invaluable contribution fabricators can make through their craft, we hope to foster an unbroken design-to-production workflow for future projects through a unified language of computational design.

THE NEW DESIGN TEAM
—

As all our team members, regardless of their capabilities in 3D and algorithmic design, are designers, we are beginning to see the development of a new culture and language for collaboration within project teams. Project architects either are working directly inside associative models, or they speak the language

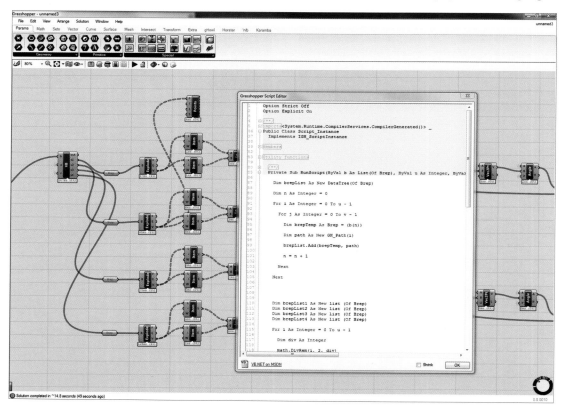

Figure 11. Symbolic diagram showing the wiring of geometric associations and a custom script.

well enough to direct the team to work within this new design methodology. The symbolic diagram, a graphic device common in associative modeling tools and intended as a representation of the design's rule systems, enables design discussion among team members. [Figure 11] All team members are beginning to recognize the power that lies in abstract algorithmic notation.

Although more common in early competition and concept stages, this working method is also applied in further phases of a number of our projects with the aim of directing fabrication. By embedding the intelligence of fabrication methods and material properties into algorithmic design models, teams are able to design workflows that blend concept and fabrication, which supports Grimshaw's long tradition of integrating design and production. All consultants can be creative forces in shaping the design at inception. Early inclusion of data received from consultants, whether environmental or structural, helps to make the associative model an even richer design space. While we have yet to utilize this more comprehensive workflow method from start to finish on a project, competition-level studies where a single associative model has been shared between architect and structural engineer have yielded compelling results worthy of future exploration.

New design team structures, built upon early collaboration and shared digital models among all team members, are essential to implementing this workflow in active projects. The distributed model for the CDU was recently expanded to include all four Grimshaw offices globally. Questions about geometry, fabrication, analysis and software can now be posted to the group for feedback, effectively resulting in a crowd-sourced collection of solutions for review. Using Web 2.0 technologies in a collaboration-based intranet, like micro-blogs for posting quick questions and news, and wikis for the documentation of internally developed systems, enables conversations across the offices on newly found software and methods, and furthermore fosters the collaborative design of new internal design systems. [Figure 12]

In our quest for integrated workflows between designer and consultant, between digital model and fabricated element, we should approach design from both top-down (form and program) and bottom-up (component and fabrication) directions. We can and should embed performance and material fabrication criteria upfront into the model, in order to work within a well-formed design space. Computational design should be intrinsic—a tool that enables us to express our core thinking and approaches to design. It will inherently be unique—a design process, as expressed in digital tools and workflows, that represents and supports individual approaches to design. Algorithmic modeling should not be treated as a style, but instead as part of a new digital design methodology—a tool for achieving design concepts based on First Principles.

ENDNOTES

—

1. Google's 20 percent time is a management philosophy that allows software engineers to spend one day a week developing new projects or working on projects they are personally interested in that are outside their primary job description.

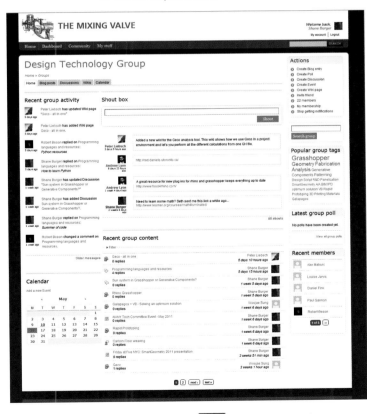

Figure 12. Screenshot of Grimshaw's social and collaborative intranet prototype, showing micro-blogging, forum and wiki pages.

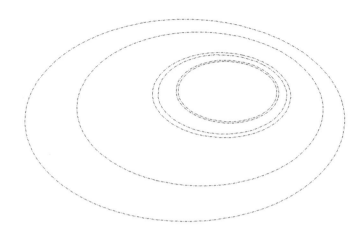

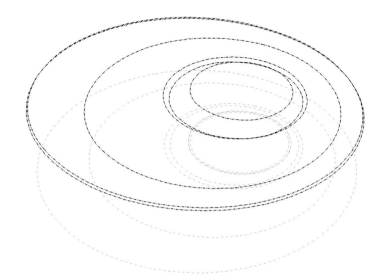

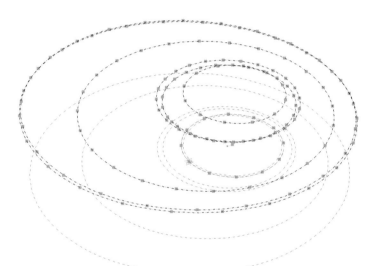

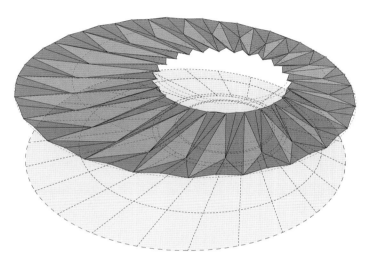

MUSEO DEL ACERO
WORKFLOW CASE STUDY ▶

The design of the Museo del Acero in Monterrey included the adaptive reuse of a decommissioned steel foundry and a new gallery addition into a series of exhibition, workshop and educational spaces. Digital workflows were used on the new circular gallery and the cladding design of the large cast hall to generate the design, refine the geometry and link to fabrication processes.

Workflow 1a (top left). The folded steel plate roof for the gallery addition: concentric and offset circles were projected on inclined planes.

Workflow 1b (top right). Inclined circles were subdivided from those initial circles to set folded plate nodes.

Workflow 1c (bottom left). Planar surfaces were created between folded plate nodes. Location and radius of all circles, location and angle of inclined planes, and number of plate nodes were all adjustable

in real time by a custom-designed control system.

Workflow 1d (bottom right). The final geometry of the roof was created by connecting the nodes generated in the previous steps. Because it was parametrically linked, changing one piece of the geometry would automatically update the rest of the model, allowing a continuous feedback loop to be developed between the architects and the structural engineers.

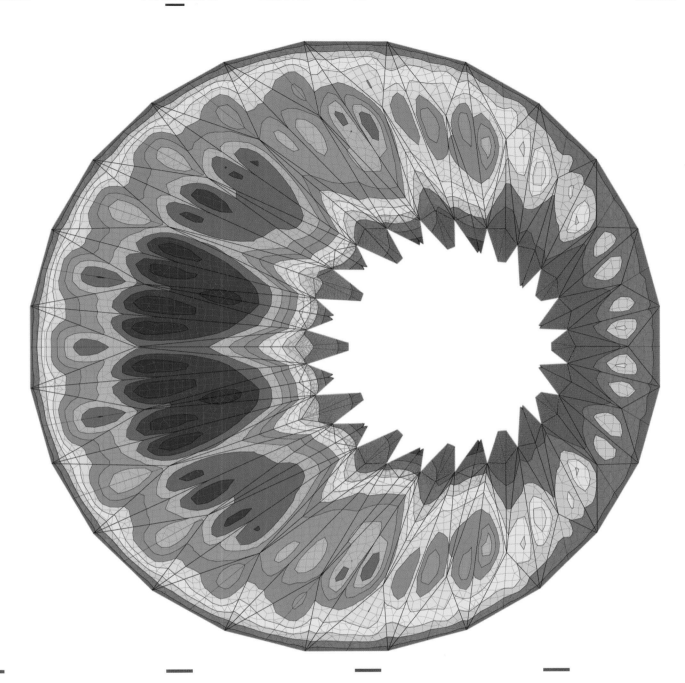

Workflow 2. The parametric
model could be exported out
and run under a structural
finite element analysis program to determine structural
and material requirements.

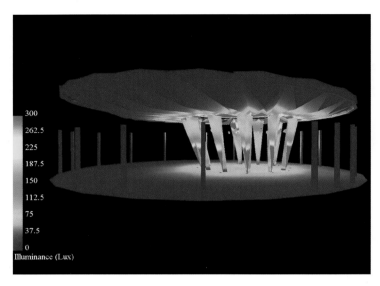

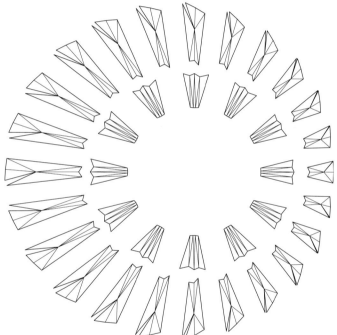

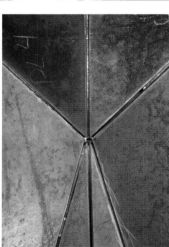

Workflow 3 (top left). The same model could also be exported out and tested in an artificial illumination and acoustics simulation to determine the lighting and sound attenuation requirements.

Workflow 4 (bottom left). The model was then broken apart into buildable components and the geometry could be unfolded to be developed for fabrication.

Workflow 5 (top right). The gallery addition and louvered facade under construction.

Workflow 6 (bottom right). The patterns for the folded metal plates were developed directly from the unfolded model and fabrication mock-ups were produced at smaller scales to check the structural integrity.

Workflow 7. The folded
metal plate assembly became
both structure and roof.
Construction on site proceeded
with temporary structural members in place until the assembly
was situated properly and could
become self-supporting.

Workflow 8. The expressive
form of the surface structure
plays into the museum's focus
on the history and application of steel in building and
industry.

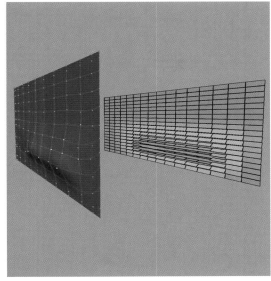

	1	2	3	4	5	6	7	8	9	10	11	12	13	14	15	16	17	18	19	20	21	22	23	24
A										0	0	0	0	0	0	0	0	0	0	0	0	0	0	0
B							0	2	5	10	16	21	25	28	30	31	32	31	29	25	18	7	0	0
C							0	2	8	16	25	34	40	45	49	50	51	50	45	41	29	12	0	0
D			0			0	0	3	10	19	30	40	48	53	57	59	60	59	55	43	35	14	0	0
E			0		0	0	0	3	10	20	30	40	48	54	58	60	61	60	56	48	43	14	0	2
F			0	45	0	0	0	3	9	18	28	37	44	50	53	55	55	56	55	52	45	32	13	4
G			0		0	0	2	6	12	18	23	31	37	42	45	46	47	46	43	37	27	11	0	5
H			0		0	0	2	6	12	18	24	29	32	34	36	36	36	35	33	29	21	8	0	6
I			0		0	0	1	4	8	13	17	20	23	24	25	26	25	24	20	15	6	0	0	6
J			0	0	45	0	0	1	3	6	9	11	14	15	16	17	17	17	16	14	10	4	0	6
K			0	0	45	0	0	0	2	3	5	7	9	10	10	11	11	11	10	9	6	2	0	5
L			0	0	0	0	0	0	1	2	3	4	5	6	6	6	6	6	6	5	4	1	0	4
M			0	0	0	0	0	0	0	1	2	2	3	3	3	3	3	3	3	2	0	0	0	2
N			0	0	0	0	0	0	0	0	0	0	0	0	0	0	0	0	0	0	0	0	0	0
O	0	0	0	0	0	0	0	8	15	15	15	15	15	15	15	15	15	15	15	15	10	0	0	10
P	13	13	13	13	15	15	15	28	30	30	30	30	30	30	30	30	30	30	30	30	15	10	10	20
Q	25	25	25	25	28	30	30	38	45	45	45	45	45	45	45	45	45	45	45	45	33	20	20	29

	25	26	27	28	29	30	31	32	33	34	35	36	37	38	39	40	41	42	43	44	45	46	47
A	0	0	0	0	0	0	0	7	18	27	33	35	35									0	0
B	0	0	0	0	0	0	7	18	27	33	35	35										0	0
C	0	0	0	0	0	0	11	29	42	51	57	60										0	0
D	2	3	3	2	0	0	12	32	47	57	64	69										0	0
E	6	7	7	6	2	0	12	31	45	55	62	67										0	0
F	8	10	10	8	4	0	10	26	39	48	54	58										0	0
G	10	13	13	10	5	0	8	20	30	37	43	46	37	38	39	40	41	41	42	42	56	30	30
H	11	14	14	11	6	0	5	15	22	27	31	35	37	38	38	40	30	30	31	25	20	20	20
I	12	15	15	12	6	0	4	10	15	19	22	24	26	27	28	29	30	30	30	20	16	12	12
J	11	14	14	11	6	0	2	6	9	12	14	16	17	18	19	19	20	20	20	20	16	9	6
K	10	13	13	10	5	0	1	3	5	7	8	9	10	10	11	11	12	12	12	12	9	6	6
L	8	10	10	8	4	0	0	1	2	3	3	4	4	5	5	5	5	5	6	6	3	0	0
M	6	7	7	6	2	0	0	0	0	0	0	0	0	0	0	0	0	0	0	0	0	0	0
N	2	3	3	2	0	0	0	0	0	0	0	0	0	0	0	0	0	0	0	0	0	0	0
O	10	10	10	10	10	0	0	10	15	15	15	15	15	15	15	15	15	15	15	15	8	0	0
P	20	20	20	20	20	10	10	20	30	30	30	30	30	30	30	30	30	30	30	30	28	15	15
Q	29	29	29	29	29	20	20	33	45	45	45	45	45	45	45	45	45	45	45	45	35	30	30

Workflow 9 (top left). For the exterior louvered façade, a design system was developed through a 3D associative model using a control surface (at left), enabling real-time visual adjustments of louver rotation. Louver rotation was then finetuned within constraints and aligned with programmatic requirements. For example, openings aligned with the architect's desired sight lines from inside the building.

Workflow 10 (bottom). Louver rotation values were live-linked to Excel and exported to a spreadsheet for use by the subcontractor.

Workflow 11 (top right). The contractor was then able to hand-adjust the louvers in place, following the printed-out schedule.

———

Workflow 12 (above left).
Completed roof of gallery
addition.

———

Workflow 13 (right). Completed
project with gallery addition
in foreground and louvered
façade behind.

———

WORKFLOW TEAMS
—
EDITOR'S NOTES

The transformation of working methods through digitally integrated workflows suggests new hierarchies within existing office structures as well as new models of practice. Many firms focus on these workflows as a means to increase efficiency—the primary motivation behind BIM—while others focus on exploring new design potentials, largely driven by parametric or associative modeling, where efficiency is more of a by-product than a goal. The workflows discussed by Shane Burger belong to this more creative array of processes and have enabled an office like Grimshaw Architects to advance their office philosophy of design and technology integration such that structure, material and production methods become the foundation of creative thinking. For Grimshaw, the design potentials of associative modeling, more than the management potential of BIM, are driving new working relationships between project team members.

Over the past decade, the division between architectural designers and digital technicians spawned an increasing number of outside specialty consultants and elite programmers dedicated to designing digital workflows for offices. However, this division is beginning to disappear as architects recognize the design potential of these new tools. In more technologically progressive offices, this digital expertise is internal and rapidly moving from back office research and development to an essential ingredient of project teams.

The evolution of the Computational Design Unit at Grimshaw Architects and the rapid integration of its members into design teams is representative of these new team structures. The CDU has typically worked on special projects largely outside of the day-to-day office work, with the goal of developing tools or techniques that might be useful for specific parts of a project.[1] Originating as more speculative, the research work of the CDU has quickly become an invaluable resource for many projects. This has created a new dynamic between project designers and computational designers and has resulted in the members of research groups being positioned as an integral part of project design teams. While previous developments in digital technology such as CAD and explicit 3D modeling simply shifted the manual process of drawing to the computer with little or no impact on design processes or team structure, associative modeling affects the underlying creative thinking process by, as Burger describes it, "embedding the designers' thinking into an active model". This capturing of design intent, along with the ability to include technical constraints often not addressed until construction, anticipates workflows where the design system develops in tandem with the design intent as well as a team structure where the work of computational designers is an extension of the work of project designers.

When the algorithmic logics of digital models define the design space of possible solutions, they become an intricate part of the design process. While standard design software is intended to be generic enough to work for any design approach, the custom scripts and workflows developed by Burger and his team are intended to support the specific design approach of their office—a strategy also utilized by other offices presented in this book including Morphosis, UNStudio and Buro Happold. This strategy recognizes the interdependencies between design and technique that develop with digital workflows and the new types of collaboration and skills required. The accumulated knowledge of senior architects with years of design and construction experience can be combined with the programming skills of younger designers.[2] This dynamic is manifest in the scene of Shane Burger sitting with Sir Nicholas Grimshaw exploring design options through custom-designed digital interfaces. While this still maintains a distinction between types of designers and their respective roles, a further development of project teams will occur when project designers begin to use basic programming techniques themselves. Project design and computational design will become intertwined.

Designing design, for Grimshaw, is the process of applying creative instincts and human judgment to the decisions that set the rules of parametrically structured design space. The creative effort of a typical analog design process, culminating in the discrete decisions that define a building, is frontloaded to the design of a design system. The enhanced design system offers a higher level of creative exploration (what Burger refers to as "playful") through complex relationships that would be impossible without computation. While this is "natural and intuitive" for an office like Grimshaw, it poses a challenge to architects surrounded by data and technology but with no workflow to drive it.

—

1. Similar types of computational research groups are common in larger offices and constantly evolve as the technology advances. Examples of current versions include SMART Solutions at Buro Happold, the BlackBox Studio at SOM and the Smart Parameters Platform at UNStudio.

2. Another version of this type of collaboration is the new working relationship between traditional and computational designers outlined by Marty Doscher in "Disposable Code in Persistent Design" in this volume.

WORKFLOW CONSULTANCY
—
SCOTT MARBLE AND JAMES KOTRONIS

James Kotronis is the US-eastern Regional Director at Gehry Technologies.

The Fish pavilion design by Frank Gehry for the 1992 Olympics in Barcelona marked a turning point in the relationship between design, assembly and industry. It initiated digital processes in architecture that have evolved into the more comprehensive workflows being used today. With this project, technologies were deployed that were new to the design and construction industry, including scanners for digitizing 3D form, CNC machining for fabricating parts from this digitized information and GPS to locate reference points in space for site assembly of these digitally fabricated parts. After several years of refining these processes internally, Gehry Technologies (GT) was launched to offer this service to the industry at large. Reliant on proprietary software called Digital Project (derived from Catia, a powerful parametric software used primarily by the aerospace industry) and on the working protocols developed for previous projects, GT pioneered a new type of "workflow consultancy" that began the arduous task of stitching together an industry that was fragmented by decades of disciplinary isolation.

Since that time, many other versions of digital workflow consultants have emerged in an attempt to leverage the potential of digital tools to link existing sectors of the industry and bring in new sectors in response to the growing demand for intelligent processes and intelligent buildings.[1]

The work of GT initially addressed procedural problems that hindered an efficient translation of formally complex design to fabrication and construction. A "brute force" rationalization of geometry for constructability at the outset, solutions evolved into an intricate digital workflow that integrates formal design intent, site constraints, material behavior, assembly design, shipping constraints, cost parameters and schedule coordination, as represented by the Burj Khalifa Tower Office Lobby Ceiling. This workflow design was flexible enough to allow project-specific factors to be incorporated when appropriate. For instance, in the Burj Khalifa, the veneer mapping was incorporated into the workflow model to solve the aesthetic challenge of a uniform distribution of grain appearance across a large surface, a task that otherwise would have been left to chance and likely resulted in substantial material waste. In order to incorporate as much information into the model as possible, the process often involves physical prototypes or tests to identify the limits of material behavior and use them as parameter contraints within the model, in order to define the range of viable design options. Experience from expert craftspeople can also be integrated into the model, in a form of knowledge engineering[2] where rules are extracted from hand sketches and informal exchange about the specific parts of the project.

Highly unique designs combined with complex project conditions, like in the Broad Museum by Diller Scofidio + Renfro, are encouraging more architects to engage in the workflows developed by GT. Although GT has explicitly positioned itself not as a design consultancy but as a technical facilitator (as to not confuse GT with Gehry Architects), there is little doubt that the knowledge and input they provide to projects have a significant impact on final architectural results. Most of their staff are trained as architects and represent a new generation of designers, a generation who sees much less of a distinction between the design intent and the technical means to achieve it than did the previous generation of architects.

The attempt by GT to avoid any confusion with the role of the design architect is the result of a lingering, but questionable culture of the Sole Designer, a culture that continues to be a primary source of identity for architects. As the writer Keith Sawyer notes: "We're drawn to the image of the lone genius whose mystical moment of insight changes the world. But the lone genius is a myth; instead, it's group genius that generates breakthrough innovation."[3] The type of infastructural integration and interactive workflows developed by GT offer an opportunity to push towards this model of open and inclusive work. This will identify and challenge bad ideas, by testing their robustness through the means and methods to be used for their realization, but also make good ideas better in the same way, whatever their origin. The collaborative approach should not be confused with the banality of design-by-committee, which is the result of compromise, but rather should be seen as experts meeting with clearly defined positions and skills.

A by-product of digital workflows is the inventory of design scripts as well as material and procedural knowledge that have been captured in code. This raises the question of reusablity of this code. While the advantages of refining industry-wide procedural issues through the reuse and refinement of digital workflows—similar to upgraded versions of software—seems obvious, the advantages of doing the same for design processes is a more debatable issue. The work between GT and Erwin Hauer shown below illuminates some of these issues. Is there a new economy of design with digital design workflows, where a designer's "uniqueness" is captured in code and, with the simple adjustment of input parameters, reproduced in a new design? Is the act of creativity identical with the "uniqueness" of designers, or does the ability of someone else to translate this into code produce results more unique than the input? These are some of the provocative questions that are emerging with new design, assembly and industry workflows and the work of a new category of consultants, like GT, who are exploring their potential.

The three projects representing the work of GT New York were selected to show the impact at different scales and in the context of the three types of workflows presented in this book: design workflows and the development of rule-based logics that can contain design intent (Hauer Wall); fabrication and assembly workflows that can merge complex form with material and machining capabilities (Burj Khalifa Lobby Ceiling); and industry workflows that place design, construction and owner concerns into clearly defined parameters that can be adjusted, negotiated and integrated with benefits and consequences readily apparent (Broad Museum Workflow).

ENDNOTES

1. Examples include designtoproduction, whose work is presented by co-founder, Fabian Scheurer, in the contribution "Digital Craftsmanship: From Thinking to Modeling to Building" in this volume.
2. Knowledge engineering is the process of transferring human intelligence and experience into computer code.
3. Sawyer, K. (2007) *Group Genius*, New York, Basic Books, p. 7.

WORLD BANK ERWIN HAUER WALL
WORKFLOW CASE STUDY▶

Erwin Hauer's work has become a point of reference for many contemporary architects exploring issues of surface continuity and formal complexity. This project was initiated when Enrique Rosado, who studied with Hauer in the early 1990's and now works in his studio, became interested in connecting his work to digital modeling and fabrication processes. This started with the introduction of computer modeling and the addition of a 5-axis milling machine into the studio, as a step to evolve Hauer's working process through digital means. When attempts to scan some of the existing work proved unsatisfactory, Rosado began modeling the CONTINUA architectural screens and walls. Later, he connected with Ronald Mendoza in the GT Los Angeles office and they began to test some surface modeling for a new project, which then led to the GT New York office becoming involved.

This project for a large wall would extend several floors adjacent to a stair in the lobby of the World Bank in Washington, D.C. Hauer wanted to refine and evolve the form and geometry of the project based on his previous work, but at a larger scale. The role of GT was to define the essential formal logic in a parametric modeling environment, allowing quick iterations of design options and then be able to fabricate from this model. Beyond describing a static form geometrically, the project was an exercise in the art of capturing design intent—asking how an artist would want to control and manipulate a surface and creating a new digital tool with new capacities to do this.

Workflow 1 (top). Hauer's forms have evolved over decades of work and designs from past projects serve as the basis for new commissions and evolve over time.

Workflow 2 (bottom). Castings from some of Hauer's original handcrafted molds.

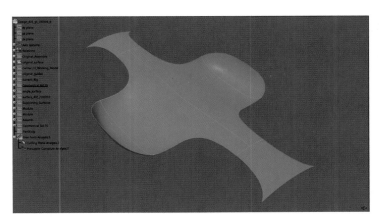

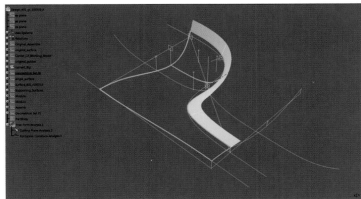

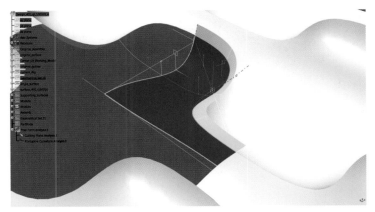

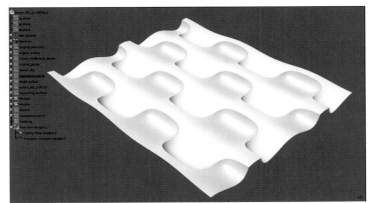

Workflow 3 (top left). Hauer's designs are expressed through surface continuity, which relies on surface tangencies. Enrique Rosada, who has a deep understanding of both the digital and physical side of the process, initially modeled the surface in Rhino but was unable to achieve these tangencies without a relational parametric modeling platform so GT brought the geometry into Digital Project.

Workflow 4 (top right). To enforce the required tangencies and lines of symmetry GT emulated Hauer's hand-working techniques to define the surface in the model to his liking. The yellow bounding surface became the point of tangency for the center surface.

Workflow 5 (middle left). Rules were established to study surface variation. In this image, the purple surface was forced to be tangent to the yellow surface, which adjusted the rig to reflect the desired variations. This rig became a means of communication and translation that made sense to Hauer while giving GT adequate control to evolve the design.

Workflow 6 (middle right). Following Hauer's descriptions of handcrafting his work, GT developed a digital rig. This repeat of the surface pattern would be used to create a CNC-milled mold.

Workflow 7 (bottom). Enrique Rosado, Erwin Hauer, James Kotronis (left to right). Although Hauer was somewhat skeptical of using digital tools to generate work that, for him, was embedded in a handcrafted tradition, he engaged fully in the technology as a way to evolve his thinking. Reviewing designs on the computer, he would perceive and comment on formal aspects that neither Rosado nor GT would notice until a physical 3D print of the surface was prepared.

Workflow 8 (top left). Using a 5-axis CNC milling machine with a large bed at Hauer's factory in New Haven, the positive part of the mold was milled in MDF. There was also the option to mill directly from stone.

Workflow 9 (top right). The design was divided into units and cast in glass fiber reinforced concrete (GFRC) from the molds.

Workflow 10 (bottom left). The units were shipped individually to the site and were combined and finished in place.

Workflow 11 (bottom right). The finished wall.

BURJ KHALIFA TOWER
OFFICE LOBBY CEILING
WORKFLOW CASE STUDY ▶

GT was brought into this project to
assist in the fabrication of an office
lobby ceiling for the Burj Khalifa Tower
in Dubai. An interior rendering of the
design, which the owner had approved,
was the main point of reference for
understanding the scope of this task.
The design concept was lost in translation from design architect to executive
architect to fabricator, which is common on a design with geometry of this
complexity. The project joint venture had
been working unsuccessfully with a local
fabricator, and decided to assemble a new
team that included Imperial Woodworks,
Rick Herskovitz from ICON Global and GT
New York. The project had to be completed
within seven months.

Workflow 1 (above left). The
Burj Khalifa Tower, completed
in 2009, is the tallest building in the world at the time
of writing.

Workflow 2 (top). In this
design rendering, the lobby
ceiling was conceived as a
series of curved surfaces
made from wood that would
weave around the building
structure and house all of
the building systems.

Workflow 3 (bottom). Global
delivery: the joint venture on
location in Dubai; the design
architect, SOM in Chicago; the
millwork fabricator, Imperial
Woodworks in Chicago; Rick
Herskovitz from ICON Global in
Philadelphia; and GT New York.
GT's Abu Dhabi team was also
accessible for on-site issues.

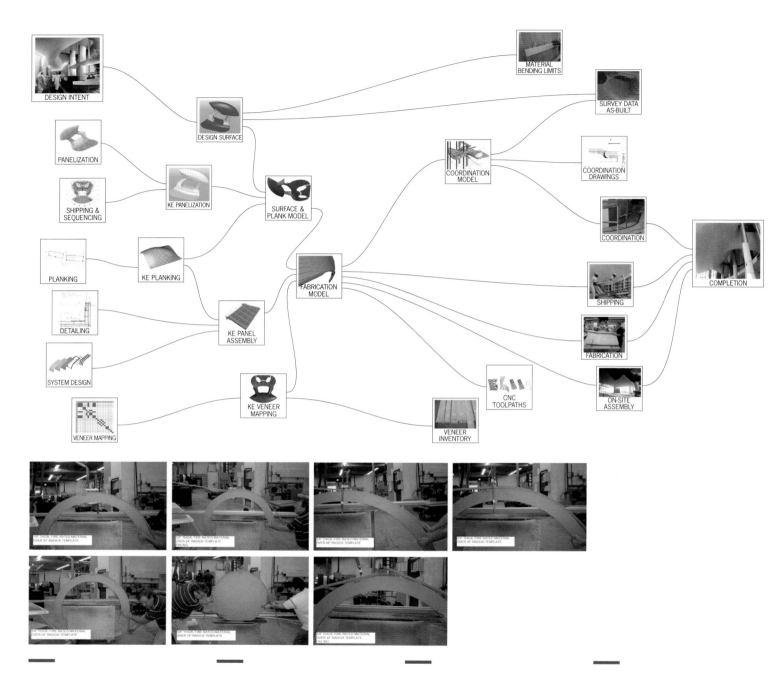

Workflow 4 (top). Diagram illustrating the workflow process: on the left are the design and creative thinking; on the right are the physical constraints of the project; in the middle part are the digital processes used to bring these two sides together. With live parametric modeling, the intent of the surface geometry was captured and layered with the physical limits of material and fabrication including the bending of wood, surface tangencies, prefabrication, panelization, shipping and site assembly. The creative thinking merged with the physical constraints through an integrated model and became actionable, testable and able to be quickly iterated as an effective workflow.

Workflow 5 (bottom). The initial step was to establish the material limits for the bending radius of the wood used for the ceiling. Based on their experience, the millworkers predicted which material thickness would bend to the required radius and then tested this by bending the material to its breaking point. This information was then incorporated into the digital model as a limiting parameter.

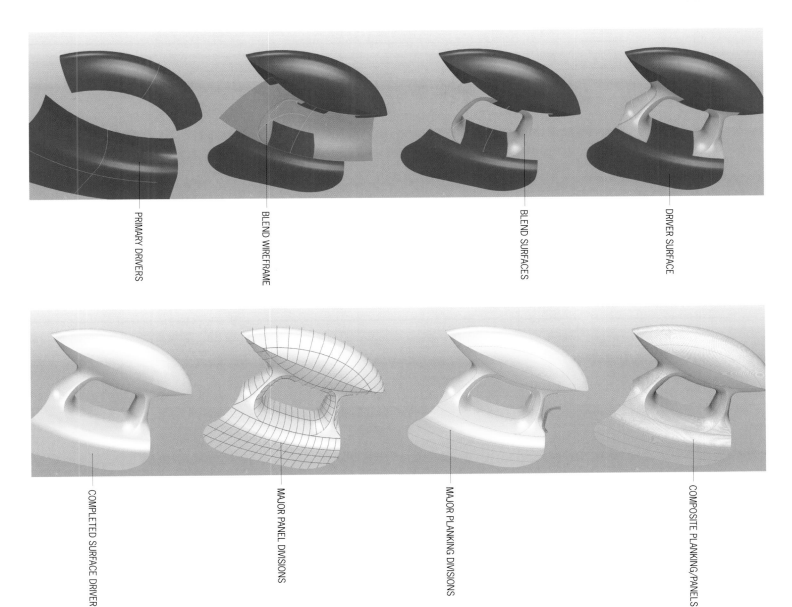

PRIMARY DRIVERS

BLEND WIREFRAME

BLEND SURFACES

DRIVER SURFACE

COMPLETED SURFACE DRIVER

MAJOR PANEL DIVISIONS

MAJOR PLANKING DIVISIONS

COMPOSITE PLANKING/PANELS

Workflow 6a (top). Design drivers: even though the project was in construction, GT had to step back to the underlying design concept and reinterpret the geometry with input from all team members. Adjusting the warped surfaces to material and fabrication constraints resulted in modeling the connecting pieces as "sweeps", which allowed fairly regular panelization (purple). The only areas of unique panelization were the arms (orange).

Workflow 6b (bottom). System drivers: once the surface was developed, the maximum substrate panel size could be overlaid to begin optimizing material usage. The design system was then tuned to fit maximum panel size with the fewest number of components to attach to the framing armature. The individual wood strip planks, which was the finish surface, were then laid on top of the substrate. At this early stage, the project moved from a conceptual idea to a high-fidelity, highly articulated surface

with actual joint lines and material properties.

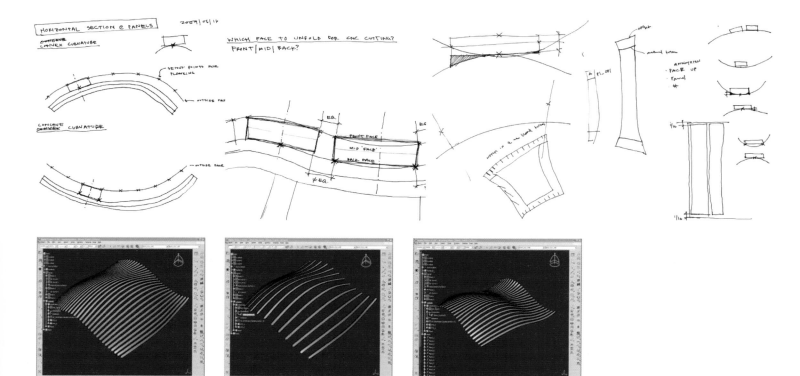

Workflow 7 (top and middle).
The bending and planking
algorithms were developed to
incorporate as many unique
conditions as possible. One
rule required the wood strip
planks to be kept parallel so
that the sides of each plank
would take up the curvature.
Rules to address detailed
nuances were often developed
through sketches before being
written into the algorithm.

Workflow 8a (above left), 8b
(above right). A full-scale
physical mock-up of the most
difficult part of the ceiling
was generated from the digital
model to test not only the
material and aesthetic goals
but also the digital workflow.
All problems identified and
resolved through the physical mock-up were incorporated
into the digital model to
refine the workflow. This step
provided critical feedback to
prepare the digital model with
the necessary information for
fabrication.

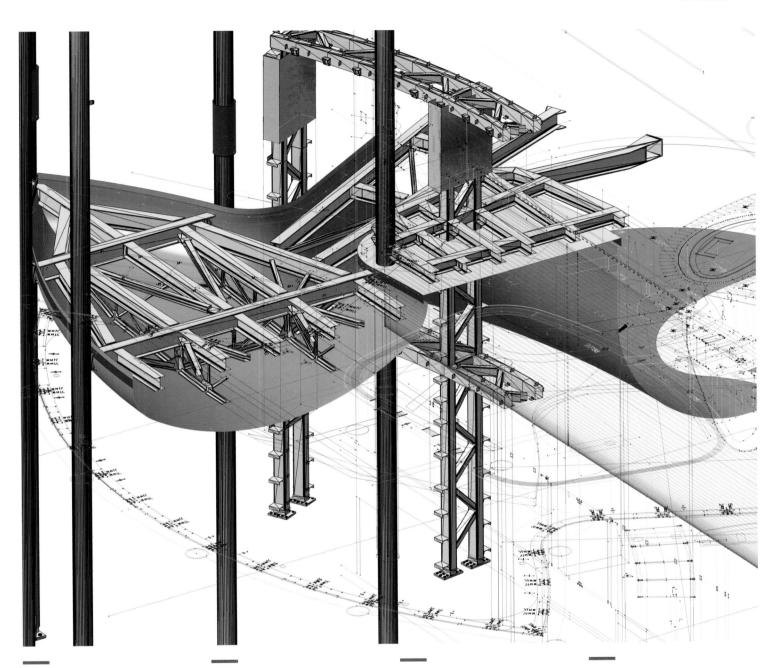

Workflow 9. Because of the
strict schedule and complex
coordination with building
systems, structural columns
and slabs, and other infrastructural elements that were
being built simultaneous to
the ceiling, progressive real-
time surveys of the existing
space were made to adjust
the "as-planned" model to
conform to these "as-built"
conditions. This went through
several iterations over the
course of the project and the
model was continually updated
to avoid on-site installation
conflicts.

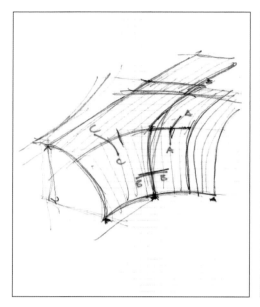

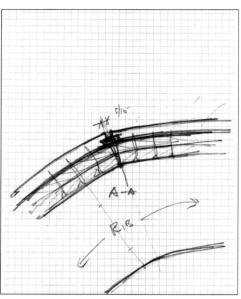

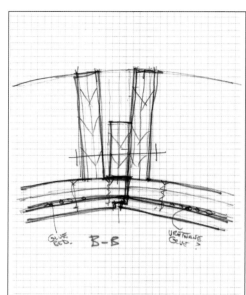

2D output for CNC fabrication

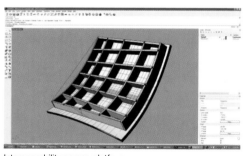

Typical panel assembly

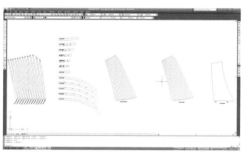

Interoperability across platforms

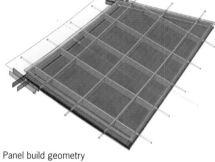

Panel build geometry

Workflow 10a (top). Much of
the digital modeling consisted
of extracting logic and developing rules from sketches of
the substructure and joints
done by the millworker.

Workflow 10b (middle and bottom). The detailed geometric
relationship between the double-
curved egg-crate framing and
surface substrate was worked
out in sketch form and then
generalized into the model.

Workflow 11. The ceiling was made up of 7,000 unique wood veneers of different lengths and widths, and the design intent was to create a uniform distribution of grain types across all surfaces. The mill-worker had no way of achieving this, so GT developed a custom script to manage this process. A spreadsheet was developed by the mill worker with length, width and visual classification for each veneer strip, also indicating which strips could not be adjacent to each other. Victor Keto, a GT automation specialist, set up a weighted selection randomization algorithm that introduced probability into an automated selection and layout process: if the veneer selection fit with its neighbors, the algorithm would use it and move on to the next; if it did not fit, it would search for another option. Three preliminary versions of the veneer layout along with the final selected layout are shown above.

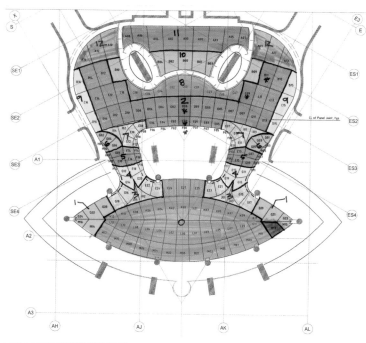

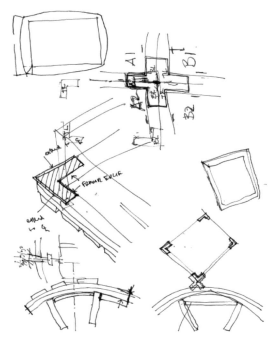

Workflow 12 (top left). The model was used to monitor and track the combination of standard and unique panels, which had different fabrication and delivery schedules in order to optimize the on-site assembly process. In a project of this complexity, it is never effective or feasible for the solution space of a parametric model to solve for all conditions. An 80/20 rule was applied, meaning that the intention was to solve 80% of the conditions and accept that the other 20% would be addressed as unique. The colors represent zones of panel types. The transition areas between the "arm" and "boat" have the highest degree of differentiation, due to the unique nature of those panels.

Workflow 13a (top right), 13b (bottom left). Jigs were designed to align the corners between four panels by controlling any spacing variation across the entire assembly.

Workflow 14 (bottom right). The jigs allowed the installers to position the panels correctly on site.

Workflow 15. The completed
project.

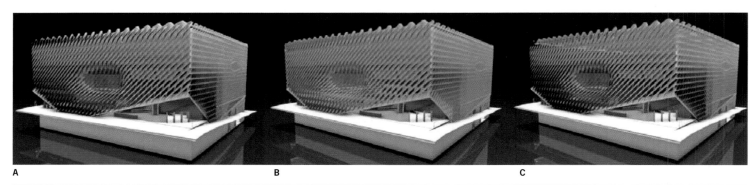

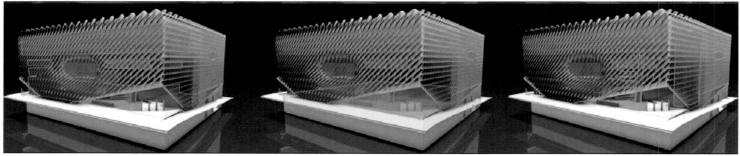

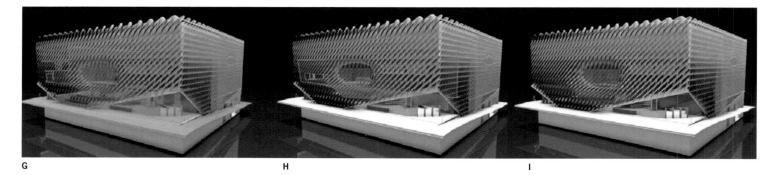

BROAD MUSEUM
DIGITAL WORKFLOW
WORKFLOW CASE STUDY ▶

The task for this project was to help synthesize the digital design workflows with the concurrent scheduling and budget demands for the Broad Museum in Los Angeles, designed by Diller Scofidio + Renfro. GT was engaged at the end of schematic design in a broad collaborative role to structure the process between the key team members and to help manage the integration of the primary building systems with the primary architectural elements.

Software interoperability continues to be one of the main causes of fragmented, silo-working environments and a significant deterrent to truly integrated collaboration. In an effort to address this, GT set up an overall workflow between the team members in a single

relational parametric modeling platform that can accept digital data in a range of file formats. This allows specialized design work to be completed in standard software that is familiar to a particular trade, but then be able to link this work into the shared parametric model. This requires the base modeling platform to have enough flexibility to match the needs and requirements of all of the different specialty platforms without losing valuable data. In this way, GT is trying to address interoperability as a design issue, not just as an exchange of generic file formats.

Workflow 1. The primary design features of the Broad Museum are a structural precast concrete veil surrounding a double-curved cast-in-place concrete "vault" that forms the entrance. GT focused on the interdependency between the primary building systems and how they come together with the veil. This diagram illustrates the building elements highlighted in blue:
A) interior vault, B) exterior façade veil, C) exterior roof veil over the gallery spaces, D) curtainwall that interfaces with the façade veil, E) parking garage below.

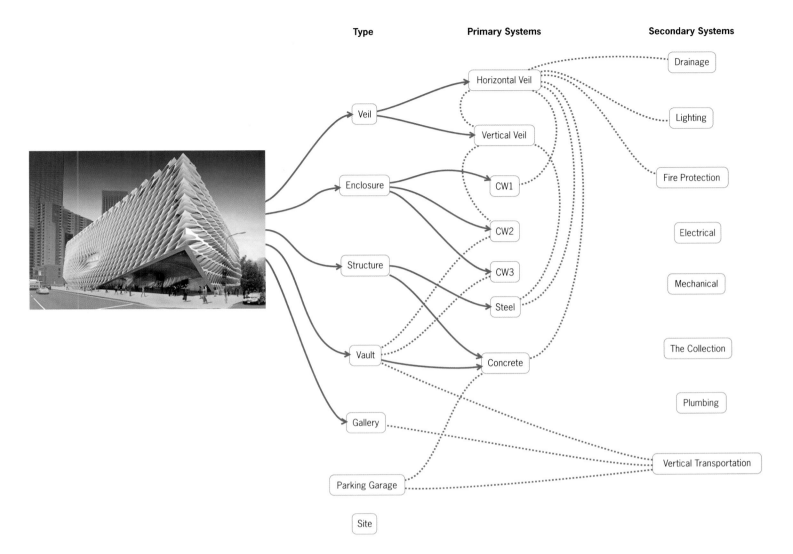

Type   Primary Systems   Secondary Systems

F) vertical circulation that ties into shear walls penetrating the vault.
G) superstructure that interfaces with the veil.

Workflow 2. The diagram of the building elements linked to their primary and secondary systems emphasizes the importance of integrating the architectural and engineering efforts. The integrated parametric model helps coordinate and achieve both the aesthetic/qualitative and the technical/quantitative goals of the project, by fully understanding the impact that each would have on the other and orchestrating their interdependencies.

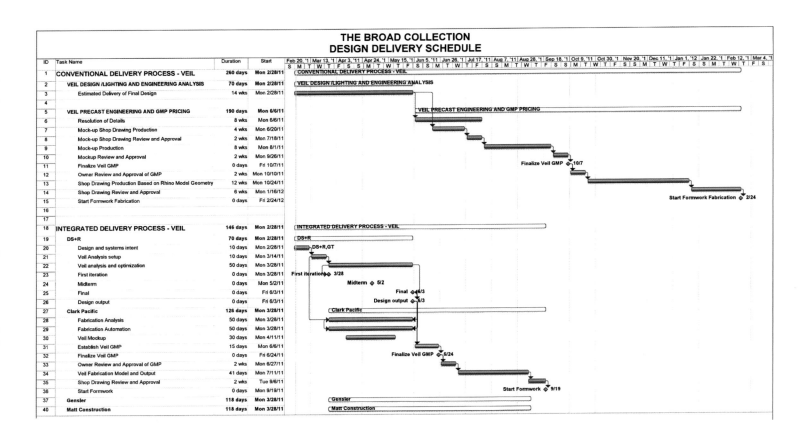

**THE BROAD COLLECTION
DESIGN DELIVERY SCHEDULE**

Current Delivery Process

| DD | CD | GMP | Fabrication Eng/Doc | Review | Fabrication |

Integrated/Concurrent Delivery Process

Synthesis	CD
(review)	(review)
Fabrication Analysis	GMP	Fabrication Eng/Doc	Fabrication

Workflow 3 (top). The initial schedule (top), derived from a conventional delivery process, created significant perceived risk because many high-risk tasks would not be occurring until late in the schedule, when any change would have greater consequences.

Workflow 4 (bottom). Developed after a month-long buy-in process where all team members met and voiced their concerns, an integrated delivery process (bottom) front-loaded critical fabrication and constructability steps that would inform the design and avoid later changes. The accelerated schedule summary emphasized the overlaps between the various team members.

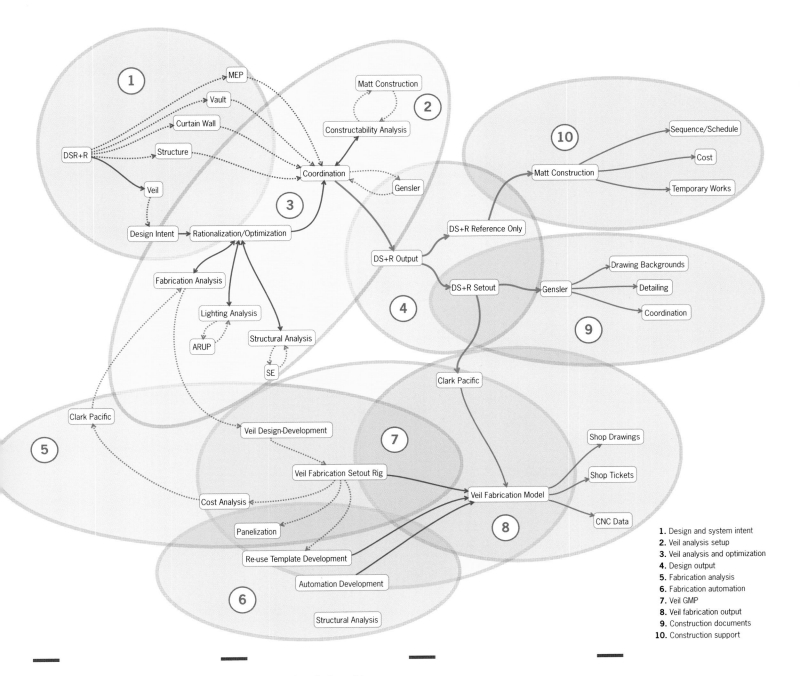

1. Design and system intent
2. Veil analysis setup
3. Veil analysis and optimization
4. Design output
5. Fabrication analysis
6. Fabrication automation
7. Veil GMP
8. Veil fabrication output
9. Construction documents
10. Construction support

Workflow 5. During this buy-in process, a workflow diagram of a concurrent design, engineering and fabrication process facilitated the discussion among the team members. For instance, during the design development of the veil around lighting and structural issues, information is being sent to the precast subcontractor to develop their fabrication processes and perform real-time cost analysis. The workflow was broken down into ten tasks as represented by the shaded ovals. The blue lines indicate design information; the red lines indicate fabrication and pre-construction information; and the green lines indicate the delivery of construction documents.

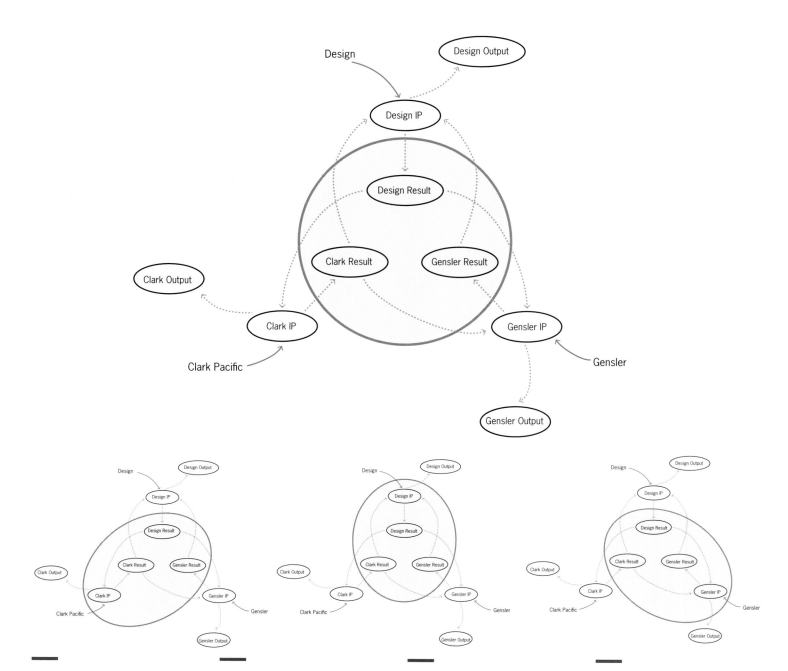

Workflow 6 (top). The three key team members—the design architect (DS+R), the executive architect (Gensler) and the precast fabricator (Clark Pacific)—operate within their internal working environment and then periodically publish modules of information to share and link to the integrated parametric model. This framework allows each member to maintain their intellectual property without sacrificing a high-level collaborative relationship. This extends the traditional BIM structure where interaction is limited and used primarily for clash detection.

Workflow 7 (bottom). These three diagrams show the link between each team member and their internal workflow to the collaborative integrated workflow.

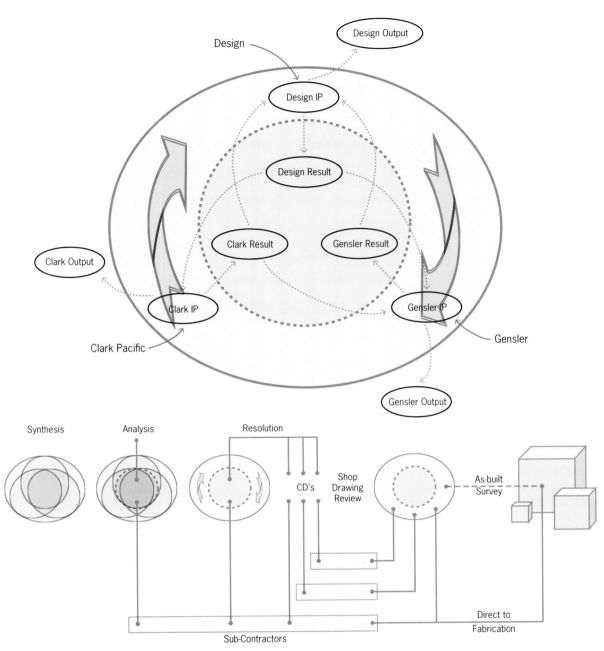

Workflow 8 (top). The role of GT is to maintain a holistic, systems-level view of the overall process to set project goals and optimize the work-flow to achieve those goals. For instance, each key design decision would have input from each team member, weighted towards the objectives of one or more member, and then multiple solutions could be evaluated and a decision made by the whole team.

Workflow 9 (bottom). GT systems-level view, shown as evolving over the course of a project in steps that reflect a traditional process. In the first step, synthesis, the main system interdependencies are identified and captured in a relational parametric mod-eler that is flexible enough to perform rapid design iterations. This occurs during schematic design. In the sec-ond step, analysis, multiple team members conduct their own internal analysis and then provide feedback into the integrated parametric model to structure and stabilize

the core parameters. All of the systems are in the model at this point, which allows the team to see the global repercussions of any design adjustment. At the third step, resolution, all team members reach a consensus, allowing each to extract the neces-sary output from the model to actually manifest the proj-ect. This is where contracts come into play and design and fabrication data are final-ized and issued (represented by the blue bars). Depending on the subcontractors, some workflows might be more traditional, requiring shop

drawings, while others, like for instance the fabrication of the veil, will utilize file-to-fabrication CNC processes. In either case, the workflows are digitally integrated and the fabrication information has already been coordinated, tested and evaluated.

THE SCENT OF THE SYSTEM

JESSE REISER & NANAKO UMEMOTO

Jesse Reiser and Nanako Umemoto are Principals of Reiser + Umemoto RUR Architecture. Jesse Reiser is Professor of Architecture at Princeton University.

It is widely assumed that the architectural innovation of the 1990s was made possible by the computer, but this is only a partial truth. Certainly, new technologies made possible linkages between design and the economics of production that had never before existed, yet the real breakthroughs were conceptual and aesthetic before they were technological. The politico-aesthetic ground was laid in the aftermath of exhausted strategies to produce architectural difference (deconstruction and collage) over and against modernism's homogeneity, through Deleuzian concepts like continuous variation and corresponding architectural models such as Jeffrey Kipnis's theory of intensive coherence.[1] In short, the architectural desire to produce difference through similarity pre-dated its technological employments.

Today's current infatuation with scripting is no exception, where in the name of bespoke algorithms practitioners hope for an architecture that will be, at long last, more fully intentional, tractable and rigorous. To be sure, scripting is a useful addition to the digital toolbox when it is used to explore well-defined design concepts, but in the worst case it becomes a substitute for active judgment. Inertia takes over and architects fool themselves into thinking that repetition—simple or complex—is a form of rational thought. There are many aspects and applications of computational design and analysis that are becoming common today; the risk is that the seduction of these tools creates an illusion of rigor that obscures the role of active critical assessment. The challenge for the future development of computation in architecture is the use of

discretion to know when and how it should be applied to design.

In our work, computation is used as a tool to work through aesthetic and architectural agendas. One of the primary benefits of using digital tools during the design process is the increase in speed of feedback—of being able to visualize changes quickly. The use of scripts allows us to speed up the design process to a point where we can streamline mechanical processes and complete the project with a small team. However, there is a limit to what computation as a design tool can achieve before the results become mechanical.

With this in mind, we can discuss our design for O-14, our recently completed office tower in Dubai, and its particular relationship to design, analysis and fabrication methods. The design began with a primarily aesthetic desire to see drifts of forces flowing down the building—these could have been painted or sketched—but as we attempted to develop scripts to simulate selective modulation, the desired effect was lost. We tested ways to automate the effects of the building's gradient hole pattern but the result was not responsive enough and became too mechanical—you could smell the system through the unthinking inertia of the script. When these design ideas were turned into rules, the rules necessary to produce the local conditions became so numerous and specific that the time needed to generate each iteration was no longer efficient, so eventually this approach was abandoned.

We were much more interested in the sensitive shifts and continually changing gradients that could be produced in a watercolor wash or charcoal drawing as an expression of the painter. These effects would be more localized and precise. In the end, the shell geometry, subjected to the iterative process of structural

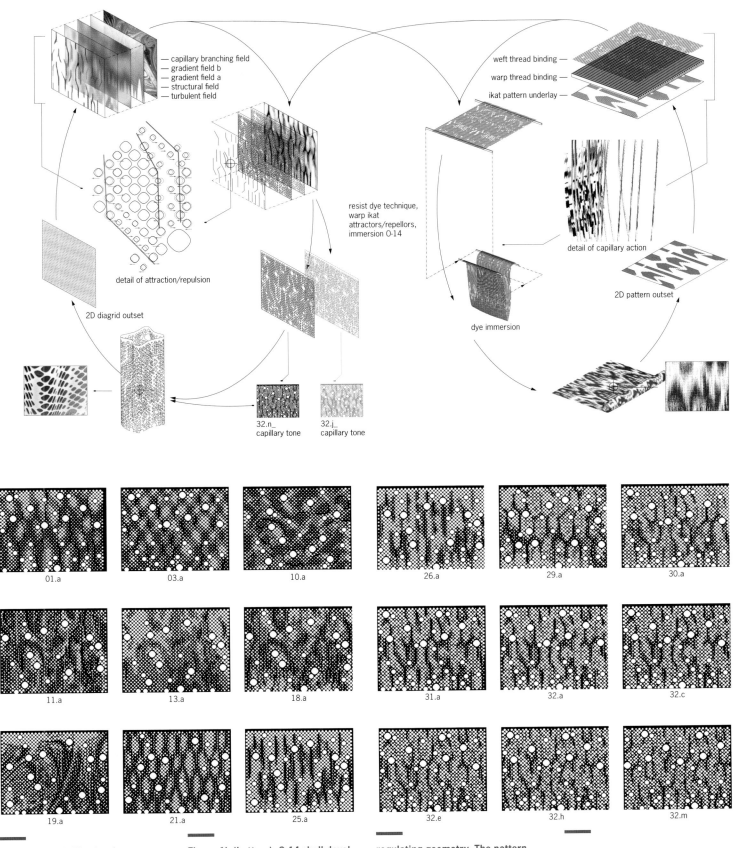

Figure 1a (top). The development
and recombination of the O-14 tower
shell pattern, as compared with the
layering processes of Japanese Ikat
weaving techniques.

Figure 1b (bottom). O-14 shell development, highlighting in sequential
order 14 of the primary 32 families
of perforation iterations, thereby
further emphasizing that the design
of O-14 is not tied to the overall

regulating geometry. The pattern
seeks to attenuate the monotony,
while still preserving the sense of the
sublime and the monumental.

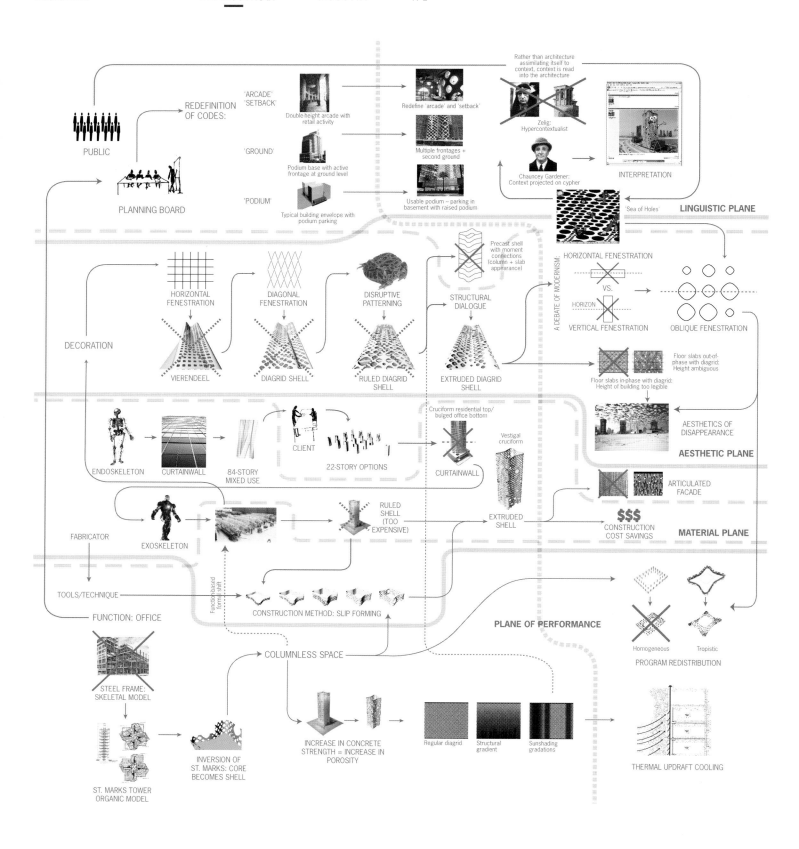

Figure 2. The design of O-14 is a combination of different tracks of influence; linguistic, aesthetic, material and performance. In this way, the appearance of the shell is neither a pure rationalization of structure, nor a purely aesthetic pattern, nor a sustainable solar screen and heat chimney.

analysis and architectural modification, was created using five sizes of holes and Photoshop filters. We were not tied to a specific tool, and in fact much like the artist has to originate sensations in their own medium rather than representing them, the painterly effects in O-14 needed to be re-originated as architecture; it is not simply a representation of a painting. [Figures 1a, 1b]

Considering the issue of how to derive design through computation, it is a question of how (and if) one can elicit new sensibilities through rule-based systems. Michelangelo's contempt for textile weavers was widely known; he considered them to be at the bottom of the hierarchy of the arts, because he considered their work to be repetitious and unthinking. It is much easier to find rules for objective performance than for intuition or serious cultural production. It is absolutely possible to derive mathematical formulas from a Mozart sonata but debatable whether you could run the process in the reverse and come out with a Mozart. [Figure 2]

Figure 3. The concrete shell of the O-14 commercial tower provides an efficient structural exoskeleton that frees the core from the burden of lateral forces and creates highly efficient, column-free open spaces in the building's interior.

O-14
—

O-14 is a 22-story-tall commercial tower, perched on a two-story podium, that comprises over 300,000sqft of office space for the Dubai Business Bay. It is located along the extension of Dubai Creek, occupying a prominent location on the waterfront esplanade. [Figure 3] With O-14, the office tower typology has been turned inside out—structure and skin have conjoined to offer a new economy of tectonics and of space. The concrete shell provides an efficient exoskeleton that serves as the primary vertical and lateral structure of the building. This frees the building core from the burden of lateral forces and creates highly efficient and flexible column-free open spaces in the building's interior.

The shell is organized as a diagrid, the efficiency of which is wed to a system of variable-sized openings that always maintain a minimum structural requirement by adding material locally where necessary and taking away where possible. The efficiency and flexibility of this system enabled us to create a wide range of atmospheric and visual effects without changing the basic structural logic, allowing for systematic analysis and efficient construction methods. A common misreading of O-14 is that the diagrid pattern is a direct materialization of the structural forces on the shell. This approach would have yielded a much more aesthetically homogeneous result. Certainly, the structural logic of the gravity-loaded exoskeleton had to be taken into account, but the redundancy inherent to the diagrid gave us a tremendous amount of expressive freedom. [Figure 4]

AESTHETIC EXPRESSION VS. STRUCTURAL RATIONALIZATION
—

Modeling and analyzing the shell of O-14 was a key part of the design. In our initial meeting with the structural engineer, Ysrael A. Seinuk, we showed two different options for the openings: orthogonal and diagonal. [Figures 5a, 5b] Their recommendation was to avoid the orthogonal, as its structural consequence would result in many small Vierendeel frames, while the diagonal option offered the benefit of channeling both gravity and lateral loads to the base of the building. This was consistent with our aesthetic interests and gave us more opportunity to pursue the aesthetic objectives of the design. The collaborative process began with Reiser + Umemoto generating a 3D model

of the shell, indicating preliminary locations of the openings. This first iteration of the shell geometry was subject to a structural analysis program but deliberately run "weak", i.e. tested in a low-strength concrete so as to exaggerate the formation of the stress patterns. This index of invisible forces was selectively enhanced or diminished in the geometry of the next iteration, so as to propagate the desired density pattern of solids and voids in the overall shell. The size and location of these openings were adjusted accordingly, resulting in a modulated grid pattern. Comments on the model were then sent back to the architect to determine the architectural implications of these changes, after which the architect revised the model to send back to the engineer for more analysis. This process took several iterations, until the final design of the shell's apertures, elements and grid pattern fulfilled both the architectural and structural requirements. [Figures 6a, 6b]

When considering the expression of O-14, one must keep in mind the development of structural technologies from the load-bearing logics of masonry to the vector-based logics of

steel. The shift from arch-and-wall to column-and-beam techniques signified a shift in thinking about matter, in which the structural logics within building components became freed from the "excessive" material surrounding them—the ability to more accurately calculate structural forces resulted in an economy of material. The logical extension of this shift led to the pursuit of an ideal structural form—the development of the I-beam, truss, space frame, cable and anchor point system, etc.—which was the precursor to the machine-aesthetic and the modern concept of functionalism—including its eventual degradation into the baleful High Tech and currently to the highly optimized yet culturally reductive phase of performance architecture. In this spirit, high Modernism has been shaped by the dialectic between the generic and the accidental: wherein the generic is classical and impersonal and the accidental is singular and unique. Our design method attempts to circumvent this dialectic by assuming that the repetition of the Modernist diagrid can be modulated in such a way as to produce singular architectural

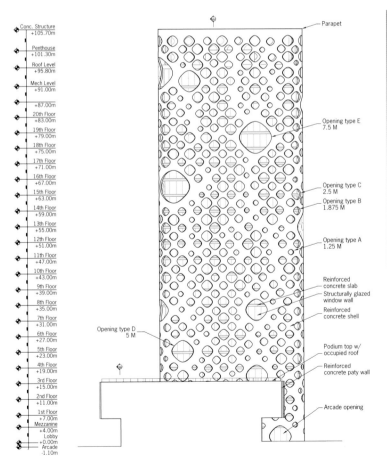

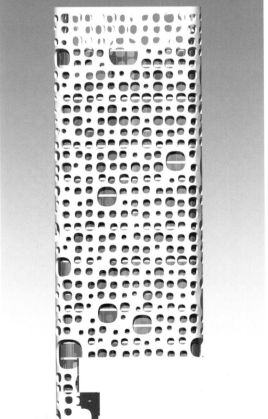

Figure 4 (facing page). The shell is organized as a diagrid, the regularity of which provides a certain over-structuring. While the shell changes its performance locally based on the actual forces, a fictional exaggeration of the pattern was used to emphasize the appearance of structural forces.

Figure 5a (above left). The redundancy inherent to the diagrid system provides an efficient and flexible platform within which a wide range of atmospheric and visual effects could be explored without changing the overall basic structural logic.

Figure 5b (above right). This early orthogonal pattern was discarded in favor of the diagonal pattern, as the original scale-less quality was lost and the building appeared markedly shorter and less slender.

features, thus overcoming its homogeneity while retaining its systemic coherence.

The diagrid of O-14 is neither arbitrary nor structurally ideal—each perforation reads independently and as part of a combinatory pattern. This approach assumes an active management of the relationship between the building geometry and its material behavior; however, it avoids the twin traps of either the simple optimizing ethos of structural rationalism, or its hypertrophied version: structural expressionism. The design of O-14 compounds these ideas beyond just the appearance, porosity and effects generated by the façade, extending to the uses and functions of the office spaces within, where the program is intended to locally reorganize itself in relationship to the ever-changing gradient of apertures.

In opposition to what one might consider the inherent expressive qualities of the tower topology, the façade pattern of O-14 is not tied to an overall regulating geometry and attempts to defy a rational reading of force transfer. The pattern seeks to attenuate the monotony associated with office towers, while still preserving the sense of the sublime and the monumental. The deliberate lack of alignment between the perforations and the floor plates obscures legibility and challenges an easy reading of the building's height and scale. [Figure 7]

There is a graphic desire driving the design process, a desire that overrides the structural and environmental logics. The modulation of pattern works like camouflage, becoming disruptive and de-materializing the tower block. The shell's pattern changes as its relationship to the viewer changes, and when combined with additional patterns of light and shadow, produces a sort of virtual form. Because of the effects of this virtual form, the actual form of the building can be simplified and respond to the logics of production methods, structural analysis and economy.

There was a constant negotiation between four different tracks of design criteria: material, aesthetic, linguistic and performative. These were not equal in their influence. The graphic articulation of the façade took precedence over the others, resulting in "over-structuring" the shell, to the point where optimization was no longer important. The shell became a fictional index of forces in the end—something akin to the anatomical license in nineteenth-century neoclassical painting[2]—where upon close inspection, the pattern is slightly off, creating a vivid and visceral impression of the force flows in the shell. The pattern cannot be fully understood through a single lens and is a form of very precise fiction. If we had considered the index of forces only from a structurally

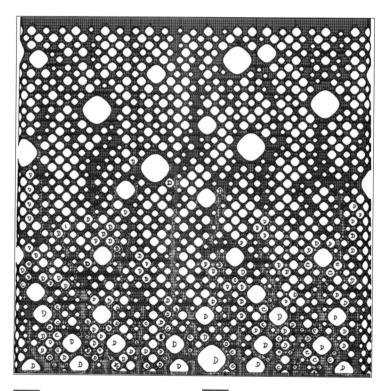

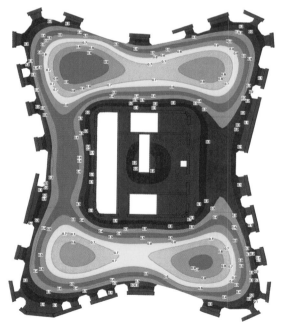

Long-Term Deflection LC: Deflection Plan
Scale = 1:200
Vertical deflection plot

.1 .2 .3 .4 .5 .6 .7 .8 .9

Figure 6a (above left). Structural analysis of the unrolled O-14 shell. The sizes and locations of the openings were carefully coordinated in order to make the wall effective in channeling both gravity and lateral loads down to the base of the building.

Figure 6b (above right). Structural analysis of a typical floor plate.

optimized perspective, they would not have been particularly expressive of anything other than structure.

SUSTAINABILITY/ENVIRONMENTAL EFFECTS
—

Likewise, the sustainable aspects of the design were derived from a desire for aesthetics as well as performance. In addition to serving as its main architectural feature and the primary structural system, the perforated concrete tubular shell is also an environmentally smart *brise-soleil* open to light, air and views. Our first design iterations had the floor slab edges directly in contact with the shell, but this, like the initial orientation of the openings, over-emphasized their horizontality as they were directly registered on the façade. To reinforce the aesthetic desire for scalar ambiguity, the slabs were separated from the shell except at selective connection points, which made them recede in space. Since the locations of the openings vary throughout the façade, the connections between the floor slab and the shell are different at every floor. This created a space between the glass window wall and the shell, which was later increased to 1m for more pragmatic reasons, to fit a window-washing track onto each slab edge. The gap between the main enclosure and exterior shell had the additional benefit of creating a chimney effect,

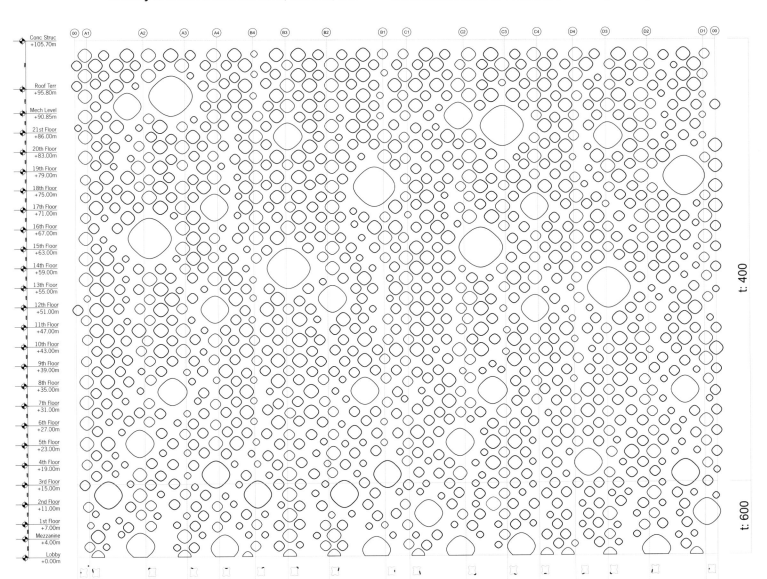

Figure 7. Final O-14 unrolled shell line drawing illustrating perforations, slab connections, parking column grid and elevation markers.

which effectively cools the surface of the glass windows behind the perforated shell. [Figure 8] This passive solar technique became an integral part of the cooling system, reducing energy consumption and costs by more than 30%. Once we became aware of the dynamic of the gap, we refined it by minimizing the width of the structural connections (the tongues) between shell and slab. The evolutionary biologist Stephen Jay Gould calls this a process of *exaptation*, where novel performance arises from the (geometrical) by-products of other primary operations.[3]

CONSTRUCTION METHODOLOGY
—

In order to construct the perforated exoskeleton, a slip-form construction technique was utilized where modular concrete forms moved up along the building axis, preventing costly dismantling and setup of formwork with complex shapes. Self-consolidating concrete was used to flow between the intricate matrix of reinforcing bars and polystyrene void forms used to shape the openings. [Figures 9a, 9b] Our original thought was that by limiting the openings to five sizes, we could work with a limited number of reusable forms made of a flexible material, such as rubber, which would be able to repeatedly bend to conform to the tower's plan geometry. This idea proved incorrect, however, as the cost of the actual reusable molds, as well as the effort required to recycle them, would have been greater than the cost of milling each mold individually out of a disposable material like polystyrene. The geometry of the molds were complicated by the curving surface of the shell, so we offered to provide separate digital files to the fabricator to mill each mold. [Figure 10] However, the fabricator chose to redraw each one individually by hand, using the standard arc notations for the inside and outside surface of the shell and then projecting between them to generate the thickness. Thus after all the planning and precision, the success of the project was due more to the superb craftsmanship of the contractor than the ability to digitally control all aspects of the process, from design through construction. [Figure 11]

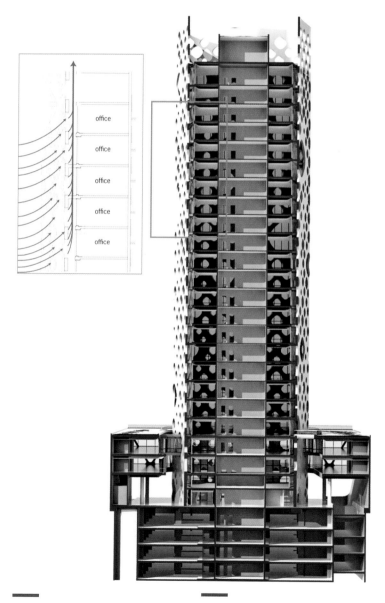

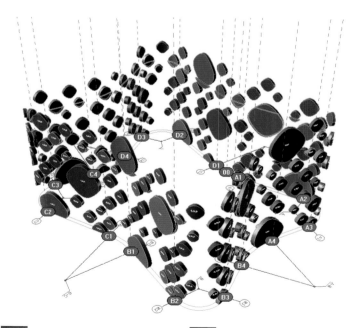

Figure 8 (above left). The gap between the exterior shell and the window wall creates a chimney effect, reducing energy consumption by more than 30% over typical curtainwall alternatives.

Figure 10 (above right). 3D models of each polystyrene void form were tagged and made ready for CNC production; however, the formwork company chose to provide hand-drawn shop drawings, calculating the projected geometry themselves.

ENDNOTES
—

1. *Dubai Next: Face of 21st Century Culture*. Exhibition curated by Rem Koolhaas and Jack Persekian.
2. For instance, Jean-Auguste-Dominique Ingres painted what would appear to be extraordinary living beings through the exaggeration of features that upon cursory inspection would appear entirely natural; if one were to reconstruct the body from the paintings however there would be additional vertebrae or distended limbs - the people would be monsters if they were actually living, although they were very precise, realistic depictions in the painting.
3. Stephen Jay Gould, "The Pattern of Life's History", pp. 56-57, from *The Third Culture*, John Brockman, 1995.

Figure 9a (top left). Polystyrene void forms (pills) were woven into the rebar meshwork prior to the concrete pour. After the pills and rebar mesh had been constructed, the steel slip-forms were placed, and the shell and slabs were cast-in-place floor by floor. Self-consolidating concrete was used to ensure penetration all the way into the meshwork.

Figure 9b (bottom left). Two sets of slip-forms were used in tandem, and as each upper floor was cast, the lower one was raised, reset and readied for the next pour.

Figure 11 (above right). The ground-level restaurant and retail podium next to the public esplanade—the chimney effect creates a pocket of cool shaded space in the relentless heat of Dubai.

INDETERMINACY
—
EDITOR'S NOTES

"As compared to twentieth-century expressionism, which foregrounds the formal and emotive characteristics of architecture as the product of a purely personal sensibility, we regard expression as the properly impersonal capacity of matter and material systems, in which human will and intentionality play a part but are not the sole determinants. The architect is, in effect, neither a passive observer of determined systems nor a determined manipulator of passive material, but rather, the manager of an unfolding process."[1]

In one of our first meetings to discuss the topic of this book, Reiser + Umemoto warned that they might be a skeptical voice among the other contributors. While they value the pragmatic benefits associated with computation, they are also suspicious of its tendency to reduce architectural expression to a cause-and-effect aesthetic. Their concern applies equally to the recent trends towards performance-driven design and to

the earlier formalism pioneered in the 1990's that was often nothing more than an index of a project's generative logic. Reiser + Umemoto's work developed during this earlier period, when digital design research was largely removed from material concerns. Even though they are often associated with this period, their work has always been grounded in a negotiation between their craft sensibility and a deep understanding of matter and material systems as active, evolving processes—processes that exist in a state of potential as much as a state of fact. The question for them is how, and if, digital workflows can further this negotiation by allowing an even deeper understanding of material systems.

Although digital workflows are most often seen as a singular discrete operation with well-defined parameters bracketed by inputs and outputs, multiple workflows can act in parallel and connect to external databases that might indirectly impact a design operation, acting

more as an influence than an input. In other words, digital workflows can expand the capacity of a design process to build a knowledge base around a given task. Reiser + Umemoto have relied on the organizational capacity of the diagram for this[2]—as a technique to negotiate between precedent typologies, social critiques and other project conditions, and the architect's role of critically assessing these conditions to explore and uncover novel design solutions. Their phylogenetic diagram for O-14 (Figure 2) is instructive in this regard. Unlike many of the operational workflow diagrams in this book that depict the flow of digital data across the timeframe and among the participants of a building project, this diagram combines the influences of "linguistic, aesthetic, material and performance criteria" in a non-linear, relational manner. It defies the logical structure of a purely digital workflow. Influences as divergent as building massing scenarios, anatomical structural models, aesthetic theories, and material and

construction techniques are nodes within a thought process with no clear beginning or end.

A comparison of the contributions of Reiser + Umemoto to David Benjamin,[3] who is part of a younger generation of designers with a more acquiescent position towards computation, serves to highlight a recurring theme throughout this book: the limits and potentials of digital workflows. Benjamin's work is based on the use of optimization algorithms as a technique for design exploration. In a creative misuse of multi-objective optimization processes, he attempts to generate multivalent architectural effects by inputting diverse, often conflicting objectives into algorithms that search for design solutions. Optimization is not used to find a single local maximum—its conventional application—but rather to explore many local maximums, all of which satisfy the multiple design objectives, but with controllable trade-offs. Reiser + Umemoto find an overtly systemic reading in any algorithmic process that reduces the resultant output to the limitations of the inputs. Their design for O-14 had multiple goals: to produce a wide range of atmospheric and visual effects; to avoid visual homogeneity while retaining systemic coherence; and to defy a rational reading of structural force transfer. Their means of achieving this were to develop very precise and almost rule-based objectives: to separate structure from internal program; to create a structural diagrid with variable-sized openings; and to avoid alignment of diagrid holes with floor slabs. When considered together, however, these objectives result in what they refer to as a "precise fiction"—"it cannot be fully understood through a single lens". While Benjamin seeks similar disjunctions, his process relies exclusively on algorithms—the very process that creates the problem for Reiser + Umemoto. They remain unconvinced of algorithmic design and are focused on the distinct realms of human

thought not approachable through computation. Shared, however, is their re-evaluation and repositioning of the architect in the context of new digital workflows.

Reiser + Umemoto's reflection on the creation of a Mozart sonata most clearly reveals their fundamental question about the role of computation in architecture. As a tool of analysis, computation can provide insight to better understand the nature of something that already exists, but as a tool of creation or origination, even with its daunting power of combinatory processing, it will at best merely mimic the subtlety of human thinking.

—

1. Reiser + Umemoto (2006) *Atlas of Novel Tectonics*, New York, Princeton Architectural Press, p. 104.
2. There are many types of diagrams in architecture, so it is important to qualify this term. In the introduction to Reiser + Umemoto's *Atlas of Novel Tectonics*, Sanford Kwinter describes the diagram as "an invisible matrix, a set of instructions, that underlies—and most importantly,

organizes—the expression of features in any material construct… It determines which features (or affects) are expressed and which are saved".
3. See "Beyond Efficiency" by David Benjamin in this volume.

DESIGNING

AND INDUSTRY

WHAT DO WE MEAN BY BUILDING DESIGN?

—

PAOLO TOMBESI

Paolo Tombesi is Chair of Construction at the University of Melbourne.

You can teach a man to draw a straight line... and to copy any number of given lines or forms with admirable speed and perfect precision... but if you ask him to think about any of those forms... he stops; his execution becomes hesitating...; he makes a mistake in the first touch he gives to his work as a thinking being. But you have made a man of him for all that. He was only a machine before, an animated tool... And observe, you are put to stern choice in this matter. You must either make a tool of the creature, or a man of him. You cannot make both. Men were not intended to work with the accuracy of tools, to be precise and perfect in all their actions. If you will have that precision out of them, and make their fingers measure degrees like cog-wheels, and their arms strike curves like compasses, you must unhumanize them...
—John Ruskin (1853), *The Stones of Venice*[1]

... All the improvements in machinery, however, have by no means been the inventions of those who had occasion to use the machines. Many improvements have been made by the ingenuity of the makers of the machines, when to make them became the business of a peculiar trade; and some by that of those who are called philosophers or men of speculation, whose trade it is not to do anything, but observe everything; and who, upon that account, are often capable of combining together the powers of the most distant and dissimilar objects.
—Adam Smith (1776), *An Inquiry into the Nature and Causes of the Wealth of Nations*[2]

AN AGENDA FOR THE STUDY OF THE BUILDING INDUSTRY
—

In 1966, the year Robert Venturi published *Complexity and Contradiction in Architecture*,[3] an Argentinian architect of Italian origin, Duccio Turin, delivered *What Do We Mean By Building?*[4]—his inaugural address as London Master Builders Professor of Building at the Bartlett School of Architecture in London. In the lecture, one of the defining moments of the modern construction discipline, Turin set out to provide an intellectual harness for scholarly reflection on building and a "dispassionate analysis of the functions actually performed by the participants in the building process, quite independently of their professional labels, their technical qualifications, or their particular training". For Turin, "it was unlikely that the professional structure (in place at the time) would change radically in the near future", and this would make it "inevitable to continue to speak of architects, engineers, quantity surveyors, contractors, subcontractors, etcetera, for many years to come". He warned, however, that "these names will become increasingly meaningless to describe the real contribution made by those taking part in the process". As an antidote against self-complacency, he pointed to the need of coming to terms with the distinct components of the building industry, building detailed evidence of their existence, agreeing on concepts and verifying macro-scale connections with the economy. To these ends—he suggested—it was necessary to exploit the available data in order to organize critical descriptions of the industry, whilst developing in-depth investigations of selected aspects of the processes of production it encompassed that could help envisage the impact of the various actors' inputs and the variables as well as predict future structural changes in the industry. But, he recognized, there was no need for, or chance of this happening at once; on the contrary, building should be approached and structured in a Newtonian way, by defining a "general framework where existing and future knowledge would fit in beauty and order".

Twenty-five years on another architect, Ranko Bon, this time the editor of the journal *Construction Management and Economics* and Bovis Professor of the same discipline at the University of Reading in England, built upon Turin's seminal lecture for his own inaugural address—What Do We Mean By Building Technology?[5]—in which he pushed the idea of exploring building-technological constellations even further. In his speech, Bon explained how the economic structure of a "territory" can be read through the variety of inputs that are required and available to produce the local building output. Buildings, as he put it, are "bundles of goods and services" brought together in reflection of a specific albeit extended geography and, thus, in light of a complex social framework. For this reason, "there can be no such thing as steel" per se, but rather a variety of contributions, resources and sets of machinery that allow steel to be manufactured and erected. Not unlike Turin, Bon praised the role of critical imagination in making assumptions about technological paths and possible futures. Since "we can understand more than we can explain", it is not unfeasible to suggest and explore patterns of change that as yet elude economic models.

If one considers the framework outlined by Turin and Bon, a clear methodological agenda emerges, an agenda for the study of the building industry that is as valid today as it was in the 1960's and the 1990's, particularly because it does not rest on a set platform, but seeks a deeper understanding of the complex dependencies of the discipline rather than a validation of any preconceived theses. As Turin explains, it is only after selecting the terms of reference and sketching a picture that one can decide what matters on the subject, eventually to set the compass for further analysis and development. Bon reinforces this approach by focusing on how data can be compiled, filières revealed and functioning hypotheses suggested. While Turin's ambition is defining the field conceptually, Bon's concern is teasing out its actual components.

DEFINING PROFESSIONAL RESPONSIBILITIES
—

Field and components (or context and technology), however, say nothing about the processes employed to conceive building products and implement production. Since construction is a transformative industry, what determines the outcome of the work is not the simple presence of options and opportunities but rather the actual linkages established between distinct components, the nature and ordering of these linkages, the choices behind their selection and the relationship of power among the actors making these determinations.

Both Turin and Bon, in fact, felt the need to complement their analyses with examinations of the building procurement process and the decision-making landscape in which it developed. Turin, in particular, published an influential essay—*Building as a Process*—in which he explained that buildings can be developed according to several approaches, which differ from one another in relation to where design emphasis (or innovation) is placed vis-à-vis product standardization—in the initial idea, the building components, the overall structure or in work patterns.[6] The value of this index extended beyond the four categories, and lay in its suggestion that the analysis of the process cannot focus simply on abstract stages of project development and theoretically assigned functional roles, but must always consider building actors' changing or contingent positions of influence in the overall project configuration, and their consequent intellectual contributions to the process. Decision-making pressure is indeed exerted on particular aspects of the process, depending on contributors' industrial origin and profile, but the space available to them is also constrained by the space available to others, depending on the specific types of project configurations as well as the objectives (or design intent) embedded in such configurations.

By highlighting the rich socio-technical nature of project coalitions and the way in which decisions are added, transferred and further developed across the project, Turin essentially did away with the simple design/construction dichotomy that characterizes the professional tradition in architecture and building and replaced it with an industrial network connecting practices with roles, and roles with cultural agendas. In fact, the workflow templates contained in the essay were not labeled by stages according to the separation between design and construction but rather in light of the expected use of the output of each work stage: user requirements, brief, product design, building design, production information, production, assembly, consumption. [Figure 1] Within each output column, a black dot identified the agency (e.g. user, client, professions, contractor or manufacturer) who is in control of the defining aspects of the task at bay, and therefore charged with interpreting and translating contributions, both their own as well as those of other actors. These, in turn, were highlighted by arrows leading in and out of the functional boxes. Corresponding flow diagrams were not entirely linear, contained information loops that varied in scope and/or players, and featured implicit parallel design tracks (as in the case of the "product design"/"production information" tasks in Figure 1, to which "professions" and "manufacturers" contribute in different capacities). Project-related technical dynamics and transactional patterns, in other words, were thought to be network-based and determined by the social distribution of knowledge, social origin and the social allocation of power.

Since the publication of that text, Turin's socio-technical reading of the building process has supported and eventually been metabolized into a particular area of construction scholarship, by and large concerned with industrial organizational studies and technological innovation. By contrast, however, and more importantly, his suggestions regarding the multiplicity and interactions of actors and design-related activities have not been picked up by the conventional framework of practice, which, as I have argued in previous fora,[7] has maintained linear workflows, task separation and functional specialization as fundamental organizational structures. In part, this has to do with the need to simplify (or curb) the level of social and information complexity found and manageable in project-based work, particularly in the absence of a technological framework that could help nurture, coordinate and use the information properly.

Today, a unique combination of technology *push-and-pull events* may have created the appropriate conditions to reconsider Turin's intuition and the challenges it poses for the architect. As Gray and Hughes suggest in *Building Design Management*,[8] the "pull" is likely to be found in the dramatic increase of specialist knowledge required in construction, determining—but also deriving from—more articulate views of how buildings should behave, both individually and as stock. The consequent variety of contributing organizations has given rise to design processes that are scrutinized through a plethora of lenses, require continual exchange and refinement of hypotheses, decisions and knowledge, and make information supply logistically cumbersome. On the other hand, the connective and analytical power generated by the introduction of digital technologies and information processes in the Architecture, Engineering, Construction and Owner-Operated (AECO) sector seem to have engendered (or "pushed") an interest in reconsidering how individual actors integrate with project teams and industry structures, how the sub-fields of process, policy and technology relate, and how information artifacts (e.g. drawing representations, models, prototypes, schedules, charts, bills of quantities) can fulfill meta-design needs.[9]

Yet, from an architectural point of view, the interest in engaging digitally with the other aspects of the building process and cycle appears selective, and concerned mostly with those that are instrumental to streamlining design procurement, rather than expanding the scope of the building process or questioning its premises. With few notable exceptions, the majority of academic and industry-driven discussion on computer-aided design and visualization deals with updated versions of traditional professional responsibilities—the integration of pre-construction activities, the

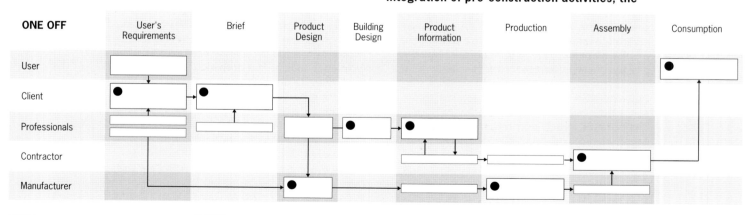

Figure 1. One of the four diagrams of the building process published in D. A. Turin, *Building as a Process*, showing decision-makers, information contributors and information flows in "one-off" building projects.

simulation of product behavior—and partly with process management. Component fabrication and assembly sit comfortably (and possibly conveniently) as natural craft extensions of object-based modeling, yet far less effort has so far been placed on the development of tools that allow for coherent and extended production/product planning beyond discrete systems or trades. It is uncommon, for example, to come across parametric connections between architectural form and ease of building maintenance, technological innovation and construction safety, materials procurement and environmental performance, site organization and built quality, building systems selection and labor resources, detailed solutions and trade skills at hand. Building Information Modeling (BIM) and CAD-CAM synergies are expected to dilute the risks of cultural dislocations or insufficient labor training, by detecting the potential for physical clashes and by streamlining manufacturing. Yet neither strategy seems to have, for the moment, what it takes to verify design decisions as they relate to site activity, localized craft and tacit knowledge (or lack thereof): most BIM visualizations offer 3D experiences of each part of the building object, but only as constructed—after human intervention, in a sense. CAD-CAM systems optimize a world of production that pre-dates the building site, at best indicating on-site handling patterns for the components and materials supplied.[10]

A number of questions, then, come to the fore, theoretically as well as practically: is the dialogue between digital processes and actual construction maximized by treading lightly on the non-virtual aspects of building work, i.e. the skills of the people that will construct what is envisioned, the physical processes that will have to be carried out, the material batches that will be supplied, the errors that can be made throughout? Is there value in bringing the simulative and reactive potentials of digital tools to bear onto the social dimension of construction activities, or vice versa? If so, how can one define a design environment that extends to, or allows engagement with, the entire building process, context and outcome?

DESIGNING DESIGN
—

One possible way of responding to the last question is to suspend, temporarily, the accepted meaning of design in building and return to fundamental definitions that associate design not to the task performed by a set of professional categories, but rather to a generic activity that defines a specific course of action, on the basis of understood conditions and rules (however partial or rationally bounded these may be).[11] It is useful not to lose sight of the fact that design in this sense is usually interpreted as "preceding work", i.e., what comes prior to, and determines the execution of, the production process. In other words, it designates the space where goals are set, implementation strategies laid out and a related organization put in place. Under this light, design fulfills a double function: 1) It envisions the solution to a problem (be it the strategy to be followed, the object to be produced and/or the condition to be achieved); and 2) It conceives ways to organize the necessary means to achieve such a solution. Within a divided organization of labor, of course, design gains a further connotation, because the distribution of responsibilities requires that identified solutions and defined courses of action be communicated by and to the various actors who contribute to the process, so as to ensure consistency among separate activities. To this end, design needs to incorporate a representational dimension, which defines design intent and product characteristics as well as implementation procedures. Design has to structure information.

Sketched in these terms, it is possible to say that the idea of design as a reflective, instrumental service to production is present within any activity that can be described as a problem-defining/problem-solving/information-structuring process. And if we look at the instances wherein activities consistent with this notion of design inform the building project and process, we realize, even intuitively, that design must expand beyond its current limited application to define and engage at least six dimensions, which can be described, indicatively, as follows:
– building opportunity generation, or what is needed to assemble resources, define stakeholders and set goals;
– building scope formulation, or what is needed to delineate, develop and control the scope of the building vis-à-vis identified objectives;
– building manufacturing, or what is needed to define and plan all the activities concerned with production of the materials, parts and components specified for the building;
– building erection, or what is needed to define and plan means and methods to assemble the building, or parts of it, on the site selected;
– project definition and control, or what is needed to define the structure of production, or the set of decisions concerning the selection of the project team, the definition of the project's

timeframe and the strategies to follow, in order to control appropriate development and implementation of the work;
– building use and maintenance, or what is needed to define the occupation patterns of the building produced, the mechanical and environmental performance of its parts, and the ability of the whole to respond to or withstand the passage of time.

     As shown in Figure 2, each of the six dimensions referred to above can be thought of as composed of sub-tasks, which demand specific operations, have specific objectives and generate specific information. The designation of these tasks must be taken with a grain of salt. Labels are naturally provisional, levels of analysis are not fixed and can be further magnified, and definitions could be sharpened. But the point is to reveal and give an analytical format to the multi-faceted, socially heterogeneous nature of design in building, and lay the foundations on which a complex approach to

both its cultivation and management can be developed, in line with the times and the technology available.

AUTONOMY, INTERDEPENDENCE AND UNCERTAINTY
—

If one follows the hypothesis proposed, building design can be conceived as composed of a host of different tasks, spread across official project inception and management, professional design, manufacturing and building production operations. It involves actors from each phase, including not only professionals but also fabricators, component suppliers and tradesmen, among others. In the same way as "there is no such thing as steel", there is no such thing as "a building design", but rather a bundle of design intentions/briefs that are active and interacting within a socially dynamic framework. In line with previous discussions on the operational morphology of the design process,[12] autonomy

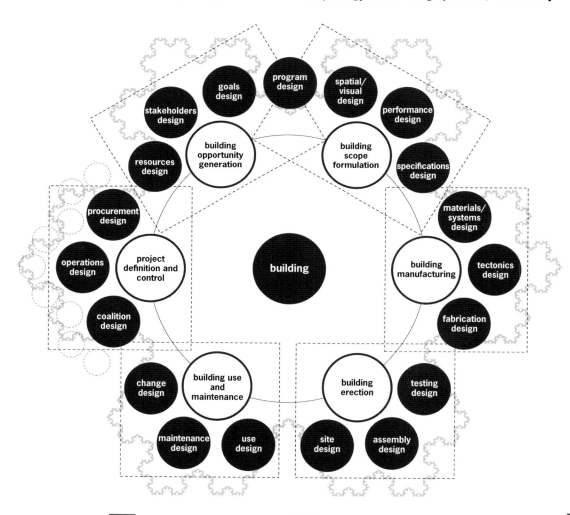

Figure 2. The different dimensions of the building cycle, wherein specific design activity must take place for goals to be set, strategies laid out and information organized. The system has fractal qualities in that it lends itself to being further subdivided into smaller areas of concern.

WHO DID WHAT

		YEAR 1	YEAR 2	YEAR 3	YEAR 4	YEAR 5	YEAR 6	YEAR 7	YEAR 8	YEAR 9

LEGEND

- DEVELOPER
- ARCHITECT
- BUILDER
- FINANCIER
- STATE GOVERNMENT
- CITY OF MELBOURNE

- COST CONTROL
- TOWN PLANNER
- STRUCTURAL ENGINEER
- SERVICES ENGINEER
- CRANE ENGINEER
- ENV. CONSULTANT

- REAL ESTATE AGENT
- PRECAST CONCRETE
- PRECAST SHOPDRAWER
- STRUCTURAL STEEL
- PLASTERBOARD
- FACADE SYSTEM

- CORE & LIFT STRUCTURE
- MAJOR RETAIL TENANT
- MAJOR RETAIL TENANT
- SERVICED APARTMENTS
- RESIDENTIAL TENANTS

Design clusters (each with rows: Advice/Information, Advice, Information, Indirect impact):

- OVERALL BRIEF
- ECONOMIC BRIEF
- PROJECT FINANCING
- BUILDING VOLUME
- URBAN SITING
- SPATIAL ORGANIZATION
- FORMAL DIRECTIONS/ OUTCOMES
- ENVIRONMENTAL PERFORMANCE
- TECHNOLOGICAL STRATEGIES

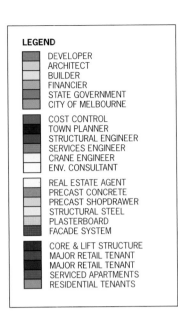

Figure 3. The division of design labor in a commercial high-rise building development in Melbourne (2008), with actors' contributions (identified by different color bars) organized by functional design clusters and duration over the life of the project.

Full thickness bars indicate information that the project team must have to further the work; thinner bars represent information that clarifies the scope of the project but does not condition the sequence of design operations.

and interdependence characterize this frame-work, since each task has to remain consistent with the internal logics of its function, while also cooperating with the other tasks towards the common goal of defining a building with a specific program and budget, at a given time and location, using determinate technologies and materials.

With respect to conventional professional descriptions of design, the structure suggested here adds an important horizontal dimension to the design development and design produc-tion process. The activity as a whole, in fact, becomes partialized not only vertically (that is, along the linear sequence of project-related operations inherited from canonical representa-tions of the building process), but also socially, at any given stage, according to networks of (sometimes decentralized) contributions that reflect the specificity of design dimensions and the knowledge required to respond to them. Within this expanded scenario, design is defined both by "flow" and by "nodes", progressively over time but also in parallel. [Figures 3a, 3b]

This scenario shapes the idea of both building and project. The building is the com-bined result of the implementation of multiple scope-specific designs; the project is the space where the gradual integration of these designs occurs, following a process of negotia-tion between objectives that are internal to each design dimension and objectives that are related to their integration. In this context, it becomes plausible to turn the conventional image of construction around and think of the building process, with all its ramifications, as a "system of design production"—a cycle, that is, within which all the information necessary to the proper implementation of the building is produced, assembled, translated and com-municated. Analytically, the Newtonian design system of sorts determined through this exercise is helpful for two reasons. First, it provides a proper index of the design challenges that exist within the building process, and a measure of the substantive breadth the design task must gain to respond to them. Second, it helps form a view of the building project that is not tied to specific actors but rather open to the recording of direct or indirect design contributions, which can be qualified in relation to the areas they impact. By creating the conditions for isolating and then bringing together the work conducted on disparate design domains by clusters of contributors, such a multi-dimensional view of design can be used as a tool to interrogate

project results and eventually intervene on the dynamics that led to them.

EVALUATING PROJECT EXPERIENCES
—

For a number of years, I have been working with the Polytechnic of Turin and the University of Melbourne on a research program spon-sored by the Italian Government and the Australian Research Council, aimed at articu-lating and evaluating the design structure of specific high-profile architectural projects.[13] One of the objectives of this program was to define and describe how decisions taken in spheres that are functionally specific affect the rest of the design as well as the outcome of the work. Analyses were organized against a view of design similar to the one suggested in this text, structured by several subsys-tems, each definable through technological characteristics, the logics employed in their selection, associated levels of innovation, detail development, external coordination needs and decision-making subjects.

For each of the case studies, a technical description was produced that could be visual-ized through heuristic categories and values, so as to make it possible to quantify the relative weight of groups of decisions on the economy of the entire building development enterprise. Through this process, representations of the project could be produced that suggest links between design decisions of different nature and the obtainment of various levels of techni-cal performance, the management of risk, the control of costs or the respect of schedules.

As shown in the spider diagrams pro-duced from the analysis of the Casa da Música in Porto, Portugal (OMA/Arup London, 1999-2005), and the Sage Music Centre in Gateshead, UK (Foster + Partners, 1997-2002) [Figures 4, 5], the impact of specific design dimensions over the fortune of the project varies greatly within and between projects. In the Casa da Música, building tectonics and systems fabrication are complex design endeavors, partly in light of the challenge to use traditional assemblies in new ways. Together with the detailed definition of the use of the building, they have the strongest impact on the design process. By contrast, the build-ing's technical performance and fitness for use are affected most greatly by the selection of building materials, the composition and work of trade specialties and the involvement of the expert client. Risk relates mostly to the way the work was coordinated and approved (that is, the design of operations, stakeholders coalitions and goals), whereas cost control is tied to as-built quality and maintenance needs. In the Sage Music Centre—a British lottery-sponsored project—generation of building opportunity and formulation of building scope are tightly connected, because financing brings specific design covenants and project requirements along. In this case, building use and flexibility are as important as, and complementary to, form-making. Cost control is mainly a function of the typological and erection logics of the building, with fabrication decisions impacting the path of the project significantly. In the end, the technical performance of the building is determined by the nature of the client, the architectural form developed in response to constraints and the composition of the technical project team coalition. Many of the project risks are abated by approvals and design review protocols (e.g. operations and procurement design).

Examining these and other examples through the method outlined leads to important conclusions concerning building design. The first is that quality cannot be pursued simply through the design of the "architecture" as conventionally considered, because it is a function of the attention paid to each and every one of the design challenges contained in the building process: developing the same program through different perspectives makes its resolution more sophisticated as well as more robust. Hence, for a thorough level of quality to be attained, one must be willing to engage with the web of relations that exist between design sub-tasks as well as consider the effectiveness of the resources invested. The second conclusion is that an objective assessment of the work required to this end is not only feasible within the framework created but also useful to suggest modifications to the procedures examined or in use. In fact, the identification of simple patterns in each project makes it possible to highlight areas of design concentration or design scarcity, areas where problems of procedural, technical or conceptual nature have emerged, and areas that have shown to require particular attention or links with other areas. On this basis, it becomes plausible to speculate (almost by design but by taking advantage of empirical evidence) about ways to manipulate the entire framework in order to achieve determinate results, either by exerting pressure on certain areas and releasing pressure from others or by connecting sets of design issues/dimensions.

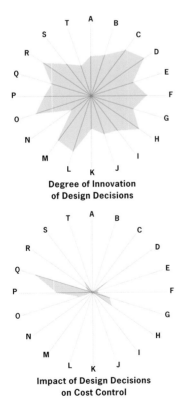

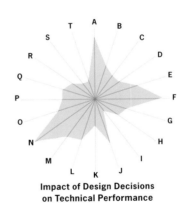

A. Commissioning
B. Financing
C. Program
D. Space and boundaries
E. Performance/specifications
F. Building materials and systems
G. Production and fabrication
H. Assembly
I. Site organization
J. Testing
K. Approvals
L. Control and management of operations
M. Design coalition
N. Construction coalition
O. Building use
P. Building change
Q. Building maintenance
R. Design development
S. Work coordination
T. Contractual relations

Degree of Innovation of Design Decisions

Impact of Design Decisions on Project Development

Impact of Design Decisions on Technical Performance

Impact of Design Decisions on Cost Control

Impact of Design Decisions on Risk Management

Figure 4. Spider diagrams of the nature and impacts of different types of design activity in the Casa da Música project, Porto, 1999-2005. Each spider diagram is constructed around a set of specific heuristic values, the intensity of which increases away from the center. Main design consultants: Rem Koolhaas, OMA/Arup London; main contractor: J.V. Somague/Mesquita.

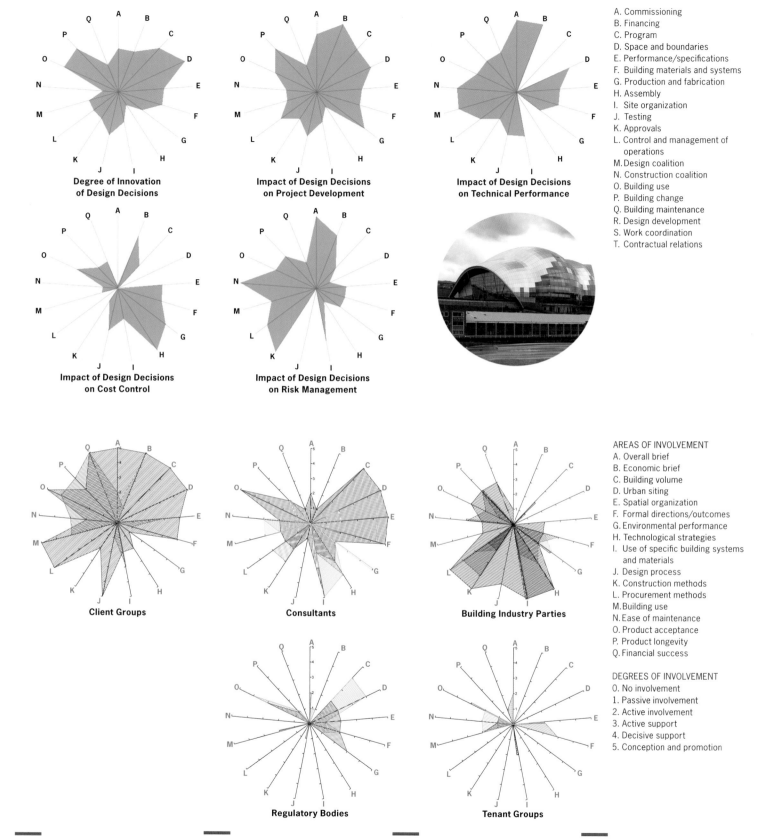

A. Commissioning
B. Financing
C. Program
D. Space and boundaries
E. Performance/specifications
F. Building materials and systems
G. Production and fabrication
H. Assembly
I. Site organization
J. Testing
K. Approvals
L. Control and management of operations
M. Design coalition
N. Construction coalition
O. Building use
P. Building change
Q. Building maintenance
R. Design development
S. Work coordination
T. Contractual relations

Degree of Innovation of Design Decisions

Impact of Design Decisions on Project Development

Impact of Design Decisions on Technical Performance

Impact of Design Decisions on Cost Control

Impact of Design Decisions on Risk Management

Client Groups

Consultants

Building Industry Parties

Regulatory Bodies

Tenant Groups

AREAS OF INVOLVEMENT
A. Overall brief
B. Economic brief
C. Building volume
D. Urban siting
E. Spatial organization
F. Formal directions/outcomes
G. Environmental performance
H. Technological strategies
I. Use of specific building systems and materials
J. Design process
K. Construction methods
L. Procurement methods
M. Building use
N. Ease of maintenance
O. Product acceptance
P. Product longevity
Q. Financial success

DEGREES OF INVOLVEMENT
0. No involvement
1. Passive involvement
2. Active involvement
3. Active support
4. Decisive support
5. Conception and promotion

Figure 5 (top). Spider diagrams of the nature and impacts of different types of design activity in the Sage Gateshead Music Centre project, 1997-2002. Main design consultant: Foster + Partners; main contractor: Laing O'Rourke.

Figure 6 (bottom). Spider diagrams of the nature and impacts of different types of design activity in the Sage Gateshead Music Centre project, 1997-2002. Main design consultant: Foster + Partners; main contractor: Laing O'Rourke.

For the way in which this design edifice was constructed, however, connecting design dimensions means connecting the panoply of contributing actors in a way that enables participation, cross-scrutiny and information transfer. [Figure 6] In other words, proper technical design clusters can emerge if effective feedback loops are in place. But since, as explained earlier, building design domains span across planning and realization stages—encompassing a context, that is, where objectives and instructions can change on the basis of contingent and often unforeseeable situations—the nature of design data must be dynamic and inevitably provisional. To design a building well, the ability to respond and adapt to the developing context of the work by modifying existing information is as important as the ability to simulate its final state, predict its behavior at the outset and incorporate different views in its definition.

The level of operational agility implied by these remarks determines an important distinction between the use of this conceptual framework as a critical yet simple analytical tool for evaluating project experiences and its use in professional and building practice. As Bon suggested in his professorial address referred to earlier, we can theoretically understand the value of particular ways of working even without practicing them. Similarly, we can appreciate the advantages of conceiving building design as a complex network of sub-domains, specialized design contributions as well as negotiated practices and push for the cultural adoption of the model. Yet, for all the reasons brought forward until this point, it would be almost impossible to make this system materialize into actual patterns of work without a supporting scaffold that allowed ongoing compilation, elaboration, mining, distribution, monitoring and visualization of data within a timeframe short enough not to disrupt temporal development routines. This is, in my opinion, where digital infrastructure can come to the support of work that attempts to build complexity into designed artifacts and design processes. As Michael Benedikt has noted,[14] working digitally is not about simplifying design procedures and streamlining production, but rather about using the power of computing to expand design boundaries and to create and manage greater product complexity through stronger, more precise, and yet more fluid connections between (at present often distant) problem areas.

THE ARCHITECTURE OF DESIGN
—

Necessary though they may be, digital apparatuses are not sufficient for the construction of product complexity. Building projects are not all the same, nor are they the predictable result of the application of complex taxonomies. Even aside from their appearance, the space and weight allocated to each of the dimensions introduced in the previous pages changes according to many factors including the occasion, the context, the brief and the actors. While every building imbues decisions affecting the various aspects, every building also implies a different combination of those decisions, produced on the basis of established priorities, analytical judgment and preferred strategies.

In a recent publication with Jennifer Whyte on the management of design in building,[15] I have proposed that built examples be read and discussed against their ability to reflect a specific ordering of design dimensions. For instance, the Ara Pacis Museum in Rome, designed by Richard Meier & Partners and completed in 2006, is a building where the attention devoted to the architectural image and some of the materials and the systems selected seemingly does not extend to the more prosaic fit-out elements, the design of the interface between systems, their maintenance, the workmanship required on-site throughout the building assembly process, or the use of functional spaces. [Figure 7] A similar hierarchy between visual design, complex specialist design, construction design and program design can be seen at Federation Square, the institutional complex opened in Melbourne in 2002 by LAB/Bates Smart, where the degree of resolution of the highly intricate triangle-based outer façade of the main building is much higher than the environmental and functional design of the workspaces behind it. In this case, the asymmetry is also a reflection of the prevalence of urban design over other spatial dimensions, the absence of building use design and the way in which the procurement process was planned and stakeholders identified. [Figure 8] At MIT's Simmons Students' Hall in Cambridge, Massachusetts (Steven Holl Architects, 1999-2002) the construction of the building envelope tells the story of a skewed relationship between building design, systems design, assembly design and testing, with the structural façade proving difficult to assemble due to the challenging labor conditions produced by an otherwise sophisticated conceptual solution. [Figure 9] At Southern Cross Station, Melbourne's main train interchange designed

Indicative hierarchy of specific design dimensions in the economy of the project (default—considered—conditioning—topical, from smaller to larger diameters). Red circles identify design dimensions with important mutual relationships for project procurement and outcome.

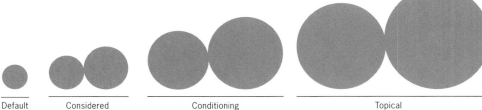

Default   Considered   Conditioning   Topical

1. Program
2. Spatial/visual
3. Performance
4. Specifications
5. Materials/systems
6. Tectonics
7. Fabrication
8. Testing
9. Assembly
10. Site
11. Use
12. Maintenance
13. Change
14. Coalition
15. Operations
16. Procurement
17. Resources
18. Stakeholders
19. Goals

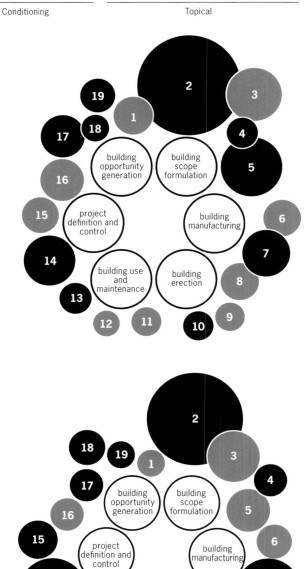

1. Program
2. Spatial/visual
3. Performance
4. Specifications
5. Materials/systems
6. Tectonics
7. Fabrication
8. Testing
9. Assembly
10. Site
11. Use
12. Maintenance
13. Change
14. Coalition
15. Operations
16. Procurement
17. Resources
18. Stakeholders
19. Goals

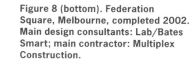

Figure 7 (top). Ara Pacis Museum, Rome, completed 2006. Main design consultant: Richard Meier & Associates; main contractor: Maire Engineering.

Figure 8 (bottom). Federation Square, Melbourne, completed 2002. Main design consultants: Lab/Bates Smart; main contractor: Multiplex Construction.

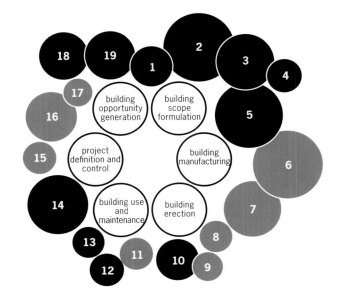

1. Program
2. Spatial/visual
3. Performance
4. Specifications
5. Materials/systems
6. Tectonics
7. Fabrication
8. Testing
9. Assembly
10. Site
11. Use
12. Maintenance
13. Change
14. Coalition
15. Operations
16. Procurement
17. Resources
18. Stakeholders
19. Goals

1. Program
2. Spatial/visual
3. Performance
4. Specifications
5. Materials/systems
6. Tectonics
7. Fabrication
8. Testing
9. Assembly
10. Site
11. Use
12. Maintenance
13. Change
14. Coalition
15. Operations
16. Procurement
17. Resources
18. Stakeholders
19. Goals

Figure 9 (top). Simmons Hall, Cambridge, Mass., completed 2002. Main design consultants: Steven Holl Architects, Arup, Nordenson & Associates; main contractor: Daniel O'Connell & Sons.

Figure 10 (bottom). Southern Cross Station, Melbourne, completed 2006. Main design consultant: Grimshaw Jackson JV; main contractor: Leighton Contractors.

by Grimshaw Architects, site, assembly and procurement design threatened to disrupt the success of the environmental solutions imagined for the building when, shortly after the opening of the facility to the public in 2005, serious internal air pollution problems emerged. Eventually, it became clear that the problem did not reside in how the fumes exhaust system had been modeled and designed, but in the fact that delays in the construction program had deferred the erection of a wall needed for this section of the terminal to work, environmentally, as planned. [Figure 10]

The fact that functional designs must be brought into a mutual relationship to yield meaning and value to the process brings us back to architecture and its connection to design. In a work context amplified by the power of digital tools, architecture cannot be taken simply as the culturally inflected production of built form and space realized through the provision of a proper plan—i.e., architectural design. Rather, it must be interpreted as the architecture of the design system—or the orderly, strategic arrangement of its parts, done with a view to establishing relevant linkages, structuring proper interfaces, ensuring consistency between selected intellectual streams, setting the sequence of decisions and enabling coordination against defined criteria. The apparent similarity between this notion of architecture and the idea of system architecture employed in Information Technology is misleading, because the architectural organization of the design system is not simply the result of internal operational goals and logics but also the eventual reflection of a system of external, non-technical values. The architecture of design, in a sense, may take the shape of a value-free procedural agenda, but it will always imply a conceptual (or professing) narrative underneath it.

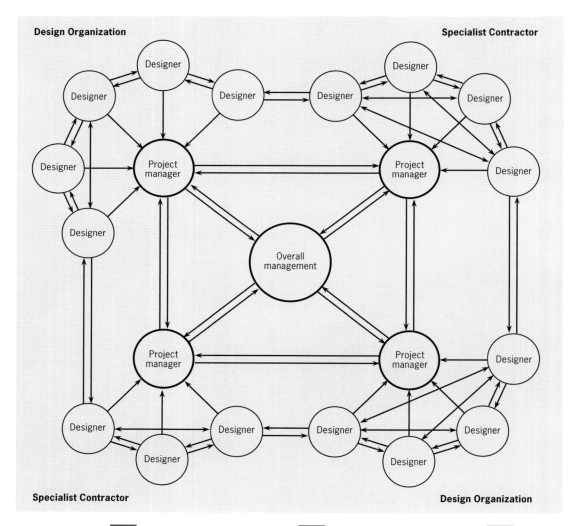

Figure 11a. The representation of design as an information flow management issue, where project management facilitates the flow but does not establish strategic contacts between design agencies. Diagram adapted from: Gray, C.; Hughes, W.;

Bennett, J. (1994) *The Successful Management of Design.* CSSC, University of Reading.

Still, accepting the terms of this proposition blurs the boundaries of design management and project design. Since the procurement of any building project requires a number of autonomous design dimensions to be concurrently active within the construction field, the architecture of ordered relationships between design processes in relation to explicit value ranges, understanding and judgment of the project's aims, available resources, socio-technical context and development timeframe must be established and also sustained in terms of information flows and monitoring. At this point, however, a professional question emerges: if the challenges built into the definition and management of the contemporary design process concern the strategic recomposition of sets of decentralized practices, what sort of agency has the cultural profile, the technical ability and the social sanction to act in a true, all-encompassing critical and managerial capacity? In other words, who should design the project (rather than the building)? Who should manage the development of the various designs (rather than the procurement of the construction artifact)? And is this different from managing information?

THE TECHNOLOGY OF ARCHITECTURE
—

Answering these questions within the framework of contemporary practice and the picture outlined in this publication presents a double challenge. On the one hand, there is little doubt that the functional mandate, the cargo of expertise implied and the cultural inclinations required to act as the architect of the design project as sketched in these pages make it difficult to fill the role through existing profiles (other than when these are defined via extended, multi-disciplinary coalitions). Traditional architects—a devil's advocate would say—hardly have the power today to cover, professionally, all the issues depicted in this framework, particularly in light of the fact that their agency function within the normal process has been reduced or challenged by the rise of other professional profiles. Moreover, the technologies increasingly available to govern the system of contributions and to assess project performance could reduce the need for the type of experience-based judgment traditionally required from professions like architecture, which are fiduciary, i.e. based on the translation of client expectations according to public value systems rather than on the application of formal (and neutral) knowledge

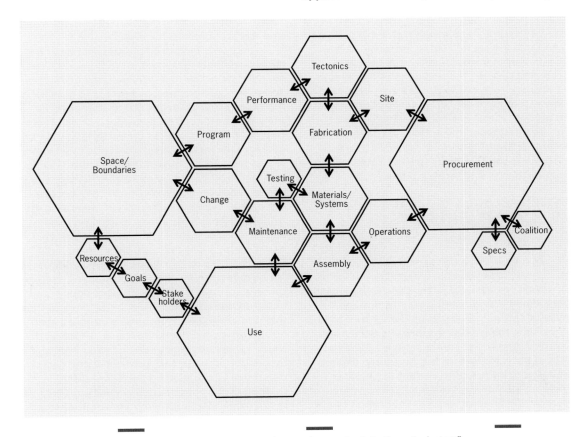

Figure 11b. The representation of design as a work structure with adjacencies and connections that need to be established and ordered by the agency in charge of designing the design. The critical point here is not simply the flow of information but the definition and facilitation of links between specific design dimensions, which reflect the goals and context of the project. Diagram adapted from: Nicolini, D.; Holti, R.; Smalley, M. (2001) "Integrating project activities: the theory and practice of managing the supply chain through clusters", *Building Research & Information*, 19, pp. 37-47.

relying on quantitative indicators—the province of expert professionalism.[16] If, as Scott Marble states in the introduction, digital infrastructure and the ensuing type of process connectivity make vast amounts of descriptive and analytical information instantaneously available to project operators; if this information can help define, simulate and assess design options, extend design prescriptions beyond representation to include manufacturing instructions, monitor the implementation of the routines selected, and automate and employ dynamic feedback, then interdependence can be celebrated while uncertainty can be written off, not because it has become external to the process of building but because it can be identified and responded to. In a sense, the very availability of technology with a high capacity to integrate the conception of the building object and the management of the building process creates both opportunities and tensions between professional design duties and project management functions (or build-and-design ambitions). When simulation and coordination capacity can be aided so greatly by digital apparatuses—something not socially pre-assigned to architects—the thought of replacing professional judgment (i.e. traditional architects) with technical managers and reusable data repositories can become plausible, possibly in the direction indicated several decades ago by the fathers of artificial intelligence. This, of course, depends on how the cluster of design functions is conceptualized, and whether the acts of synthesis that are at the very core of design work are performed only within each subset or across them. In the first case, overall project coordination could be assigned to an information manager; in the second it would have to be replaced by a true design proposition that required authorship (rather than guardianship). [Figures 11a, 11b]

DESIGN ARCHITECTURE AND ARCHITECTURAL DESIGNERS
—

This is in fact where the connection between design architecture and architectural design/designers comes back to assign more relevance to design professionals than a technology-based view would justify. The reason for it is simple. Irrespective of the knowledge-integrative nature of building-related digital tools, it is not the ability to generate and retain complex information that matters in the end, but rather the choices underlying its specific production. Against a technological framework potentially capable of connecting building design elaboration to any

content areas, an agenda for the inclusion and control of design variables (or the weighting of design dimensions) must be selected that can be wide but cannot be endless. Since buildings cannot be developed by following infinite, neutral lists of variables—because place, program, use and other contingent constraints matter after all—value judgment must be passed on what is to be included in each specific development of a project or digital information network, and which priorities are to take central stage. To manage information is different from giving it meaning. The moment a meaningful agenda is defined, inevitably to the advantage of certain issues and the detriment of others, the architecture of the system produces intent, thus taking a clear cultural, or value-based, direction. The architects of the system become political actors (when not activists), because they have to respond to the necessity to order or select from the multiplicity of design dimensions and carry the burden of existing in a true polytechnic world. As such, the architectural act suggested in these pages is not simply about the procedurally efficient integration of different disciplines and data sets, but it is about defining the active terms of a continuously re-formable discipline. In order to explain what "we mean by design" we must also determine what "we mean by architecture". This is something that carries consequences, and therefore responsibilities.

Under this light, the task and the role of the design architect/architectural designer become socially important but intellectually cumbersome, because the design process in a digitally advanced world cannot be simply normative but must also be selective: decisions can and therefore ought to be made on the growing plethora of relevant design issues/platforms that, with a few exceptions, were seldom part of traditional architectural canons or cultures. In fact, many of the areas that can inform the architecture outlined above have not received much interest or enjoyed much purchase in architectural discourse or academia this far, even though decisions originating from within them have the potential to carry significant implications far beyond architectural form, building system clashes, critical path detection or energy consumption assessment. If we go back to the diagram of design dimensions introduced earlier [see Figure 2], architectural decisions on which spheres to connect could yield thorough fitness-for-purpose across whole-of-life cycles, determine occupational health and safety in relation to the construction or the future use of the building, establish clear connections with ecological footprint policies, support supply-chain planning and waste minimization goals and deal with labor capacity building issues. The present unlikelihood that these aspects are explicitly part of the design rationale employed by the majority of current practitioners, digitalized or not, means that the three issues behind the thrust of this publication—the design of design, the design of assembly and the design of industry—should perhaps be joined by at least one other: the design of a professional educational system that recognizes the inclusive potential of digital processes but also the cultural limitations of existing curricula, and which, on this basis, would seek to nurture and facilitate reflective debate and exchange under the aegis of the architectural project.

ENDNOTES
—

1. Ruskin, J. (1853) *The Stones of Venice*, Book 2, Chapter 6, New York & London, Garland Publishing Inc., 1979, p. 161.

2. Smith, A. (1776) *An Inquiry into the Nature and Causes of the Wealth of Nations*, Book 1, Chapter 1, London, Penguin, 1986, p. 115.

3. Venturi, R. (1966) *Complexity and contradiction in architecture*, New York, The Museum of Modern Art Press.

4. Turin, D. A. (1980) What do we mean by building? *Habitat International*, 5 (3/4), pp. 271-288.

5. Bon, R. (1991) What do we mean by building technology? *Habitat International*, 15(1/2), pp. 3-26.

6. Turin's article was first published in the *Proceedings of the Bartlett Society* in 1967, and then republished in *Building Research and Information* 31(2), pp. 180-187, 2003.

7. Tombesi, P. (2010) On the cultural separation of design labor, in Bernstein, P.G.; Deamer, P. (eds), *Building (In) The Future: Recasting Labor in Architecture*, New Haven, Yale School of Architecture and New York, Princeton Architectural Press, pp. 117-136; Tombesi, P. (1999) *The Carriage in the Needle: Building Design and Flexible Specialization Systems*, Journal of Architectural Education, 52(3), pp. 134-142.

8. Gray, C.; Hughes, W. (2001) *Building Design Management*, Oxford, Butterworth-Heinemann.

9. See, for example: Coates, P.; Arayici, Y.; Koskela, L.; Usher, C. (2010) The changing perception in the artifacts used in the design practice through BIM adoption, *Proceedings of the 18th CIB World Building Congress*, W078—Information Technology in Construction, CIB Publication 361, pp. 212-223; Gu, N.; London, K. (2010) Understanding and facilitating BIM adoption in the AEC industry, *Automation in Construction*, 19(8), pp. 988–999; Linderoth, H. (2010) Understanding adoption and use of BIM as the creation of actor networks, *Automation in Construction*, 19(1), pp. 66–72; Succar, B. (2010) Building

information modelling framework: A research and delivery foundation for industry stakeholders, *Automation in Construction*, 18(3), pp. 357–375.

10. Pietroforte, R.; Tombesi, P. (2010) Physical mockups as interface between design and construction: A North-American example, *Proceedings of the 18th CIB World Building Congress*, W096—Architectural Management, CIB Publication 348, pp. 95-107.

11. In its broadest and most literal meaning, design comes from the Latin "designare", e.g. to represent by means of signs, to project, to devise, to mark out.

12. Tavistock Institute (1966) *Interdependence and Uncertainty*, London, Tavistock; Winch, G. (1989) The construction firm and the construction project: a transaction cost approach, *Construction Management and Economics*, 7, pp. 331-345.

13. Paolo Tombesi, In the shadow of the Sydney Opera House: An analysis of the innovation role of public buildings in different socio-technical environments, *MIUR Brain Return Programme*, Polytechnic of Turin, 2005-2009.

14. Benedikt, M. (2007) Eighteen proposals for revaluing architecture, in Tombesi, P.; Gardiner, B.; Mussen, T. (eds) *Looking Ahead: Defining the Terms of a Sustainable Architectural Profession*, Manuka, ACT, The Royal Australian Institute of Architects, pp. 301-308.

15. Tombesi, P.; Whyte, J. (2011) Challenges of design management in construction, in Cooper, R.; Junginger, S.; Lockwood, T. (eds) *Handbook of Design Management*, Oxford, Berg Publishers.

16. The terms of the discussion between professionals as agents of formal knowledge and professional as trustees of socially important knowledge can be picked up in: Boggs, C. (1993) *Intellectuals and the crisis of modernity*, Albany, State University of New York Press; Brint, S. (1994) *In an age of experts: the changing role of professionals in politics and public life*, Princeton University Press; and the various contributions to Ray, N. (ed) (2005) *Architecture and its ethical dilemmas*, Milton Park, Routledge, particularly O'Neill, O. (2005) Accountability, trust and professional practice—The end of professionalism? pp. 77-88.

SOCIAL INFORMATION MODELING (SIM)
—
EDITOR'S NOTES

While the majority of contributors have addressed the themes of this book in the context of a unique architectural or engineering practice, Paolo Tombesi is responding in the context of industry at large. He is less enamored with the design and production of complex architectural projects through digital technology and more concerned with the social implications of this technology and its effect on larger trends in industry. More specifically, his work, here and elsewhere, attempts to establish a theoretical basis for defining, understanding and evaluating the underlying structure of the design and construction industry. This unique field of research offers essential insight into designing the future of industry but is almost unheard of in the USA, with the rare exceptions of some engineering and business schools; it is completely absent from architectural education. The generic diagrams showing endless versions of new industry organizations under the influence of BIM and IPD seem trivial in their

insight, depth and vision relative to the analysis and framework suggested by Tombesi for imagining how information technologies might expand the criteria for decision-making at the formative stages of a project.

For architects, digital technologies take the form of design and analytic tools informed by, and sometimes literally driven by, data and information. What Tombesi is questioning is the nature of this information. When he considers the reach, dependencies and consequences of mobilizing the resources necessary to realize a building, it becomes apparent that design and construction are part of a social ecology that extends far beyond what is addressed by current industry definitions. While there have been advances in the development of digital tools and workflows for integrating design information, the information has been limited to the physical description of the building. Architects, however, have always been responsible for

both designing the physical forms of buildings and reflecting on the social and cultural consequences of these designs. Arguably, new categories of information to better inform this responsibility are available and accessible through digital communication tools, yet they are slow to make their way into the design workflows of architects.

As digital workflows continue to evolve, architects should be asking more difficult questions and demanding more from the tools at their disposal. New categories of design information should be driving the development of new digital tools to integrate and analyze this information. The critique of CAD, in retrospect, is that it only streamlined the process of drawing that had existed for years, but otherwise made no fundamental change to the knowledge base or the design capacity of architects and engineers. BIM runs the same risk unless more is demanded from it. For instance, if the framework as outlined by Tombesi for analyzing and

understanding buildings, technology and design, with its expanded descriptions of the components, processes and players within industry, developed into a design tool, it might become a "Social Information Model" supplemental to the Building Information Model. This would exploit information modeling as an open-ended technology capable of expanding the reach and responsibility of industry, offering whole new categories of design input.

Tombesi's version of an information-rich working environment suggests new categories for the dashboard of outputs from a digital model, which currently focuses on the most direct attributes of a building such as cost, environmental performance and material usage. These categories might include information pertaining to the labor force required to produce a particular building component, such as the geographic location of manufacture relative to the final installation site. While the building site would likely not be a variable, the manufacturing site could be, and if the information model had access to data from several possible factories around the world, which might include working conditions as well as schedules and costs, these factors could be weighted as variable inputs based on the values of the design team to get a resulting output. The formal complexity of design proposals, that to date has been a primary driving force behind the use of advanced parametric modeling, could be supplemented by and measured against the social complexity and consequences of actually building the design proposals. In current practice, these nuanced categories of social information get simplified and abstracted into the single metric of the one-time financial cost to build a project.

In addition to the current industry focus on streamlining working processes and increasing procedural efficiencies of building, Tombesi offers a broader challenge to the promise of digital workflows to go beyond the procedural to the social—to expand the ambition of design to access and capture information that defines the social consequences of buildings.

SHIFT 2D TO 3D

THOM MAYNE

Thom Mayne is Founder and Design Director of Morphosis Architects and a Professor at UCLA.

We are clearly confronting a change in architecture and how it is realized, brought about by digital technologies. 3D digital design tools afford the ability to work on both the form and its organizational logic at the same time. With procedures that are themselves malleable and persistent, the design process consists of iterating through changes to form, organization and technique. At the same time, today's technology is powerfully accurate and allows us to rapidly build and test the work in virtual form well before it is ever constructed. Advancements in materials and innovations in construction processes allow us to strive for higher levels of performance. Feedback is incorporated into both the model's organizational logic as well as its forms. With parametric modeling, performance and form evolve together, almost as an integrated organism. The result is, on the whole, a progression of knowledge which begins abstract and ends specific, a seamless gradient from concept to reality.

DESIGN
—

The first shift in Morphosis's design process from 2D to 3D took place rather suddenly in 1990-91 when I realized that the future of architecture would be developed digitally. The second shift occurred a decade later when we began to use BIM, which would radically change the working environment. We understood this directional change as necessary, not optional; as essential, offering unprecedented possibilities. Had we not followed this instinct, we would never have produced the work that we have.

The computational shift into 3D paralleled and propelled a conceptual and pragmatic shift in our work, which occurred with Diamond Ranch School when we moved from small to large-scale work, a circumstance which required that we navigate increased organizational complexity.

The standard approach, originating in plans and sections and then proceeding into technical detail design—a linear approach—receded as we began to conceive of our projects in 3D digital models. This methodology has evolved and now involves operating on a project model whose parts and regions each exist in varying degrees of specificity. Making successive iterations over the model sends some design regions out exploring additional options, while other regions lock onto particular solutions. In subsequent iterations the thinking will change, and where some parts of the models need more specificity, some need to explore more options. This non-linear workflow affords an increased flexibility along the way.

Parametric modeling resulted in an acceleration in the design process. We found that we could move fluidly between scales and levels of detail as we came up with new concepts, instead of moving linearly from schematics to design development to construction. Traditionally, the amount of work required to maintain a project's technical detail meant that as more detail was added, the slower the changes could be propagated. Now, we can produce a design and continuously shift it in response to any number of generative influences. Parameters and rules associated with fabrication economy, for instance, can be encoded into the design models. As design changes are made, there is a built-in attentiveness to constructability.

Parametric modeling also ramps up our choices, exponentially, and allows us to expand the combinatory language we have always used. By virtue of the experience of more iterations, of exercising more options, the way that the architect relates to the design medium and tool has been altered. Similar outputs and qualities can emerge from these singular systems; and so, the operator—the architect—must be forceful in locating his authorship. Slow, deliberate drawing is replaced with virtuosic selecting and editing. These generative processes with their ability to handle a vastly more complex set of variables generate their own outputs that go beyond our own preconceived range of possible points of departure. Willful acts of controlling the behavior of these programs generate serendipitous outputs. Importantly, design drives the selection of the tool as well. The key is control, choosing the right software for your aspirations in relationship to the demand of any particular stage of the design process. If the software does not generate a suitable range of choices, you have to change the software.

New computational processes radically expand the power of the process. The role of the designer is two-fold: to develop the input logics and behavior of generative processes, and to evaluate and discriminate among the resultant options. These generative processes with their ability to handle a vastly more complex set of variables generate their own outputs that go beyond our own preconceived range of possible points of departure. Willful acts of controlling the behavior of these programs generate serendipitous outputs. The generative processes and the outputs selected from them are not ends, but are part of the architect's broader design process—dynamic high-performance idea generators collaborating over time with designers in a broader design process. It is this territory between chance and willfulness, between determinacy and possibility that the digital technology allows us to explore, which in turn allows us to rethink what architecture is, what organization is, what coherency is.

DELIVERY
—

The architectural product is completely dependent on the reliability of your delivery and your investment in the building. It became obvious that the means of delivery (the plans, sections, 3D drawings, models, renderings) were all different outputs of the same thing, especially with the emergence of 3D printers. Once we build the digital model, our MEP and structural teams use it to produce a plausible mechanical or structural idea within few days. And like Xerox outputs, the physical models can be distributed to different collaborators like the structural or mechanical capacities. For the Shanghai Giant Group Campus project, we did the skin, GFRC, structure and other large components all in a 3D environment; none of them had drawings. The drawings would have been absolutely useless to them.

The evolution of the computer environment and digital production techniques has broadened architecture as a discipline. Technology enables us to control the nature of our own creative process, as well as the realization of what we design. The architect's responsibility has expanded from design to include performance, construction, fabrication, installation... the entire process. At the same time, technology is transforming contractors' processes, including how they plan and how they make buildings.

Some fear an exposure of the architect to more risk with their expanded role. This fear is situated in a practice where a firewall has been instituted between the perils of designing and the perils associated with executing those designs. In reality, the more significant risk to the architectural profession is that architects will experience an increasingly smaller role. Morphosis never faced these risks because our work has always been about the complex interactions that produce something; never about the thing itself. We started with small-scale projects, making them and constructing them; we have always been builders. Thirty years ago, we were working at a level of craft where we began collaborating with the subcontractor from the pre-schematic phase. With BIM, we have been able to return to this initial level of engagement, working with the manufacturer to strategize fabrication during the first phase of drawings.

The practice of architecture is an integrative act. Information sourced from many specialists and forces emanating from many directions are synthesized by architects into a single work. The sharing of information between architect, engineer, fabricator and contractor erases the divisions between design and realization. The 3D environment facilitates this integration and coordination across specific areas of responsibility. This environment enhances the spirit of cooperation, resulting in improved two-way communication. Designers are better able to incorporate contractors' input into their work, and contractors can contribute to the design process while gaining a better sense of design intent so they can reinforce its integrity as they execute the built work.

Starting with the San Francisco Federal Building, we were able to implement this method from the beginning of design development, throughout the pre-construction and construction stages. At the middle of the construction document phase, we brought in the subcontractors to assess the most critical architectural components in terms of cost modeling and risk management. For the double skin, we developed a complicated, kinetic assembly in a complete 3D environment with very tight tolerances. We gave our 3D model to the subcontractor; they developed it at the level of connections, simplifying it to make it viable for their own construction process.

Modeling the building in very explicit terms—free of assumptions and ambiguity—improves clarity, lowers risks, reduces reliance upon monies reserved for contingencies and saves costs. These savings can pay for any extra work required to execute these 3D models, and in successful collaborations, can even pay for the architect's fee.

EXPLORING ADVANCED CONCEPTS
—

Digitally integrated construction methods, new modes of fabrication and new modes of construction planning also enable more integration in the architectural process. These new highly and rapidly configurable production methods produce customizable building elements that replace standard products selected from a catalog. Rapid re-tooling provides a greater capability for producers of buildings to collaborate during the project's design process.

Digital integration allows us to explore more advanced concepts, producing complex forms not otherwise realizable. We have been able to work with builders who collaborate with us in the digital environment, on projects such as 41 Cooper Square, the Cahill Center for Astronomy and Astrophysics at Caltech and the Shanghai Giant Group Campus. For the Cooper atrium web, we worked with the contractor and subcontractors to resolve details digitally as much as possible, in order to streamline the process on a largely handmade building. For Caltech's complex geometries the integration was seamless: Morphosis's control geometry was embedded into the subcontractor's detail models from which they digitally cut the parts, prefabricated the framework in the shop and then assembled it on site. In Shanghai, we collaborated with the builder on a similar digitally integrated fabrication process for the building's parabolic cones and complex forms.

Now, we are working on experimental projects, developing new techniques with manufacturers. Currently, for the Perot Museum of Nature and Science in Dallas (see Workflow Case Study, p. 212), we are developing large, precast concrete panels, organized in a complex, randomized pattern. Digital tools have allowed us to generate the panels' irregular arrangement, their three-dimensional, non-orthogonal forms, and their patterns of light and shadow in relationship to the sun. Initially the precast concrete fabricator had no idea how to make these

complex panels. We worked with them to prototype the panels and to adapt their standard processes to create a more innovative product. We are now working so closely with the fabricator that they are literally an extension of our office. There is a constant feedback mechanism. This one aspect of the building in itself becomes an entire project, and the process of collaborative invention is leading to new types of products, processes and projects.

We are also building the Phare Tower in La Défense, Paris—our most complicated work to date, which will be the tallest building in Paris (see Workflow Case Study, p. 216). We have now moved far beyond the old school of thought, to develop a high-performance tower at the upper end of complexity, at an enormous scale, which would be absolutely impossible without advanced digital technology. With the integration of the diagrid frame, window wall and second skin, we have reached the next phase of development in our digital workflow.

The digital environment channels exponentially increased amounts of information through projects. Architects design integrated workflows between entire project teams, which have their own idea-generative capabilities. Involving the contractor at the earliest conceptual stages, the architect embeds actual, material realities into the design process. Architects are not making a design. We are informing a collaborative process of making a building.

Figure 1. 3D-Printed study models of the Perot Museum of Nature and Science, Dallas, TX.

Figure 2. The Cooper Union
Academic Building atrium under
construction.

DISPOSABLE CODE;
PERSISTENT DESIGN

—

MARTY DOSCHER

Marty Doscher is Founder and Director of SYNTHESIS Technology Integration based in Los Angeles. He was previously Technology Director at Morphosis Architects for eight years.

Transitioning from analog to digital processes was a seamless evolution of the design philosophy of Morphosis. New tools and techniques evolved in a manner that supported the priority of design ideas to drive workflow processes. The advanced computational design systems that are currently being used on our most complex projects have been developed with an emphasis on the designer's central role in guiding the processes. Balancing the advantages of systematic workflow processes with the necessary flexibility of design has been the underlying foundation of how these technologies have evolved. Such tools and techniques are developed in the context of day-to-day practice where we actively search for opportunities, within the imperatives of a given project, to move towards a greater integration of design and building. We are constantly in both research and development, and project delivery mode and have begun to develop more generalized workflows based on past experience that can carry over from project to project.

DESIGN TEAMS
—

A new type of collaborative design team has begun to evolve in architecture offices, merging the skills of architectural designers with the skills of computational designers. The first stage in the evolution of these collaborative teams was to match a conventional designer, who could explore ideas and sketch freely, with a computational designer working inside the "black box", who would automate parts of the process to increase the speed of design

feedback. In this case, the computational designer would use his design sensibilities to interpret another designer's sketch into computable terms and then communicate the results back to the team for further development. The next stage in this evolution was to encourage more members of the design team to participate in the middle-ground of encoding—being able to do basic scripting and, more importantly, to have a conceptual understanding of a rule-based design system—in order to allow a design team to speak a common language and improve communication. With this phase of development there began to be a change in the capability of all designers to identify and make use of the "computable" facets of their designs, which often included making their own digital tools. In the current stage of development, the prevailing notion of the architectural designer interacting tacitly with the "black box", disappears and designers are increasing their engagement not only with the explicit and abstract parts of their designs, but also with the discipline of code-writing. [Figure 1]

Computational design, once thought to be a special skill reserved only for those who were mathematically inclined, is now within the grasp of most designers. Those with a particularly evolved understanding of the potential for computation to transform design processes can write custom software to support a team's particular design approach, which was the case during the design of the Phare Tower. Computational design extends the capabilities and advantages of conventional design by quickly generating complex geometric output from inputs that are determined as part of the workflow design. In the later stages of a project, this rapid workflow can be expanded to include more technical information, like structural performance and energy analysis, resulting in a compressed feedback loop of valuable design criteria that is close to real-time. Analysis blends into the simulation of actual building performance, allowing design and engineering concepts to develop simultaneously.

DESIGN SYSTEMS
—

The design process in architecture can be characterized as highly idiosyncratic, driven by a group of creative collaborators and subject to numerous external forces that ebb and flow as a project unfolds. Both the creative aspect and the external constraints are often unpredictable and require a workflow with a high degree of flexibility. This has been an important consideration as Morphosis has formalized computationally driven design systems. We have approached this as an asynchronous network of loosely coupled techniques that can achieve a dynamic, adaptable and structured relationship between the technical criteria of a project and the creative aspect of design. With this approach, creativity can act either on the inner workings of the design systems, or as a stochastic influence that serves as a counterbalance to the rational

logic of these systems. Design systems operate in service of design goals.

DISPOSABLE CODE
—

The design systems employed by Morphosis are characterized by selectively utilizing custom-designed software code (here referred to as custom code) that is very often short-lived, even disposable. Custom code is intentionally purpose-built for the task at hand, to produce a specific result at a particular moment in the design of a project. This places the emphasis more on the design goals and less on the perfection of the code and encourages more spontaneous, creative thinking. Custom code often consists of authoring routines around a specific set of inputs that anticipates a designer's intuitive sense of the desired results.

Architectural designers have a masterful ability to intuit organizational logics to develop their ideas. One element where designers frequently explore these logics is the surface pattern on a building façade. A variety of patterning techniques can be applied to a given surface to explore a range of resulting designs

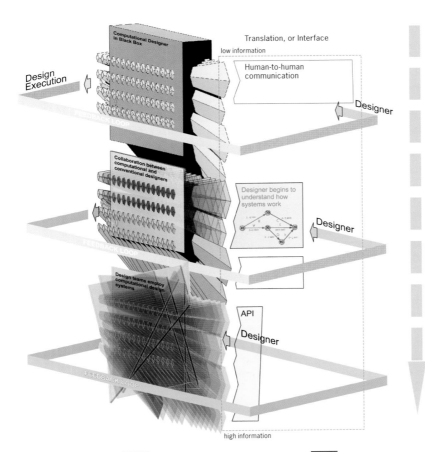

Figure 1. Evolution of a design practice integrating computational design: three stages where the communication of design intent becomes increasingly integrated into computational design systems.

and desired effects. Designers instinctively know when the pattern logic will need to change as the surface changes and can anticipate this at the outset of the design process. For instance, a patterning technique that worked for a conical surface may not work for the surface of a cube. In this case, designers will likely discard that technique and search for another that might be more suitable, instead of trying to modify the technique to suit the new surface. This describes the agility and flexibility of intuitive thinking with conventional design techniques. However, it is common for computational designers who employ custom-coding design techniques to be less willing to completely replace the encoded logic, even when it becomes apparent that it would be more effective to start anew. The time invested becomes a deterrent to working in a more flexible manner akin to how designers think intuitively.

To address this tendency, Morphosis began to structure project workflows that treat individual segments of code in a design system as disposable after it achieves its intended purpose. By contrast, the design medium—the computer model that contains the cumulative design decisions and parametric relationships of a project—remains persistent and drives the workflow. This medium is often a simple 3D geometry that contains both the output of a previous technique, and the inputs to the next technique. The medium outlives the conditional custom-coded design techniques. This approach allows flexibility for new design impulses to enter at any stage of the workflow and opens the possibility of unexpected and surprising design output—output that represents the unique advantages of combining creative imagination and computation. It also offers an alternative to the more common mode of computational design, where design intent has to be captured early in the process of setting up the logic of a design model, which subsequently allows only limited design exploration within constrained ranges of variability. For Morphosis, maintaining flexibility in the design of the workflow offsets the natural tendency of code-driven design to subvert more open-ended creative impulses in the later design phases of a project. This does come at a cost though, which is the necessary expertise of advanced programming among the members of the design team. More advanced programming allows more design flexibility within a digital workflow and this is perhaps one of the future challenges for architects and architectural education.

DESIGNING INTERFACES
—

As custom-coded techniques accumulate throughout the development of the design medium, there are situations when outputs from one do not function as inputs to another. Outputs require constant evaluation as an integral part of the design workflow before they can serve as useful inputs to a subsequent custom-coding technique. And so a critical step in this process is to rationalize the inputs and build an interface that will feed them into an ordered routine to deliver the desired results. This is not done just once, but each time the state of the medium changes, as the programmer cannot presuppose that the design will be the same from one moment to the next. One cannot presuppose that there is a consistent way to understand the implicit nature of the designer's manipulations of the medium, from iteration to iteration. Although the designer's original surfaces and patterns and those rationalized into inputs will become virtually indistinguishable, this logical re-ordering is an essential part of this workflow.

The medium of design is the workflow. It is not singular—it can include the virtual building model, physical 3D models, engineering analysis models, building information models or any other form of digital information that influences the design. This often requires designing the interconnection between the software platforms of these various systems at the level of their respective programming interfaces. Previously, the ability to connect multiple specialty design and engineering analysis platforms was limited to file-format conversion, often reducing the geometric intelligence and organizational logic of the models. Computational designers are now able to write code to not only generate results in form, but also to generate code for other

Figure 2. 3D-Printed models are used in conjunction with live 3D modeling to focus the team on specific design issues.

systems to interpret. This "meta-code" can convey organizational logics that are consistent and relevant across each respective platform. Maintaining and conveying this logic becomes progressively more important downstream in the later design and production phases of a project, to the extent that information is added to design models for specific tasks. In fact, communicating the logic of the model is often as important as communicating the design itself, especially as it relates to project execution tasks.

3D PRINTING
—

Digitally integrated design systems that shorten the feedback loop between design intent (input) and design results (output) also include 3D printing. First introduced at Morphosis in 2001, 3D printing—the low-res voxel-to-voxel physical rendering of a virtual model—has become an indispensible part of our new workflow and has enabled designers to capture their intent into virtual models, and then output physical scale models as a quick snapshot to evaluate design progress. As physical objects that can give a more comprehensive understanding of three-dimensional form, these models serve to focus the discussion of the design team to evaluate the models against the design intent. [Figure 2] With their rough texture and monolithic color, it becomes possible to think of these models as 3D sketch paper. In fact, designers often sketch with pencil on the 3D print during meetings, enabling the discussion to keep pace with the design team's creative process. The 3D-printed models are used in other ways as projects develop. Concurrent with the sketch modeling techniques where an entire building is printed at a small scale to study overall

geometry and relationship to context, projects can also be studied at increasing scales and levels of detail. Areas of complex spatial relationships forms are often 3D-printed as enlarged sectional models. [Figure 3] Multiple alternatives for wall assemblies, building skins and structural systems are printed at larger scales to study project tectonics, and facilitate communication with engineers, fabricators and builders. [Figure 4] While the amount of virtual, analytical and abstract information that accumulates within a computer model through the design process continues to expand, continually updated versions of the 3D physical model are used as the interface that integrates and reflects the efforts of all team members and supports an effective collaborative working environment.

CONSTRUCTION-READY DESIGN MODELS
—

An important progression of digital design modeling has been the continued use of these models in the fabrication and construction phases of a project. Digital production technologies allow a direct connection between the "what"(design intent) and the "how" (construction means and methods). Even if it is not in the form of direct CNC fabrication files, digitial information supplied by designers often carries the digital seeds of the work of the contractor. The contractors themselves can be more productive when they can see the design results through 3D models instead of interpreting design intent through 2D drawings. An even more significant benefit is that a well-structured digital design model conveys not only design information but also an execution framework— an organizational logic for building sequences and the primitives for proceeding directly into

Figure 3. A 3D-printed building section model of the new academic building for the Cooper Union in New York.

Figure 4. The rapid turnaround time afforded by 3D printing directly from design development models means that many alternative design approaches can be studied in parallel, each to a high level of technical detail, as in these façade component

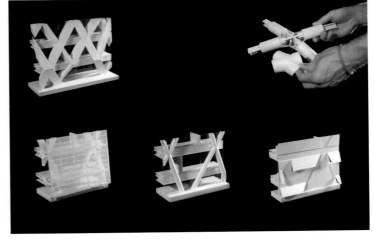

models for the Phare Tower in Paris La Défense.

fabrication and construction. While the current workflow between design and fabrication typically requires fabricators and contractors to rebuild design models provided by architects, due to both technical and legal reasons, Morphosis strives to make construction-ready design models, as we believe that this should become the future industry standard.

Pure CNC processes are not necessarily the ideal approach when developing design and production workflows for a project and through our recent experience on several completed buildings, Morphosis has evolved the notion of adapting technology to circumstances, which often involves combining human craft labor and computer-assisted technologies. This was especially true with the Cooper Union Academic Building, where processes ranged from an advanced digitally manufactured and coordinated building system for the façade [Figure 5] to a system that was used to coordinate strictly separated trades for the ceiling assemblies [Figure 6] and on to a hybrid digital and hand-crafted process for the atrium latticework. [Figures 7, 8]

INDUSTRY ORGANIZATIONS
—

The use of information technology to increase productivity arrives, not surprisingly, coupled with business pressures to produce and iterate more design options, with less time, less resources and often less fee. This condition is exaggerated when working on projects in emerging markets and in fact, a significant challenge for design practices today comes from reduced fees attributed to globalization. Highly valued building elements, often with considerable formal and performance complexity, are being produced in economies and regions where labor

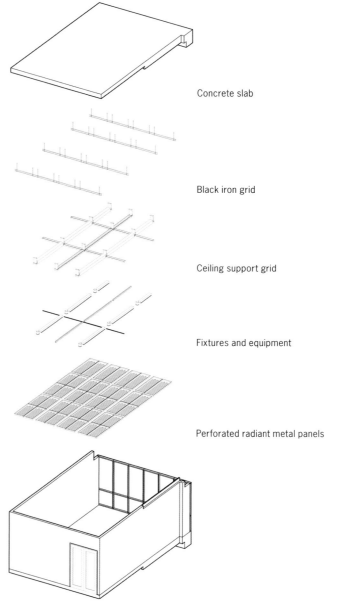

Concrete slab

Black iron grid

Ceiling support grid

Fixtures and equipment

Perforated radiant metal panels

Figure 5. The exterior envelope of the Cooper Union Academic Building utilized automated techniques for design and fabrication, involving direct digital exchange back and forth between designer and fabricator. This scope of the project was delivered under an integrated agreement involving owner, contractor, subcontractors and design team.

Figure 6. The radiant heating and cooling assemblies in the ceilings of the Cooper Union Academic Building were virtually coordinated through the model. Here, the model was important not so much for design or fabrication but for negotiating the fiercely guarded territories of the building trades in a densely packed laboratory ceiling.

costs are low, which is distorting the traditional relationship of fee structure to construction cost. Design and engineering firms are grappling with the pressure to outsource certain activities, such as BIM authoring, to reduce in-house labor cost while also maintaining high-quality services. It is costly to re-tool a design office to become BIM-proficient when these services are seen as low-value compared to the value of design.[1] Where governments permit, some firms are able to set up branch offices in these locations. Where this is not possible, partnering with a local firm is a reasonable option and while digital collaboration makes this easier, the challenge remains to effectively integrate team members in remote locations. During construction, communication and team coordination is even more challenging and in nearly every case on Morphosis projects the design staff is in the field throughout.

The act of design is a complex network of interactions across teams. The architect is becoming an integrator of increasingly complex design information generated by ever larger

and more diverse teams. This role seems to have arisen not by choice but as a pragmatic response to the growing complexity of executing built work, and the desire to get through construction process with the design as intact as possible. Challenging the outdated paradigm where building projects develop along a linear trajectory, project timelines can be rearranged to more effectively connect the network of factors, decisions and team members. The iterative design loop expands in three dimensions, similar to an intertwining double helix, to connect with other iterative loops of fabrication, assembly and construction information. These loops simultaneously place demands and offer opportunities for architects to define new roles and elaborate on workflows that leverage the value of design.

Digital communication technologies have advanced at a much faster pace in society at large than in the building industry, fueled by the rapid development of consumer-oriented virtual communities, both social and business-related. This ability to quickly connect groups of dispersed people, however, has the potential to uniquely benefit the design and construction industry, as project teams are almost always comprised of ad-hoc proto-organizations that rely heavily on quickly assembling and disassembling people around a single project. As architects, we work with self-authored software that automates design processes, we connect to digitally driven manufacturing systems and are even beginning to generate information that drives robotic systems—software is now a collaborator, not just a tool. Information, even intellectual property, flows freely across traditionally restricted borders. Accelerating cultural and technological change will continue to exert pressure on architects to develop responses specific and appropriate to our discipline. And so the evolution of design practice and the broader building industry will continue from both internal developments, from CAD to BIM to VDC, and external developments, from digitization to virtual reality to synthetic biology.

ENDNOTES
—
1. To protect its investment in re-tooling, the American steel industry has blocked efforts by companies in emerging countries to gain access to advanced technologies such as that found in mini-mills, for fear of introducing unfair competition. (Reuters, 07/06/2010, 10:11GMT, http://www.reuters.com/article/idAFN0651479520100706)

Figures 7, 8. The installation of the fiberglass-reinforced gypsum lattice in the interior atrium of the Cooper Union Academic Building was coordinated using advanced digital modeling techniques; but the field work relied not upon computer-numerical control, but upon plaster artistry. The shapes of the lattice panels were all uniquely rotated and cut, so the designer and engineer co-authored scripts to manage the geometry, then produced easy-to-read rotation template drawings for the plaster craftspeople to be read in the field. In this case, workflows shift between digital and manual.

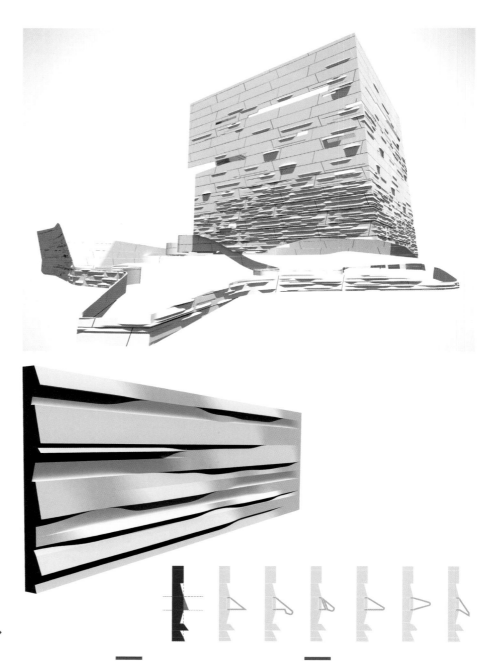

PEROT MUSEUM OF NATURE AND SCIENCE
WORKFLOW CASE STUDY ▶

The Perot Museum of Nature and Science in Dallas demonstrates the selective use of digital techniques in conjunction with the skills of craftspeople to develop an innovative workflow in support of design. The building envelope evolved from working closely with a precast fabricator to develop casting techniques that would allow maximum design flexibility within economically feasible production methods. The building's exterior cladding includes 3D precast concrete panels with nominal surface variation ranging from flat to curved in two directions. The pattern of 3D features on the face of the panels varies to enable a gradient and give a more seamless appearance to the overall façade surfaces. The array of features is designed to optimize for increasing

economy and increasing variation. Each panel is divided into a rectangular grid of identically sized modules. The design model embodies an economical system of making that translates directly to the precast contractor's fabrication and production methods.

Workflow 1 (top). Design study of the 3D precast panels of the Perot Museum of Nature and Science.

Workflow 2 (bottom). The panels include an array of 3D features on the exterior face of the panel. Designers utilize parametric tools to study variations in individual features, indicated with the red line.

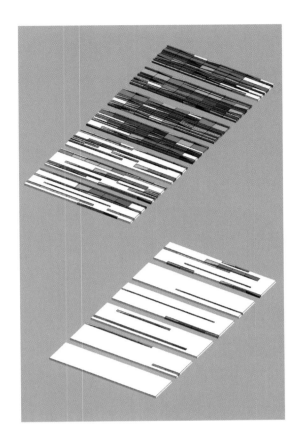

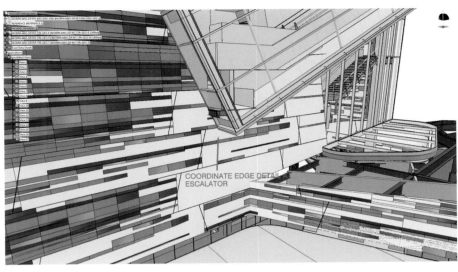

COORDINATE EDGE DETAIL
ESCALATOR

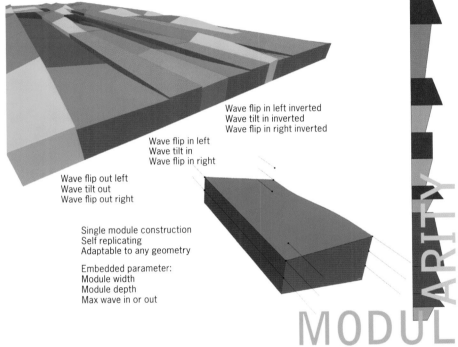

Wave flip in left inverted
Wave tilt in inverted
Wave flip in right inverted

Wave flip in left
Wave tilt in
Wave flip in right

Wave flip out left
Wave tilt out
Wave flip out right

Single module construction
Self replicating
Adaptable to any geometry

Embedded parameter:
Module width
Module depth
Max wave in or out

MODULARITY

Workflow 3 (above left).
Each panel is divided into a
rectangular grid of identically sized modules. The white
areas indicate a flat panel
with no 3D features, whereas
the colored areas represent
grid modules where a form
liner is placed to generate a
3D feature on the panel. Each
color represents a different
form liner.

Workflow 4 (top right). The
design model indicates specific and unique conditions
at the points where precast
panels are coordinated with
other building elements. The
high level of technical detail
in the model allows the design
team to resolve construc-
tability issues during the
design process.

Workflow 5 (bottom right). A
design study indicating the
method of achieving modularity of the precast concrete
panels. The colored blocks
represent the solid geometry
of a module of the precast
panel. These solids will be
created by casting their negative as a 3D form liner.

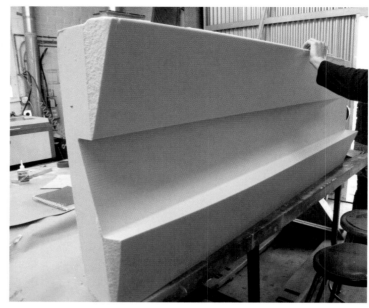

Workflow 6a (top left). Production method of a precast panel. The precast contractor inverts the design surfaces to build the form-work for casting the negative of each unique module.

Workflow 6b (bottom left). When cast, the form liners are arranged into the precast form according to the design-er's layout drawings. Several form liners can be cast in the molds, and can be reused and rearranged to form each unique panel configuration.

Workflow 6c (top right). A milled foam prototype was con-sidered for the 3D form liners but was not used due to cost. Instead, the precast contrac-tor opted to utilize their highly skilled in-house wood workers to fabricate the 3D form liners.

Workflow 6d (bottom right). Mock up of a single panel.

Workflow 7. Precast concrete
panels being applied to the
steel structure.

PARIS LA DÉFENSE
PHARE TOWER
WORKFLOW CASE STUDY▶

Drawing on the power of parametric script-ing, the design of the Phare Tower in La Défense, Paris, gathers disparate program-matic, physical and infrastructural elements from the requirements of the building and its surrounding context, and synthesizes these into a form that seamlessly inte-grates the building into the idiosyncrasies of its site while expressing multiple flows of movement. In the spirit of the Paris Exposition competition proposals, the tower embodies state-of-the-art technological advances to become a cultural landmark.

The structure and skin of the Phare Tower adapt to the non-standard form while simultaneously responding to a range of complex, and often competing, material and environmental considerations. Custom scripts were developed to integrate the work of several standard softwares so the project could progress along parallel tracks including concept design, structural analysis, environmental analysis and mate-rial as well as manufacturing optimization. Both the form and the orientation of the building respond to the path of the sun; the south façade's curvilinear double skin minimizes heat gain and glare, while the flat, clear-glazed north façade maximizes natural daylight to the interior offices. A *brise soleil* wraps the tower's continuous south, east and west glazed façades. The perception of its high-performance skin transforms with changes in light, becoming opaque, translucent or transparent from different angles and vantage points.

Workflow 1. Rendering of Phare Tower. The building's com-plex site and shape presented unique technical challenges that demanded advanced com-putational techniques to be solved. The site is bound by a train line, a highway and other infrastructure below grade that influenced the overall geometry and also required the structure to spread at the base to avoid conflicts.

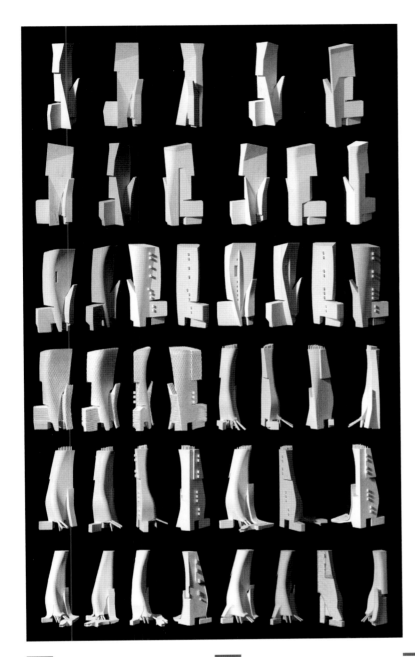

Workflow 2 (above left). 3D prints of the early conceptual massing studies during the project design competition.

Workflow 3 (above right). An overall 1:300 scale 3D-printed model, highlighting the initial pattern and shape of the building's sunscreen.

JAVA software

MicroStation

Generative component script

CATIA VB script

OBJ file

Rhino script

Rhinoceros

Digital Project

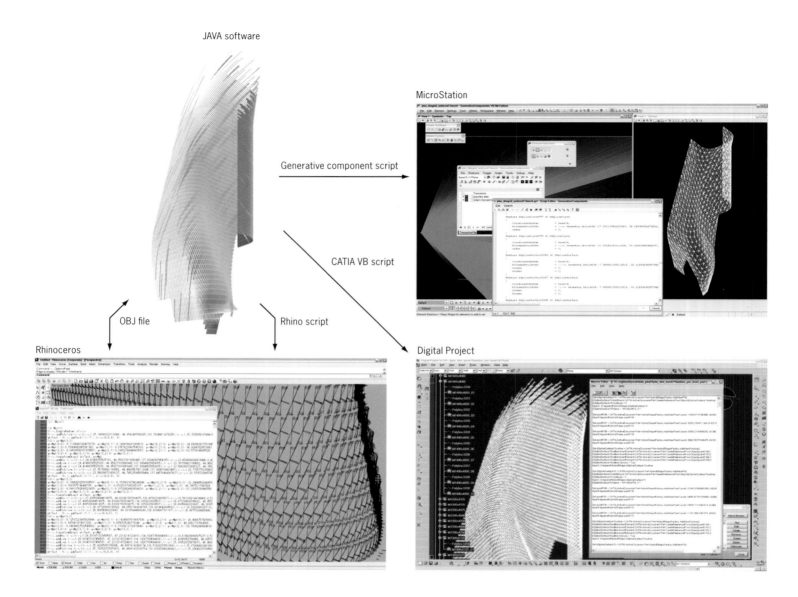

Workflow 4. Coordination of 3D data. The designer authored proprietary software in the Java language to export not just the formal geometry, but the organizational logic of the design control geometry into technical detail models. These models output scripts that can be executed in other off-the-shelf modeling software, so the consultants can continue with the technical development of the project while the design continues to progress. This process is repeatable, allowing changes to the design control geometry even after adding technical detail to the downstream models.

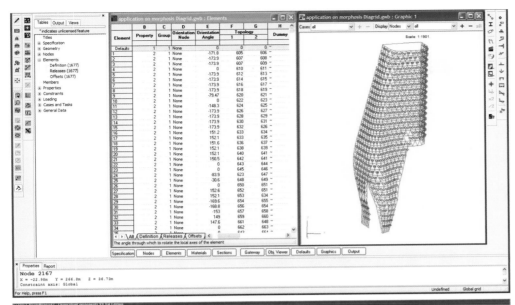

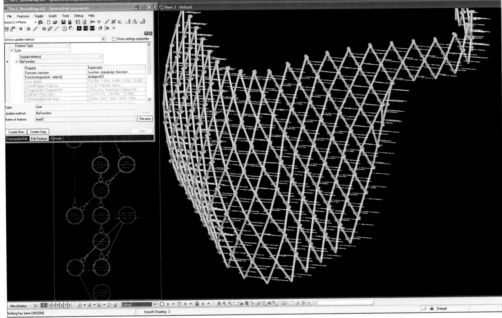

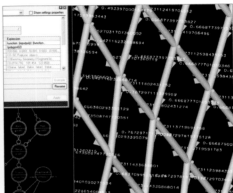

Workflow 5. Design models are integrated with structural analysis models throughout design development and construction document phases. Attributes for individual nodes and structural members can be generated from the structural models. Dimensional adjustments based on this analysis can be integrated into design models in an iterative feedback process.

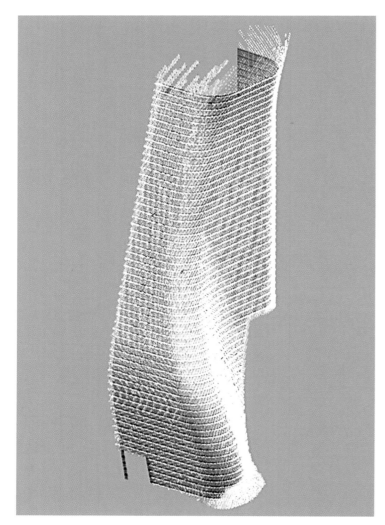

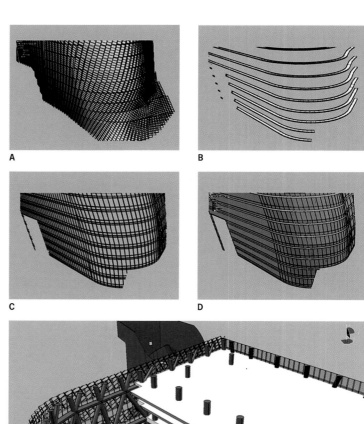

A

B

C

D

Workflow 6 (top). Overall view of the parametric model of Phare Tower envelope with each layer shown separately.
A) The suncreen mesh and panel framework;
B) the catwalks;
C) the curtainwall mullions;
D) the curtainwall with catwalks.

Workflow 7 (bottom right). Digital tectonic model of the Phare Tower. The highly technical parametric model enables a thorough study of all specific details of the project and better coordination of systems across interior finish, structure and envelope.

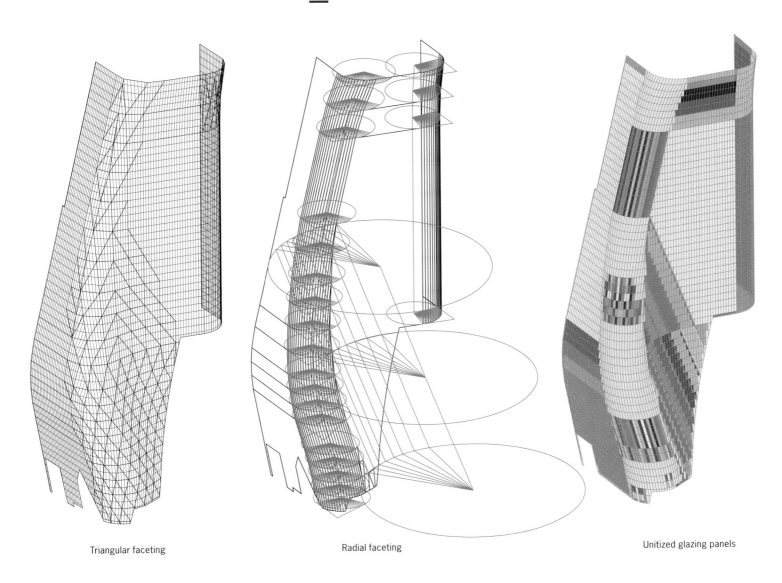

Triangular faceting   Radial faceting   Unitized glazing panels

Workflow 8a (above), 8b (following page). The glazing
panels were developed using
custom optimization scripts.
Curvature from the original
design surface was approximated into an optimally small
quantity of unique glazing
panel configurations.

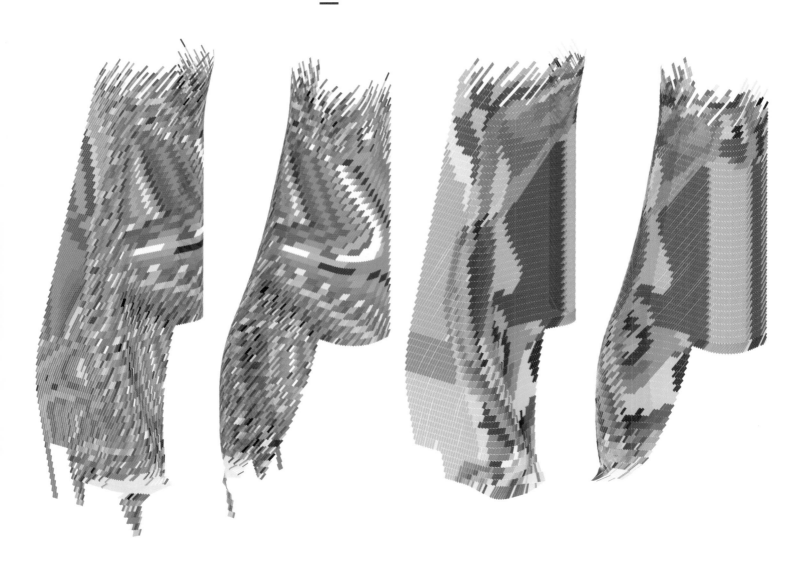

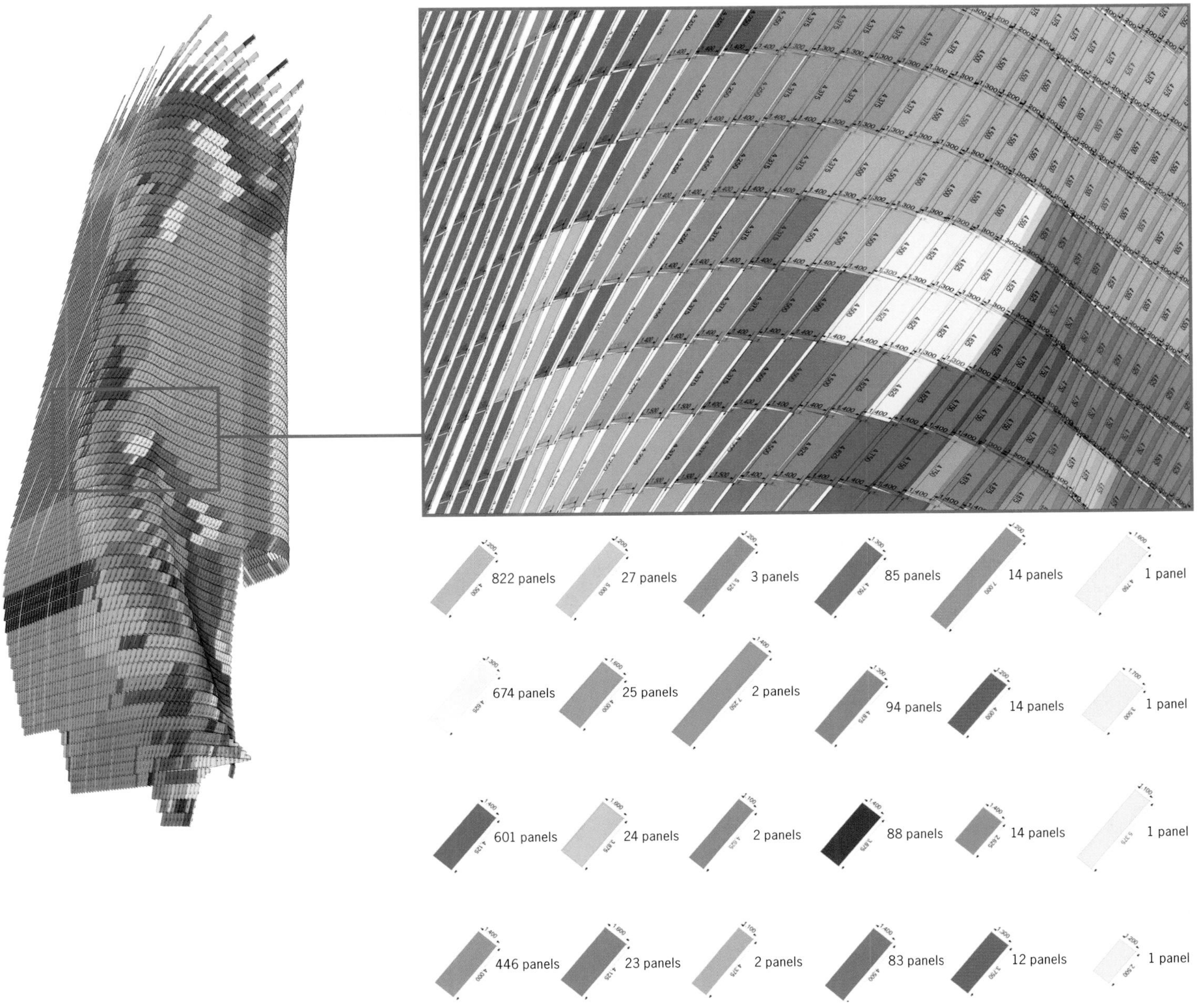

Workflow 9a (above left),
9b (top right), 9c (bottom
right). Computational optimization of exterior sunscreen.
Custom optimization scripts
were used to adjust the
layout and limit the number
of unique sizes of sunscreen
panels, maintaining the perception of the pattern while
dramatically reducing the
cost. The illustrations hint
at the millimeter level of
precision in the design model.

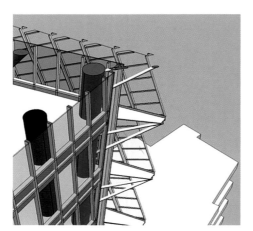

Workflow 10 (top). Integrated
digital model of all exterior
building components.

Workflow 11 (bottom).
3D-Printed detail of the metal
mesh sunscreen and structural
framework from the digital
model.

Workflow 12 (right). Full-scale
mock-up of metal mesh sunscreen and panel framework.

WORKFLOW FLEXIBILITY
—
EDITOR'S NOTES

In reflecting on the ability of digital tools to capture a wide range of architectural design intent, Dennis Shelden, the CTO of Gehry Technologies, makes the point that "there is something of an inverse relationship between the efficacy or power of a computational approach and its flexibility".[1] This simple insight speaks to one of the fundamental challenges regarding the rule-based logics of computational systems and their difficult adaptation to the provisional nature of design. It suggests that there is an ecology of computation where flexibility is a finite resource: decisions that bias one design objective have consequences that affect other design objectives. Design requires flexibility to respond to the non-linear development of ideas and as architects move towards an increased reliance on computational systems, the challenge becomes how to allocate this resource.

In the digital design workflows of Morphosis that have developed over the last two decades, it is clear that flexibility is prioritized over the efficiency of any single design system. Mayne and Doscher have worked closely together during this period to develop an approach that is consistent with the office design philosophy. For Mayne, this required few conceptual adjustments, as their work had always focused on combinatory interactions of parts rather than the end result; the interactions produced the results. Their design thinking was consistent with the relational logics of parametric design systems. Morphosis's workflows utilize particular techniques that facilitate the most fluid exchange and progression of design intent, whether it be 3D printing, explicit modeling, custom software code or hand sketching. Their unique approach to custom-created code as a disposable code that is developed only for the task at hand reinforces their emphasis on process flexibility. The digital techniques they develop are never precious and are selectively deployed when they can act as an effective method of pursuing design intent. If custom code is written to study design solutions for a particular project, it is unlikely to be applicable to another project without either significantly modifying or over-generalizing the code. Disposable, task-specific code puts the emphasis on developing the design, not the code.

Morphosis has adopted a similar tailored approach to the use of computation for construction, which often results in a combination of digital and conventional processes. "Adapting technology to circumstances" describes their process of incorporating project contingencies into the digital workflow. This was evident in their approach to the design and construction of the atrium lattice for the academic building at 41 Cooper Square, where digital techniques assisted in the installation process in response to the technology and skill level available on site. Working in collaboration with the structural engineer, Buro Happold, custom software was written to locate nodal coordinates on the lattice structure so that the site crew could use chop saws and plumb lines for site installation.

Mayne insists that they do not make drawings, they make buildings; he considers design ideas to be only as good as the delivery system, and their "construction-ready digital models" described by Doscher reflect a priority on developing workflows during design that are informed by, but also help guide, fabrication processes and construction sequences. As complex assemblies of diverse components and parts manufactured independently of each other, buildings will likely always require a significant amount of human labor, and Morphosis views this hybrid approach of blending handcraft and computational techniques as an industry-specific virtue.

Digital fabrication workflows have solidified the close working relationship that Morphosis has always maintained with fabricators and builders. By convincing their clients of the feasibility and value of using digital workflows for connecting design to manufacturing, they have managed to maintain these working relationships even as their projects have become larger and more constrained by industry-standard divisions of responsibility between architects and builders. The success of projects like the San Francisco Federal Building and the Caltrans Headquarters in Los Angeles, both subject to the onerous procurement regulations of public projects, relied on collaborating with fabricators and serve as case studies for future models of industry integration. For the Perot Museum of Nature and Science, the design of the precast concrete panels evolved from the design team understanding the manufacturing procedures and then collaborating with the fabricator to develop an efficient formwork and casting method. This resulted in new innovative processes for the fabricator and a unique design for the architect. Future developments in industry will depend on these efforts by architects to design digital workflows that align design innovation with industry innovation.

In one of our early conversations, Mayne made the often-overlooked observation that the innovative use of digital workflows will rely on new types of collaborations driven by ambitious high-performance design with equally aggressive aesthetic ambitions. Without this, digital technologies will tend to proliferate generic design solutions.

—

1. Shelden, D. (2009) Information Modelling as a Paradigm Shift, in Garber, R. (2009) *Closing the Gap; Information Models in Contemporary Design Practice*, *Architectural Design* magazine.

CONTINUOUS INTEGRATION

CRAIG SCHWITTER & IAN KEOUGH

Craig Schwitter is the Managing Director for North America at Buro Happold Consulting Engineers. Ian Keough is Associate Technical Director.

In order to realize the potential of integrated processes including BIM, and to take advantage of the full capacity of the various types of software required on complex projects, we need to be able to pass data seamlessly and efficiently between team members working on multiple platforms. The skills to create the tools to do this will belong to a new generation of architects and engineers, one that is already emerging in the Processing and Grasshopper scripters graduating from architecture programs. Those skills, while still applied mostly towards form-making, can be directed towards integrated design tools to solve practice-based workflow problems.

We need to base our workflow on three-dimensional models that incorporate the design intent of the architect, the structural and mechanical requirements of the engineers and the fabrication expertise of the contractor and specialty fabricators. In order to realize the productivity and coordination benefits espoused by integrated workflows, we will need to eliminate barriers to information sharing and fundamentally change the way that design teams collaborate where coordination is a continuous, live, process.

Efforts to make software interoperable through shared "open source" file formats have been slow to take hold in the AEC industry. Therefore, sending data between design applications is treated as something to be avoided. Designers feel as if they should do whatever it takes to contain their design within one application even if there are more appropriate tools from other applications that could do the task more effectively. Rather than waiting for software vendors to create interoperability, which might happen for those applications within their own library but is unlikely with applications by their competitors, an alternate and more flexible solution is to create yourself the tools to translate

data. This has become an increasingly common approach for Buro Happold.

For projects with highly complex geometry, there are often several applications that are utilized to design, analyze and document the final form. The challenge is to maintain the data through these numerous steps, feeding each application only what it needs, while ensuring the accuracy of data throughout the process. This level of integration is also necessary to address the fact that architectural projects are increasing in complexity and size, while timelines and budgets are being compressed. Large projects require not only the addition of the afore-mentioned skills, but also fundamental shifts in workflows that affect the organization of our regional offices and how they collaborate with other offices around the world.

Every project at Buro Happold, regardless of size, is fully modeled. Documentation is derived directly from the model so we are no longer drafting, in the traditional sense, and any 2D drawings are output from the 3D model. One of the fundamental shifts has been to use the model as the central repository to continually integrate design information from many offices. This distributed workflow has become necessary to meet the demanding schedules of large projects while allowing particular expertise from any office to be utilized on local projects. In order to support this workflow, design areas need to be carefully defined, and models carefully managed to provide a tightly coordinated design both within Buro Happold and across the larger project team.

These challenges have led Buro Happold to explore new workflows based on the concept of continuous integration. Continuous Integration (CI) is one of the central tenets of the Agile software development movement. For large software development teams working on complex applications this means frequent merging of small changes to code in order to ascertain which elements are not working well together. When taken to the extreme, this means nightly building and integration of the code base. In architecture, the use of shared 3D models is beginning to move us in the same direction. Like software designers, we realize the inefficiency of conducting post-mortem analyses of a design after the issuance of schematic design development or construction documents. But until recently, our tools and our workflows have not supported the continuous integration model. With the widespread use of Building Information Modeling (BIM), the design process is being fundamentally reorganized around quicker iterations, more up-to-date design assets and more transparency in the design process.

Unlike large software design projects where multiple parties are all working with the same technologies, it is often the case in architecture that design assets come from a number of different, non-communicating sources. In order to recognize the benefits of continuous integration, we need to be able to pass data seamlessly between applications. For Buro Happold this often means interpreting the architect's design model of curves and surfaces, generating our own analytical models and ultimately sending the data for visualization and documentation. This workflow requires both a rigorous set of protocols and a degree of flexibility to quickly address problems, because even the slightest gap in this process causes delays in design iterations, slows down the production process and can engender bad faith with our clients. For this reason, on almost every job we find ourselves writing new code or extending existing code, to make the constituent applications of the design workflow process communicate. The continuous integration process is also about integrating custom tools, integrating the expertise of fabricators into the design and integrating between our in-house disciplines. The three projects detailed here, TwoFour54, Crystal Bridges Museum of American Art and the Janet Echelman Sculptures are each exemplary of aspects of this new mode of continuous integration on projects of every scale and complexity.

INTEGRATING TEAMS: TWOFOUR54
WORKFLOW CASE STUDY ▶

This is a workflow example for a complex large-scale project with design and engineering teams located around the world. twofour54 in Abu Dhabi is approximately 7M sqft of office, residential, cultural and retail space, spread over four city blocks. Four separate architects were providing design information for the project, which had to be integrated into BIM models. By linking the models together and sharing common datums, the teams were able to assure that levels, grids and primary elements were consistently coordinated. We then applied ownership of elements to the model in order to define each participant's scope of work and also to assign responsibility to each person working on the model. For instance, engineers owned the placement of all columns, while the architects owned the locations of all slab edges. In the case of structural columns, their locations were fundamental to the structural design, so any movement of a structural column needed to be undertaken in the structural model and then coordinated with the other work.

The size and complexity of the twofour54 model made it impossible to know, when linking in an architect's revised model, what had changed. By utilizing BIM, any changes to the architectural model that might affect the structural design could be tracked with automated reports, which

Workflow 1 (above). twofour54. Exterior rendering.

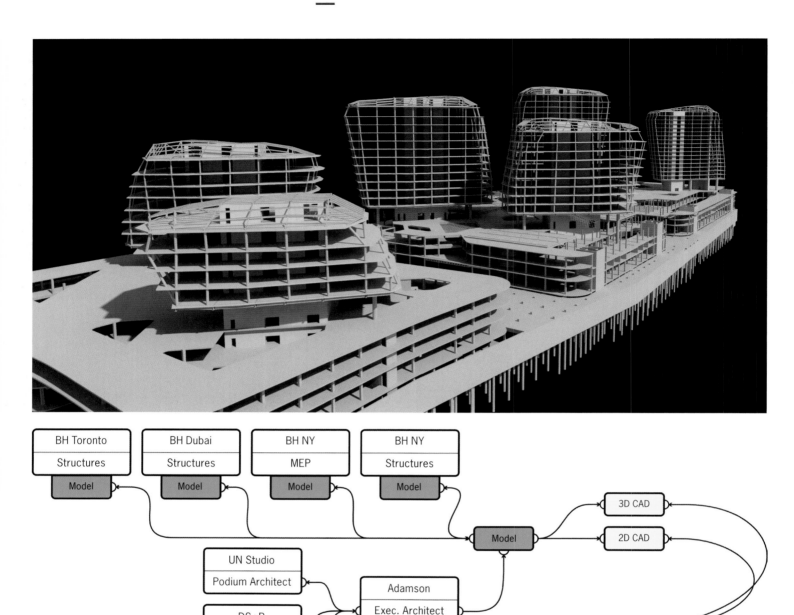

could also be used as the outline for the coordination process. Design data were being exchanged between New York, Amsterdam, Toronto, Dubai and London, spanning eleven time zones. As an example, the foundations were being designed in Dubai, the building structure and mechanical systems in New York. At the end of the day in New York, the model had to be in a state that it could be used by the Dubai team for coordination when they arrived in the office. This live approach to modeling enforced a higher standard of design, by allowing all team members to see and react to changes in real time.

Workflow 2 (top). Structural model showing columns and slabs. Responsibility of model elements was assigned to different team members.

Workflow 3 (bottom). This diagram shows the workflow between architects and engineers.

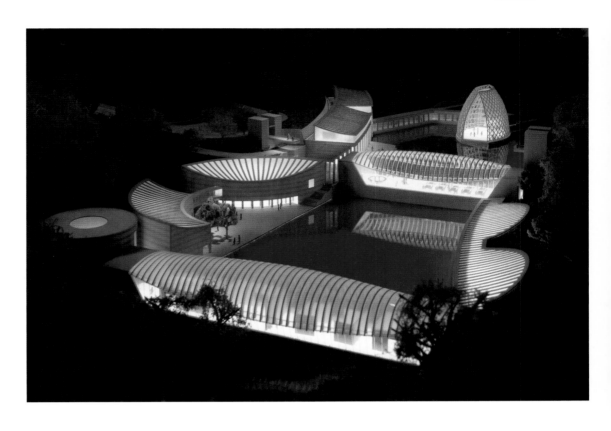

INTEGRATING TRADES: CRYSTAL BRIDGES MUSEUM OF AMERICAN ART
WORKFLOW CASE STUDY▶

Workflow 1. Physical model of museum complex.

As a mid-scale project where the emphasis was on integrating design and structural information with fabrication requirements, the workflow for this museum in Bentonville designed by Safdie Architects, required information models with extremely tight tolerances.

The museum complex consisted of several buildings with double-curved "bridge" roofs. These roofs were designed with wood glu-lam arched beams supported by 4in galvanized steel bridge cables spanning between massive concrete abutments. Construction documents had already been completed, but for many connections the two-dimensional documentation could not fully describe their complexity. For this reason many critical aspects of

the design of the structures were left undocumented, creating inadequate information for fabrication.

By defining the architect's geometry as design parameters and the fabricators' tolerances as constraints, any data extracted from the model would meet both the architectural intent and the fabricator's expectations for constructability. Building the model in this way allowed us to accommodate a very wide range of technological competencies among the various fabricators. For example, the glu-lam arch manufacturer, Unit Structures, did not use 3D models in their daily practice but were able to specify the exact number and location of data points that they would need to do their work, which could

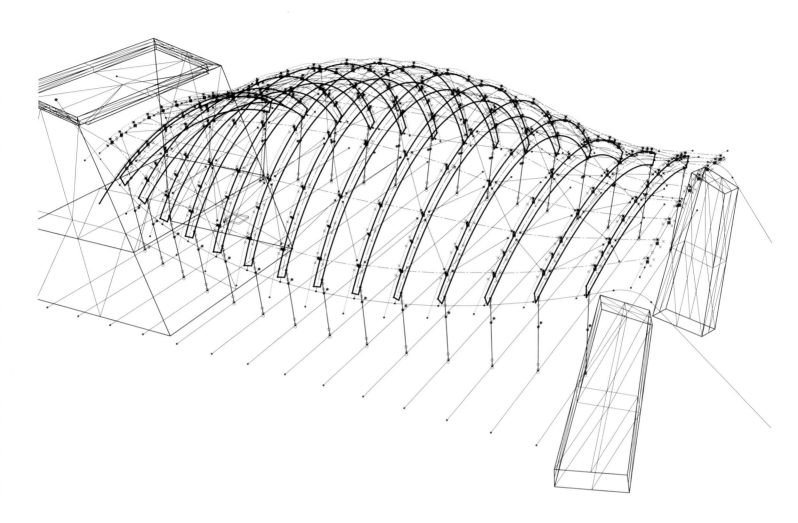

be output from the model. For most of the
fabricators, the necessary data was usually only a handful of measurements for
each component. Each conversation with
a fabricator helped to build up a comprehensive body of information into the
models that had previously existed only
as assumptions in the 2D documentation.

Workflow 2. The design geometry developed by the architect
was used to define rules to
model a wireframe skeleton of
the building. The components,
based on fabricator input,
were then "hung" on the skeleton, such that any change in
the underlying skeleton geometry would update the shape
of the attached components.

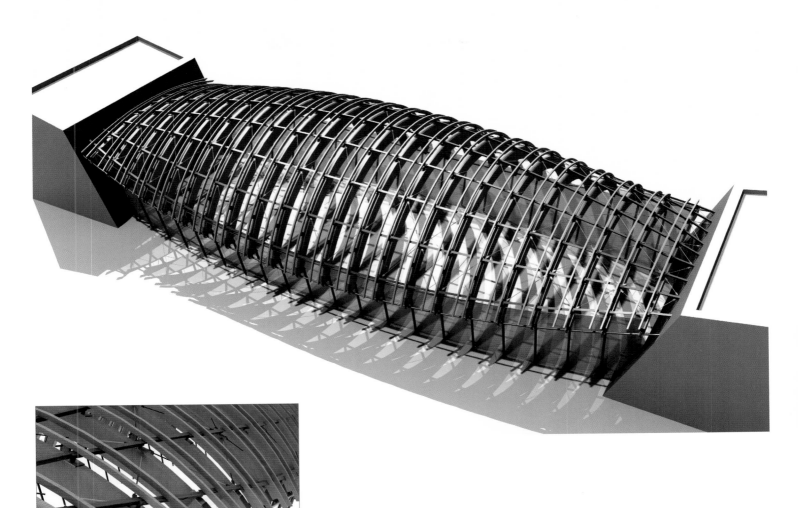

Workflow 3 (top). The roof models had an immense amount of geometry, inspiring us to create a piece of software called "Master Builder", which automated the creation of components from the underlying skeleton. The ability to easily regenerate large portions of the roof geometry lowered the design teams resistance to change. The new workflow highlighted problems which a traditional design process could not have anticipated and allowed fabricators to understand the context and complexity of their work. It enabled the architect to achieve their design intent and it reassured the client that the entire design team understood the full complexity of the problem.

Workflow 4 (bottom). As an example, the tie-rod bracing connecting the glu-lam arches utilized a double-hinged clevis attachment to adjust to the shape of the roof. Output parameters within the component would identify the length of the component and the angles of attachment for use by the fabricator. Any changes to the shape of the roof would adjust the end point locations and surface normals used to define the tie rod, and the component geometry would update accordingly. On this basis, the miscellaneous metals fabricators could pinpoint problems with the structure and adapt their tolerance recommendations.

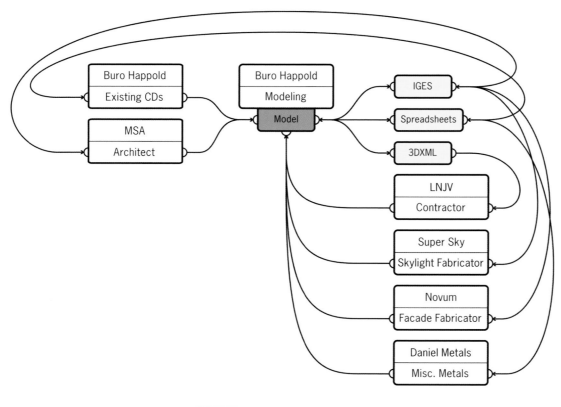

Workflow 5 (top left). A
unique numbering system
given to all elements within
the skeleton and later to
all components as they were
instantiated was critical for
communicating the building
assembly to the fabricators.
The model was delivered as a
set of 3DXml files, a light-
weight 3D model format, and as
a series of spreadsheets. The
spreadsheets contained the
exact information requested
by each fabricator for their
specific capability. No additional drawings were produced
and the original construction drawings were amended

to match the values extracted
from the model.

Workflow 6 (bottom left). Roof
under construction.

Workflow 7 (above right).
Completed project.

INTEGRATING SOFTWARE: JANET ECHELMAN NET SCULPTURES
WORKFLOW CASE STUDY▶

On a smaller-scale project, Buro Happold worked with the sculptor Janet Echelman to engineer and construct a public sculpture, "Her Secret is Patience" in Phoenix, from industrial fishing nets. The geometry was highly asymmetrical and the challenge was to create a method of patterning the nets so that they could be made on typical looms but, through the differentiation of their cell sizes, could be hung into shapes of non-constant curvature. Additionally, the netting would need to have a minimum of sag to read as close to the artist's vision as possible.

Workflow 1. Working with the architect Philip Speranza, Echelman developed a Rhino surface model of the desired shape. It became clear that a custom piece of software would be needed to distribute the net on the input surface in a way that could be manufactured, hang evenly and be transparent enough to withstand wind forces, while at the same time being opaque enough to read in bright daylight.

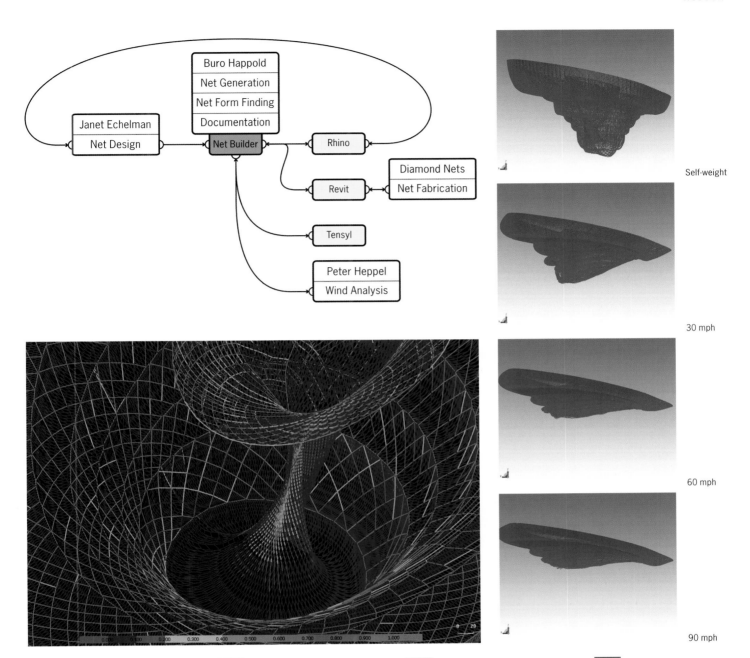

Self-weight

30 mph

60 mph

90 mph

Workflow 2 (top left). There were three software applications to be integrated: Rhino for breaking up the input surface into net elements, Buro Happold's in-house dynamic relaxation software Tensyl for conducting form-finding and analysis, and Revit for documenting the final patterns and hand-knotted assemblies of the net construction for the fabricator. As is the case with many projects, there was no common language between these applications so we developed a custom software, NetBuilder, to link the other three into an integrated workflow.

Workflow 3 (bottom left). Tensyl analysis model showing stresses in structural net.

Workflow 4 (above right). Wind studies showing deflection of net under varying wind loads.

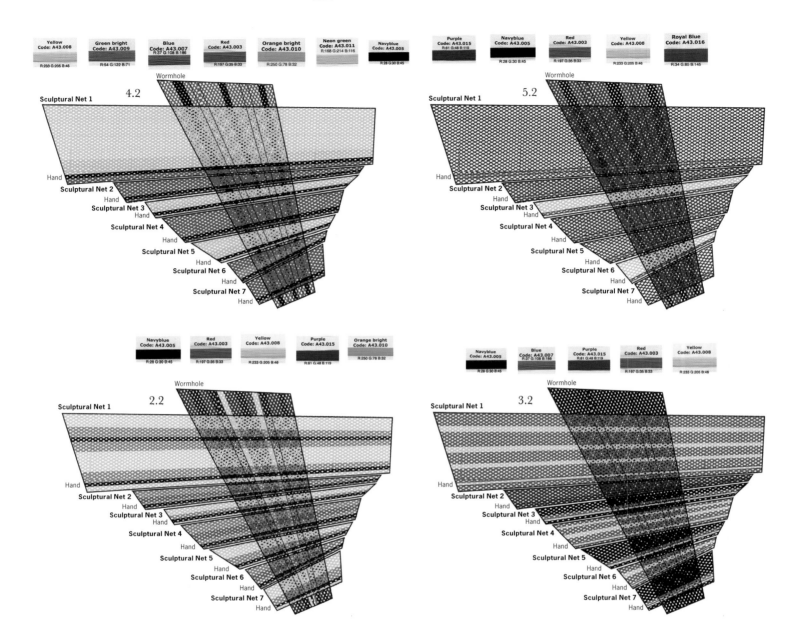

Workflow 5. Individual spool
colors were mapped onto
versions of the form found
geometry so that the software
could quickly iterate design
options that included both
shapes and color for the artist to evaluate.

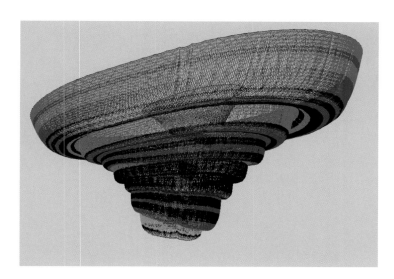

Workflow 6. When completed,
the tool could generate new
sculptural geometry, run an
analysis and output fabrication drawings in about four
hours. During each successive
iteration Buro Happold would
refine the software while
the artist was refining the
design. This became a process of optimization analogous
to the software engineering
concept of refactoring, or
the restructuring of code for
maintainability, which enabled
us to reutilize aspects of the
software for future projects.

Sculptural to Structural Rope Attachment Detail

Sculptural net edge rope, typ.

Polyester round seizing with frapping turns (ABK 3388), typ.

Structural net cinch rope, typ.

Seizings shall not be continuously connected. Seizing ends shall be finished with a reef knot (ABK 404). Sleeving shall be cut off 1/2" long at ends of seizing with a hot knife and melted to secure knots and prevent fraying, typ.

Note: Parcelling is not acceptable for rope attachment

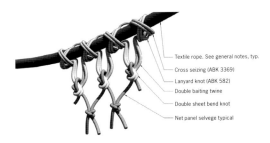

Textile Rope Net Connection Detail

Textile rope. See general notes, typ.

Cross seizing (ABK 3369)

Lanyard knot (ABK 582)

Double baiting twine

Double sheet bend knot

Net panel selvege typical

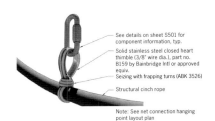

Structural Cinch Rope Hanger Detail

See details on sheet S501 for component information, typ.

Solid stainless steel closed heart thimble (3/8" wire dia.), part no. B159 by Bainbridge Intl or approved equiv.

Seizing with frapping turns (ABK 3526)

Structural cinch rope

Note: See net connection hanging point layout plan

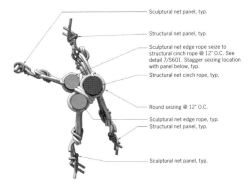

Cinch Rope Connection Detail

Sculptural net panel, typ.

Structural net panel, typ.

Sculptural net edge rope seize to structural cinch rope @ 12" O.C. See detail 7/S601. Stagger seizing location with panel below, typ.

Structural net cinch rope, typ.

Round seizing @ 12" O.C.

Sculptural net edge rope, typ.

Structural net panel, typ.

Sculptural net panel, typ.

Textile Rope Net Connection Alternate Detail

Textile rope

Double baiting twine

Constrictor knot

Double sheet bend knot

Net panel selvege

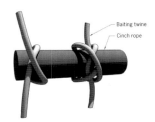

Constrictor Knot Detail (ABK 1249)

Baiting twine

Cinch rope

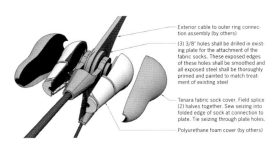

Snag Protection Detail

Exterior cable to outer ring connection assembly (by others)

(3) 3/8" holes shall be drilled in existing plate for the attachment of the fabric socks. These exposed edges of these holes shall be smoothed and all exposed steel shall be thoroughly primed and painted to match treatment of existing steel

Tenara fabric sock cover. Field splice (2) halves together. Sew seizing into folded edge of sock at connection to plate. Tie seizing through plate holes.

Polyurethane foam cover (by others)

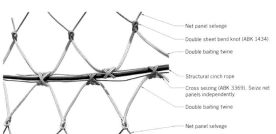

Structural Net Cinch Rope Connection Detail

Net panel selvege

Double sheet bend knot (ABK 1434)

Double baiting twine

Structural cinch rope

Cross seizing (ABK 3369). Seize net panels independently

Double baiting twine

Net panel selvege

Mesh Knot Detail (ABK 402)

Net twine

Netting template, if necessary

Workflow 7. The specification of our NetBuilder software standardized the language of the nets, with "cells", "bars", "nodes", etc. This terminology was used to name the software classes and also became the language common for the design team and later in the construction documents.

Workflow 8. No single application used for the project
held all of the final design
information; instead, the
information was read and written by the NetBuilder software
in each step of the workflow
from a series of data files.
These files allowed access
to every iteration of the
sculpture and could be read
to rebuild the 3D geometry,
the analysis model or the
pattern drawings. Numerous
other output could be generated, including fabrication
information.

Workflow 9 (above). Final
installation.

Workflow 10 (right). Completed
sculpture at night. Creating
this project with only one
software would most likely
have resulted in something
far more rational. The tools
developed here can be further
abstracted to solve challenges
on other projects, strengthen-
ing our tool kit and ultimately
paying for themselves over
several projects. Moreover, the
ability to develop custom tools
for integrating design software has engendered a sense of
confidence for what is possible
for future projects.

BEYOND INTEROPERABILITY
—
EDITOR'S NOTES

The ability of multiple software platforms to communicate is at the core of new digital workflows. Being able to reliably share digitally generated work across multiple disciplines is also the foundation of high-level integration of project teams. Industry has labeled this "interoperability", and it is currently seen as one of the most significant challenges of integrated design and project delivery. While industry in general moves towards digital standards, and software manufacturers in particular look to unify file formats to increase the efficiency of their own proprietary workflows, technologically progressive offices are designing custom workflows to support task-specific goals. Buro Happold's version of this is Continuous Integration. What distinguishes it from interoperability is the emphasis on flexibility to solve unique file exchange issues and scalability to apply these solutions to as many data sets as required to accomplish the desired task. This is demonstrated through

the diversity of the case studies presented here.

The value of this type of flexibility is discussed by several contributors in this volume as essential when working on unique problems or non-standard designs. Fabian Scheurer proposes minimal models in order to eliminate unnecessary code within a workflow;[1] Marty Doscher refers to digital designers creating "meta-code" to preserve and transfer all of the attributes and geometric intelligence of a design between platforms. Standard file formats might solve the technical problems of file exchange between software applications but as Scheurer notes, standard formats will lead to standard architecture and fail to capitalize on the universality of computers to support the flexible workflows preferred by designers.

The application of continuous integration is often more useful when bringing outside digital information, not created by a design team, into a project. Ian Keough

uses the example of laser scanning an existing building. A huge point cloud is generated that has to be edited down to the essential points and then be converted into a surface model. It can then be used as an existing conditions model. He compares this to a search engine weeding through massive amounts of data to find only what is relevant. Currently, this type of workflow is only possible by creating custom tools.[2] While standard software might be developed for certain tasks that have enough market demand, there will always be specialized tasks with limited demand that fall outside of standard software applications. Additionally, as project teams become more ambitious with accessing external data sets to address the growing demands of designing buildings, the use of custom tools to integrate these data into design workflows will become even more essential.

The information created by custom tools need not always be digital. In several cases, Buro

Happold has developed tools to extract analog output from digital workflows for use by mechanical tools or to assist in manual processes. In the net sculptures presented here, information in the digital model is translated into weaving diagrams as instructions for a mechanical loom to fabricate the nets. To assist in the installation of the atrium cage at 41 Cooper Square, Buro Happold worked with Morphosis to create tools to filter through the digital model and identify key nodal coordinates that would allow the site crew to use plumb lines to properly position the cage. As these examples show, the development of workflows that move between digital and analog can be more responsive to the unique conditions of the AEC industry. At the same time, it is a more challenging problem than that of a purely digital workflow from project beginning to end.

As an international multi-disciplinary engineering firm, Buro Happold is an influential participant in the global efforts to set policies and implement standards to improve productivity within industry today. They embrace research and experimentation to challenge these standards, in an effort to explore next-generation technologies and processes in acknowledgment that progress related to digital workflows is occurring rapidly. The work presented here suggests that industry standard workflows, while necessary, will rely on the flexibility of custom workflows to sustain future innovation.

—

1. In his essay, Scheurer also gives an overview of Industry Foundation Classes (IFC) open standards that are driving attempts to improve industry-wide interoperability.
2. This example was presented by Ian Keough at the Columbia Building Intelligence Project Think Tank in New York, 2009.

DESIGNING EDUCATION

JOHN NASTASI

John Nastasi is an architect and Founder and Director of the Product-Architecture Lab at the Stevens Institute of Technology.

"The methods and materials of design and construction will change dramatically in the 21st century as architects, engineers, scientists and manufacturers join in intense and creative collaborations."
—Sara Hart, Editor, *Architectural Record*[1]

This primary posit of *Architectural Record*'s 2003 Inaugural "Innovation" Issue suggests a redefining of the relationship between architect and engineer, long understood as cooperative but in this new millenium, becoming genuinely collaborative. Yet, there are few if any existing models in design and engineering education to explore and prepare the next generation of design professionals for these new modes of collaborative practice and thinking. In fact, existing models are conditioned to highlight silo-specialization and have developed significant departmental boundaries that hinder a productive exchange and collaborative authoring of work. While there might exist opportunities for cross-registration of coursework outside of a primary department, this does nothing to structure the collaborative condition suggested above nor carry the potential to transform the relationship between architecture and engineering and by extension, between the design and construction industry at large.

    The diminished importance of the physical and material logics of building in architectural education has resulted in the marginalization of any coursework involved with the study of the pragmatic. Structures, mechanical systems and material studies have been relegated to the edges of the architectural curriculum in both time and importance. As a result, schisms have developed between the culture of thinking within the design studio and the pragmatics of problem-solving within the means and methods courses.[2] In addition, the primary motivations

behind design concepts in architectural studios are almost always derived from outside the discipline. Since the emergence of the term "paper architects" in the early 1970's, a considerable sector of architectural education has been preoccupied with other disciplines. Recognizing that discursive investigation allowed for a broadening of possible inspirations and interpretations of one's work, meaning was understood to exist external to the physical form and all too often, was reliant on the presence of an external narrative. Occupying the majority of design discourse within the academy, external references far outweighed material resolution. Intellectual meaning existed apart from the physical condition of one's work. Is there anything internal to our own industry and discipline that has any merit? What is our own identity as Architects?

    It is from this set of experiences, observations and questions that the Product-Architecture Lab (PAL) at Stevens Institute of Technology was developed. The PAL's founding mission was to dissolve long-standing boundaries between design and engineering education and between the academy and the profession, simultaneously. This was the critical starting point for the curriculum development and continues to be the guiding philosophy today. It was understood that for a true and dramatic change to occur in the design and construction industry, future architects and engineers would have to be educated in an environment that would encourage them to re-think how they make decisions or choices outside of the normative conditions of the design academy. The program needed to be able to be disruptive on an intellectual level in questioning long-standing traditions of design process and education, which would not have been possible within the physical and intangible boundaries of a traditional architectural design school. Within the historic context of this small private engineering institution[3] and with the goals of the curriculum to focus on integrating architecture and engineering, it seemed logical to introduce a new model of design education within an institution with a long appreciation for technical innovation, as opposed to one with a legacy in design education.

...BETWEEN ARCHITECT AND ENGINEER
—

The Product-Architecture Lab opened in 2004 with the ambition to pursue the integration of architecture, engineering, product design and computation within the setting of an engineering institution. Three pre-conditions formed a critical part of this ambition: the immediate availability and direct access to core principles of engineering within other departments at Stevens; the increasing urgency of environmentally responsive buildings integrating the use of performance criteria to design and engineer expressive environments and form; and the necessity to push design computation beyond form-finding and visualization towards form resolution and fabrication. Design content, geometry, analysis, computation, materiality and fabrication would be understood and studied as one interrelated set of conditions, without the traditional departmental boundaries that would normally fragment this effort.

There was also a concerted effort to decentralize the position of the traditional design studio within the curriculum and consider design as a transparent overlay to all courses—design would not be separated from implementation but rather, would be distributed across the curriculum and applied directly into coursework on the following topics: rule-based form-finding (parametric geometry creation), engineering analysis (structural and environmental), computation (scripting and object-oriented programming), material study (analysis and design of composites) and direct fabrication (digitally linked to geometric model). [Figure 1] Design research topics within each course would also continue beyond a single semester, allowing for an extended and organic maturation of design ideas, analysis and output through the use of increasingly complex digital tools and processes that would be introduced each semester. There would also be the option of continuing research through new courses specifically tailored to the needs of the topic. In several instances, the presence of a complex design problem led to the development of advanced topic coursework in interoperability and design science through the computer science department.

In a relatively short period of time, the program has attracted a diverse and multidisciplinary set of students with various levels of design experience. Architects, mechanical engineers, civil engineers, naval engineers, industrial designers, mathematicians and computer scientists consistently form the core of the group. The steady presence of mid-career professionals from multiple disciplines re-entering the academy enhances the program's

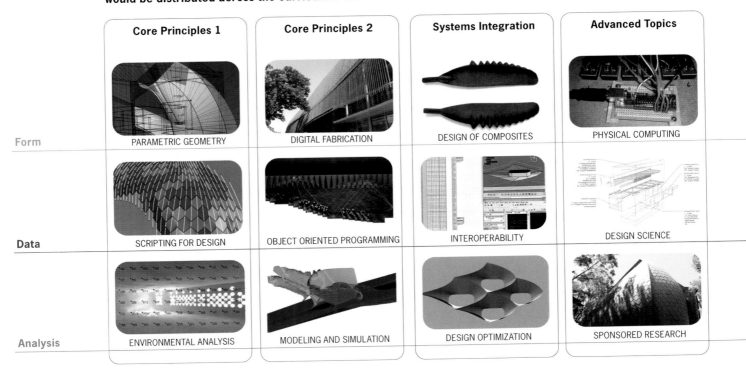

	Core Principles 1	Core Principles 2	Systems Integration	Advanced Topics
Form	PARAMETRIC GEOMETRY	DIGITAL FABRICATION	DESIGN OF COMPOSITES	PHYSICAL COMPUTING
Data	SCRIPTING FOR DESIGN	OBJECT ORIENTED PROGRAMMING	INTEROPERABILITY	DESIGN SCIENCE
Analysis	ENVIRONMENTAL ANALYSIS	MODELING AND SIMULATION	DESIGN OPTIMIZATION	SPONSORED RESEARCH

Figure 1. Curriculum Diagram for the Product-Architecture Lab (PAL), Stevens Institute of Technology.

connection to and awareness of the pressing issues within these industries.

…BETWEEN THE ACADEMY AND THE PROFESSION
—

The Product-Architecture Lab has established research partnerships with design and engineering practices in the New York Metropolitan area as a key component of the curriculum. In this model, a complex design problem and active project within a collaborating office forms the basis for student research and a bi-directional exchange. This results in a synergistic discourse in design and design processes and should not be confused with the uni-directional exchange of a typical internship program, in which students spend time in offices and "shadow" work processes with little or no input. Students consistently bring custom digital research tools and a way of thinking into the practices, resulting in an expansion of design and production capabilities beyond what these offices are typically able to accomplish. The symbiotic dynamic between the students and professionals often have a lasting impact on the structure and design philosophies of the host practices while also contextualizing and positioning the

research for further development in the more advanced courses within the PAL.

The development of advanced coursework, which has included numerical design optimization, object-oriented programming and computational interoperability, processes borrowed from the fields of mechanical engineering and computer science, provide students with the knowledge to design custom digital tool sets and working processes that are unprecedented in the AEC industry. Many of these pioneered methods formed the basis of a series of realized projects completed since the launch of the program. [Figures 2, 3]

THE RELATION-CENTRIC DESIGN PROCESS
—

"If the format of the future is digital, the content remains data. And at its simplest, scholarship in any discipline is about gaining access to information and knowledge."
—Peter Bol, Professor, Director of the Center for Geographic Analysis, Harvard University

The meta-transformation of the design industry in the 21st century, as envisioned by Sara Hart a decade ago, can be traced to the field of computer science and the origins of object-oriented programming in the 1960's. The fundamental ability to store and retrieve data within a digital file formed the beginnings of digital simulation. Coupled with advances in personal computing

Figure 2 (above left). PAL collaboration with Marble Fairbanks on the sunscreen ceiling at the Toni Stabile Student Center at Columbia University.

Figure 3 (above right). PAL collaboration with SHoP Architects on the Hangil Book House—Heyri Art Complex in Seoul.

some thirty years later, digital simulation tools became accessible to the design and engineering industry. The ability to harness, store and manipulate digital data for architectural design, while jettisoning traditional representational work methods, became the catalyst for the design research within the PAL.

The embedding of geometric relationships and physical properties of materiality into the digital kernels of a design model allow for the development of a layered and condition-based design process, shifting the focus away from the predetermination of a design solution, towards the complex understanding and construction of the problem. The use of object-oriented modeling tools allows for the conversion from static and resolved geometry to a dynamic and adaptable (parametric) geometric condition. Key geometric conditions are identified within a model as being primary and critical to the design intent and are programmed to drive or affect other secondary geometry. This interplay between driving and driven geometry forms a strategic part of the design process and fosters a deeper understanding and appreciation of geometric relationships within form. Establishing acceptable limits of adjustability within the geometric model begins to define what is commonly known as the design search space. The integration of engineering analysis, material properties and constraints associated with intended fabrication processes into the model provide a critical set of conditions that help define the design search space. Models often beginning as under-constrained studies in expressive form-finding have the potential to transition to a fully constrained and defined state of form resolution.

Research in this relation-centric design process indicates a focus away from an interest in predetermining a design solution. As a precursor to design, this process can now yield a collective set of unpredicted solutions and challenges, making the architect focus on establishing the hierarchal layers of information that structure the design problem through a complex model. The design solution, in turn, becomes the direct execution of the design problem and allows for the architect to curate selections from a much broader and often unexpected set of acceptable solutions. Early marked results in this research define a broadening role for the architect as follows:

1. *Author of design rules*: This establishes the role that logic, guidance and reasoning play in establishing and setting up the design problem. Design intent is captured in these rules, which become the link between open-ended thinking and logical reasoning. These rules allow a transfer of ideas from human intuition into digital processing, not as a reductive step but rather to extend the development of the ideas within a design process that combines intuition and logic. The critical inclusion of qualitative conditions, such as aesthetic bias, alongside quantitative conditions, such as geometric rules, analytic principles and material limitations, allow for varying degrees of balance and hierarchy in the formation of the design problem. [Figure 4]

2. *Manager of design data*: This includes setting clear and well-designed organizational strategies in the construction of the digital data set of the parametric modeling environment—the craft of modeling. This might include both the base design model and other external data sets that link to the model as either inputs or outputs. Establishing both local geometry (within individual components of the base model) and global geometry (external to any singular component but available to all subsequent components) is fundamental to a well-functioning process. Understanding the impact that certain logic sequences have on the resulting geometric output allows for subsequent iterations that are informed by the pattern recognition of these sequences. Refining the logic sequences therefore refines the design problem. Conversely, obfuscated logic sequences often hinder subsequent refinement and debilitate the design process. [Figure 5]

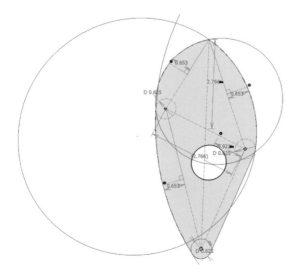

Figure 4. The architect, author of design rules. Conceptual parametric sketch for initial petal design for Liquid Sky, MoMA/P.S.1 Young Architects Installation, in collaboration with Ball Nogues Studio of Los Angeles. (Student team: Erik Verboon, Cory Brugger, Mark Pollock).

3. *Curator of valued collections of design output*: As the culminating step, curating outputs suggests that ultimately design resolution comes from the selection of a final geometric condition from a larger collective set of acceptable and highly regarded solutions. Within this new type of design process, the objective is not to author a single solution but rather a design system that can produce multiple solutions, all of which satisfy the design intent. Here, selections can be made by either the reasoning or bias of the architect or by subsequent refinement of the analytic problem, which then becomes a process of design optimization. [Figure 6]

Figure 5 (top). The architect, manager of design data. Instantiation of 2D array of entire petal catalog in preparation for laser cutting process. Liquid Sky, MoMA/P.S.1 Young Architects Installation, in collaboration with Ball Nogues Studio.

Figure 6 (bottom). The architect, curator of design collections. Final physical assembly of over 300 individual petals, each individually tagged and sequenced. Liquid Sky, MoMA/P.S.1 Young Architects

Installation, in collaboration with Ball Nogues Studio.

THE FLUID DESKTOP: COUPLING PARAMETRIC MODELING WITH ENGINEERING ANALYSIS
—

The role of the architect is broadening as a result of these contemporary work methods and nowhere is this more fundamentally understood than in the concurrent transformation of the architect's design interface; the digital desktop. In this digital working environment, a range of information feedback is available to the architect to condition the creative process of design. More than a dashboard, which is essentially a set of reactive information, the digital desktop described here is more fluid in nature. The Fluid Desktop is a collective set of interactive data that effects and is affected by any singular adjustment. [Figure 7]

The concurrent study of both object-oriented (parametric) tools for geometry creation and digital engineering analysis tools for numerical output provides an opportunity to rethink the typical linear design sequence. When coupling parametric modeling directly with engineering analysis software, direct numerical feedback is accessible for any singular geometric condition. Embedding multiple geometric parameters to a model allows for iterative analytic test cases to be run from a singular model. The awareness

and recognition of direct relationships between certain aspects of geometry and performance-based numerical output becomes apparent. Patterns suggesting logical and subsequent test strategies are often made manifest (pattern recognition). Predicting results based on prior iterations brings a deeper awareness of the relationship between digital geometry and material performance. What was previously understood as a directional and hierarchical design process is now understood as bi-directional and balanced. Design and analysis are becoming one interrelated endeavor.

However, this research also exposes limitations that each stand-alone tool presents. In order to get past an initial level of productivity, the two modes of working (geometry and analysis) need to be more intuitively integrated. Direct communication in a seamless and fluid manner could possibly diminish the limitations of each individual software platform. The integration of a genetic algorithm as a mediator between geometry creation and engineering analysis allows for an iterative link by way of a neutral third environment. This third environment is the digital bridge that connects two fields: architecture and engineering. However, the behavior of this third environment is purely computer science. The software platform

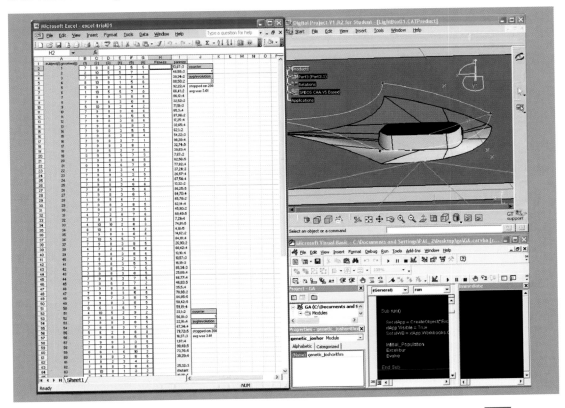

Figure 7. Sample Fluid Desktop for the Kuwait Military Academy in collaboration with SOM, showing different output components including (from left to right) environmental analysis; interoperability scripting logic; genomic logic and sequence; parametric assembly modeling.

Excel was utilized to house a series of genetic algorithms as well as resulting computational output. Mimicking the process of natural evolution, genetic algorithms define search heuristics based on design performance or fitness criteria. Automated iterations of design inputs (parametric geometry) within a range of possibilities (design space) allow for potential solutions to be evaluated at computational speeds. The implications of this research at the Product-Architecture Lab were broadening and pointing to an expansion of boundaries of the design process in both depth (the availability and abundance of data) and breadth (the multiple types of data). The suggested repositioning of the architect as author of the design logic, mediator between form-finding (design) and form resolution (engineering), and curator of the collective design solutions, was presented in 2006, at the Yale University conference *Building (in) the Future: Recasting Labor in Architecture*. Entitled "The Fluid Desktop", labor was offered anew as purely computational—the digital and algorithmic charette. The architect, now removed from the laborious tasks of manual iterations, could refocus on the authoring and management of the design rules that generate the design output, while also re-introducing bias and intuition in the curating of this design output.

ENDNOTES
—

1. Hart, S. (ed) (2003) *Architectural Record*.
2. An interesting reaction to this curriculum fracturing was the 1994 policy change by the National Association of Architectural Registration Boards (NAAB) where a singular comprehensive design studio was established as a requirement to meet accreditation benchmarks. This policy change sent reverberations throughout architectural schools as program administrators sought to determine where to place the singular comprehensive design course amongst the sequence of design studios. It was clear that the administrating board of architectural education saw an in-depth resolution of design as the key exception to the rule in curricula around the country.
3. With a respected reputation as an incubator for innovation in engineering dating back to the industrial revolution, Stevens Institute of Technology was influential in the development of the steam boat, steam locomotive and some years later, in pioneering the origin of the New York Yacht Club in 1844 and Americas Cup races in 1859. See Clark, Geoffrey W. (2000), *History of Stevens Institute of Technology, A Record of Broad-Based Curricula and Technogenesis*, Jersey City, New Jersey, Jensen/Daniels Publishers.

TOWER VIEW CALCULATOR (vCALC) AND TOWER FORM FINDER
WORKFLOW CASE STUDY▶

—

This project was a collaboration between three PAL students (Will Corcoran, Erik Verboon and Ron Rosenman) and a design team at Skidmore, Owings & Merrill on the schematic design for a residential tower in Manhattan. The client/developer's desire to increase overall tower value by maximizing the number of "spectacular views" led the student team to develop a tool that could help optimize a tower's form to maximize desired views.

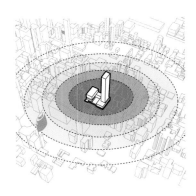

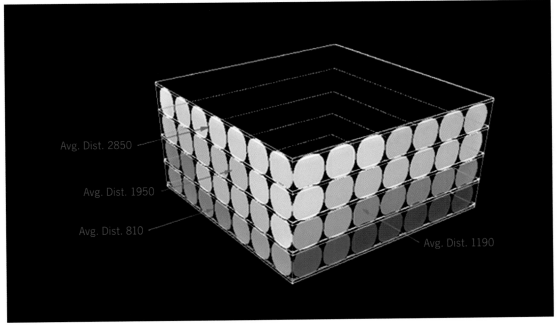

Workflow 1 (top left). vCalc: Zones of View Analysis. A custom software tool was able to map a visual representation of view quality based on the surrounding context back onto the surface of the proposed building to give designers a visible indicator of where the best view corridors lie and at what floor level the views open up.

Workflow 2 (top right). vCalc: Façade Mapping. Views are then mapped onto the building façade and valued according to distance and quality.

Workflow 3 (bottom). vCalc: View Algorithm. The design algorithm measures the view at points uniformly spaced along the proposed building façade. Every point receives a score based on average line of sight for a cone of vision emanating from that point. Points can be weighted to take into account landmarks that enhance a particular view.

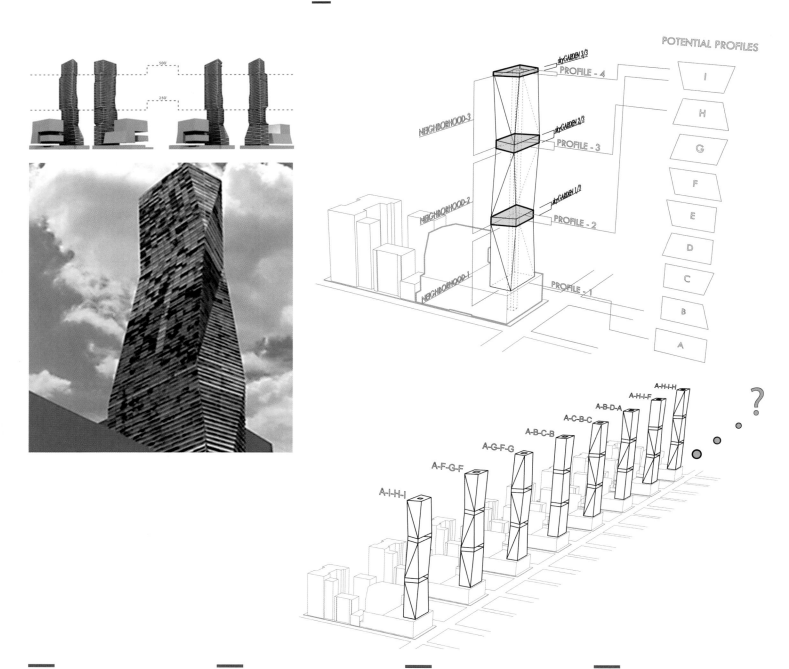

Workflow 4 (top left). vCalc: Application. The team explored two applications for the vCalc tool: the more practical application enables designers to analyze a particular tower design in order to understand how the views are behaving. The second approach was to generate floor plates and perimeter walls at multiple orientations to maximize view quality. These generated walls perform better overall than typical orthogonal walls, and effectively define an optimized "viewing envelope" that suggests tower forms that the design team might not have considered on their own.

Workflow 5 (bottom left). Tower Form Finder: Continuing Research. As a second phase of this ongoing research, Tower Form Finder was developed as an extension of the vCalc tool from the prior semester's work, in which the student team analyzed how changes to the orientation of a tower would affect the view from within an apartment unit. The results for the given site confirmed the design team's intuition that non-orthogonal walls on the north and south sides of the tower would improve the view, and that the views opened up considerably at key floor levels.

Workflow 6 (top right). Tower Form Finder: Design Logic. Given these findings, the student design team developed a workflow that could automate the analysis of a broad range of faceted tower variations. The design of this tower would be determined by choosing from a subset of nine floor plates at each of four key levels and then interpolating between those floor plates to arrive at a faceted tower composed of three "vertical neighborhoods".

Workflow 7 (bottom right). Tower Form Finder: Design Permutations. The design tool utilized an object-oriented framework that would enable the designers to input any number of floor plates and vertical neighborhoods as well as several other global parameters. The tool also allowed for sky gardens and mechanical levels at each neighborhood to give the design team maximum flexibility. Given these inputs, the tool then generated all possible tower permutations.

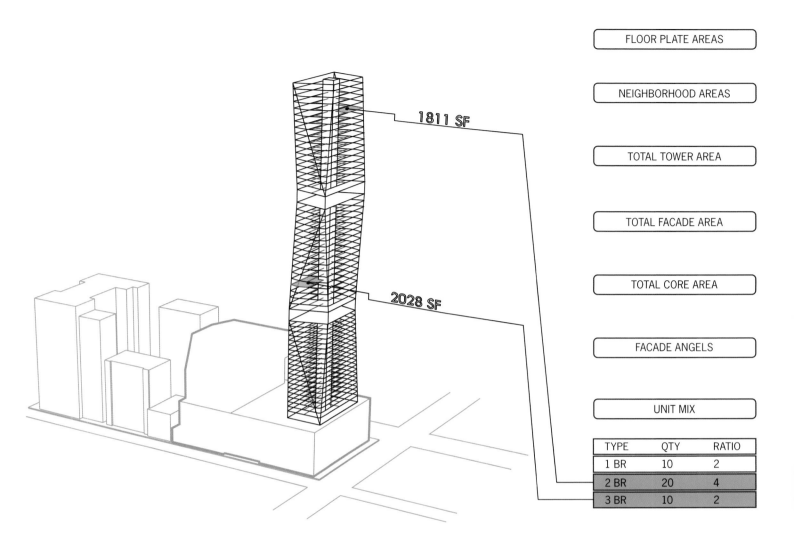

| FLOOR PLATE AREAS |
| NEIGHBORHOOD AREAS |
| TOTAL TOWER AREA |
| TOTAL FACADE AREA |
| TOTAL CORE AREA |
| FACADE ANGLES |
| UNIT MIX |

TYPE	QTY	RATIO
1 BR	10	2
2 BR	20	4
3 BR	10	2

1811 SF

2028 SF

Workflow 8 (above). Tower Form Finder: Design Outputs. The tool then analyzed each of the resulting design permutations for key metrics such as floor plate efficiency, façade to floor area ratio, to determine the best-performing towers. Finally it would allow the designers to choose from the best-performing towers and optimize them further to maximize the square footage so that it met the target ZFA.

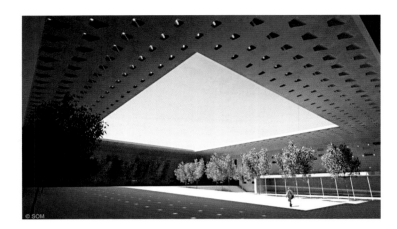

ALI AL-SABAH
MILITARY ACADEMY
WORKFLOW CASE STUDY▶

This project was a collaboration between three PAL students (Joshua Cotton, Keith Besserud and Charlie Portelli) working with a design team at Skidmore, Owings & Merrill's New York Office for the design of the Ali Al-Sabah Military Academy in Kuwait City, Kuwait. The specific task for the project was to develop a façade perforation system that minimized heat gain while creating high-quality indirect daylighting for the classrooms.

Workflow 1 (above left). Schematic design rendering of courtyard.

Workflow 2 (above right) Initial façade design. The analysis of shading and glare levels for a previously completed design provided an opportunity to question the linear relationship between geometric input and numerical output.

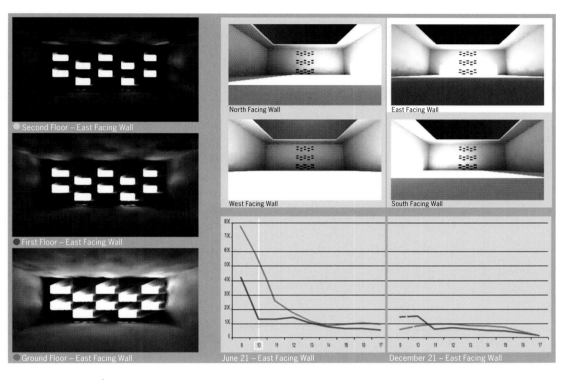

Workflow 3 (bottom). Early façade version. The student team was asked to redesign the geometry of a sculpted wall surface surrounding a typical array of punched windows that were being used as a base design across all façades of the campus buildings. The goal of the design was to minimize the amount of direct solar radiation passing through the windows and into the interior space for each of the four typical solar orientations (north, south, east and west).

Workflow 4 (top). Lighting data and visualization. Provided with design geometry and working within the capabilities of lighting analysis tools, the team produced a comprehensive set of numerical data measuring light and glare levels for a series of interior classroom spaces for each solar orientation and season.

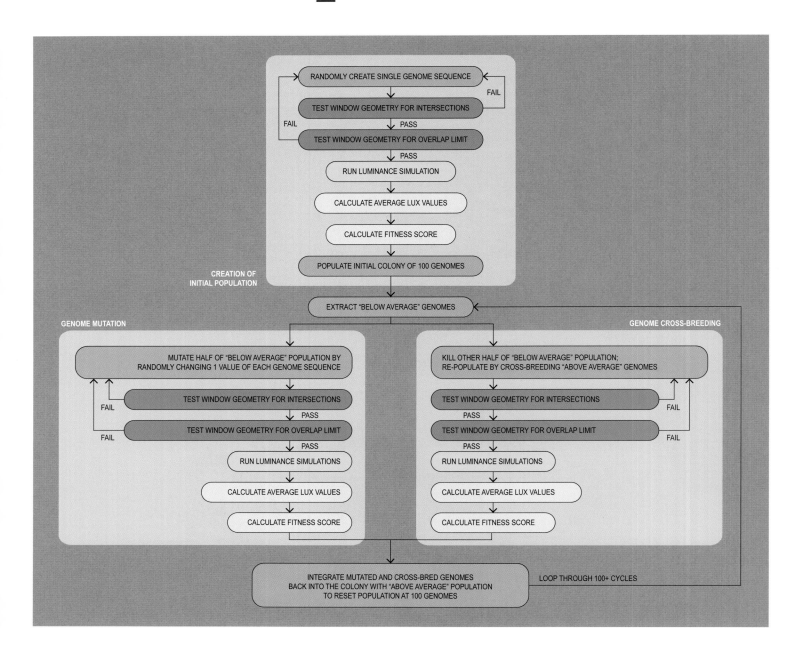

Workflow 5. Software workflow.
The student team developed
and used a genetic algorithm
that linked multiple software
programs together, including Digital Project, Speos
and Excel, to automate the
process of generating the collection of optimal designs.

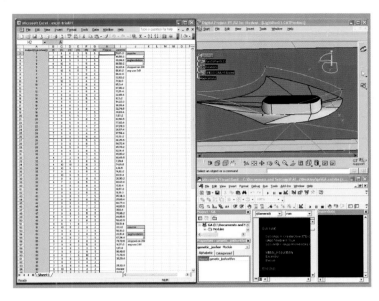

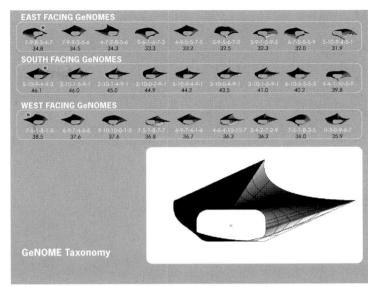

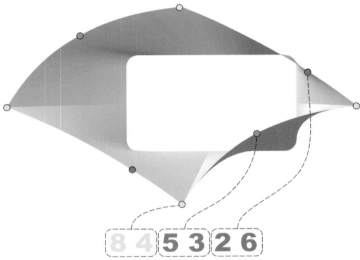

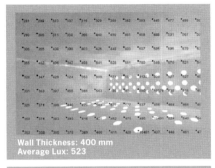

Wall Thickness: 400 mm
Average Lux: 523

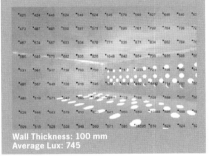

Wall Thickness: 100 mm
Average Lux: 745

Workflow 6 (top left). The fluid desktop interface allowed the team to quickly see and evaluate different collections of data simultaneously.

Workflow 7 (bottom left). Aperture logic. Catia model showing the driving parametric geometry of a sample opening. These parameters became inputs for the variations generated by the genetic algorithm. The first pair of numbers controls the positioning of the yellow vertices relative to the center of the window opening. The blue and red pair of numbers control the positioning of the center control point of a three-point Bezier curve: the first value of the pair controls the movement of the point along an imaginary straight line between the two corners of the window opening; the second value controls the magnitude and direction of its perpendicular deviation off the imaginary line.

Workflow 8 (top right). Design permutations. For each solar orientation, the design team was presented with a range of possible geometries that all performed well with respect to the goal of minimizing heat gain.

Workflow 9 (bottom right). Numeric visualization. The overlay of this numerical data on a digital rendition of the interior space offered an empirical and objective model of measuring design quality.

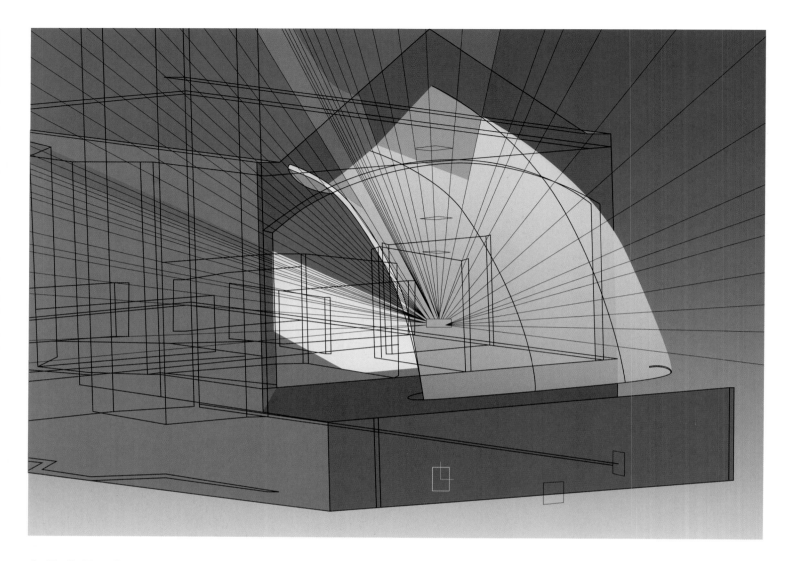

APSE CHURCH ADDITION
WORKFLOW CASE STUDY▶

This project was a collaboration between PAL students (Leanne Muscarella and Justin Nardone) and the architectural firm of Marchetto Architects on the design and fabrication of an apse church addition in Hoboken, New Jersey. The work spanned from conceptual design to project completion and incorporated content from coursework in parametric geometry, digital fabrication, environmental analysis, design optimization and interoperability.

Workflow 1. Surface model. During schematic design, a surface model of the Apse was generated in Catia with summer and winter sun angles integrated directly into the model as driving geometric parameters.

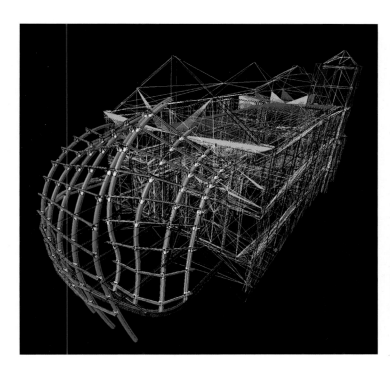

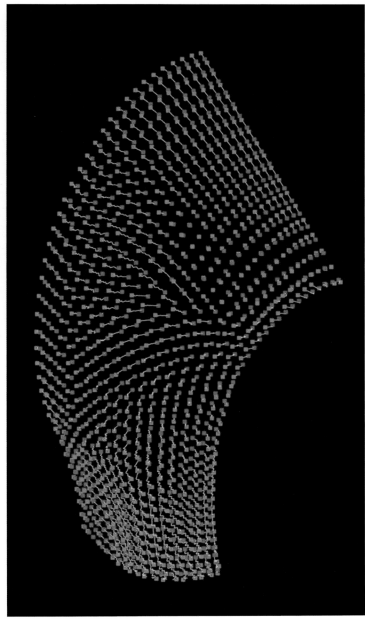

Workflow 2 (above left).
Structural model. In addition,
the model contained the full
details and assembly sequences
of structural steel components, including all radius
information for each of the
curved tubular columns and the
flat steel rib plates.

Workflow 3 (above right).
Curvature migration algorithm.
This surface model contained a
uniform point population that
was altered and optimized by
a scripted curvature migration algorithm. The script
allowed each individual point
to locate 12in square regions
of minimal curvature based on
a surface curvature analysis.
This prepared the geometry to
receive over 1,100 individual
zinc shingles across the dou-
bly curved geometric surface.

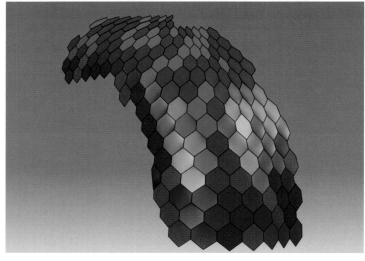
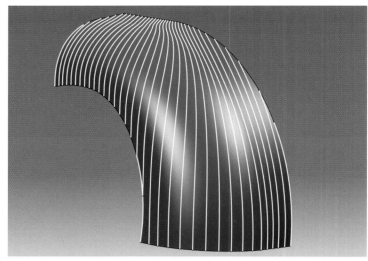

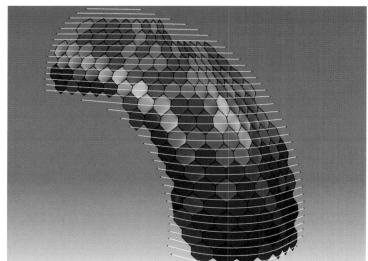

Workflow 4a (top left).
Initial shingle layout. Based
on the point locations, an
initial version of populated
shingles was generated.

Workflow 4b (top right).
Vertical drainage geometry
Overlay. At the recommendation
of the metal contractor, a
second script was introduced
to organize each columnar
array of points within four
degrees of vertical to allow
for controlled runoff of
rainwater.

Workflow 4c (bottom left).
Adjusted shingle layout. The
layout was then adjusted,
based on the overlaid constraint for minimal vertical
deviation.

Workflow 4d (bottom right).
Layout option. In the spirit
of parametric explora-
tion, student Justin Nardone
offered an alternate version
of the shingle optimization
with a horizontal bias overlay. Although this was never
intended to be implemented,
it did display the power of
object-oriented scripting to
explore design options.

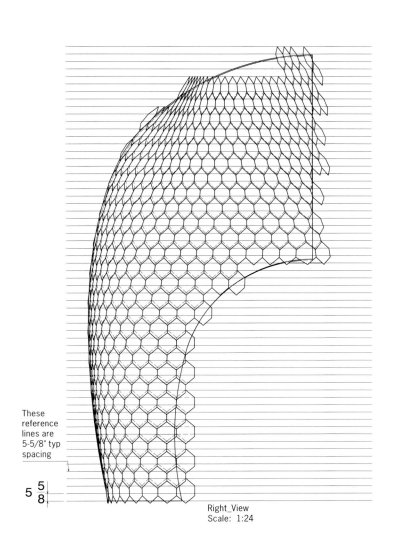

These
reference
lines are
5-5/8" typ
spacing

$5\frac{5}{8}$

Right_View
Scale: 1:24

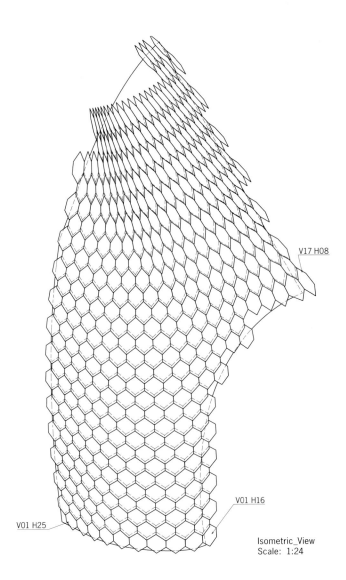

V17 H08

V01 H25   V01 H16

Isometric_View
Scale: 1:24

Workflow 5. Apse: Generated
Cutting Files. Shop draw-
ings and cutting files were
auto-generated from the Catia
model and formed the basis
for all discussions on pricing
and scope of work. The files
for each shingle were digitally transferred to Maloya
Laser, a local fabricator,
where they were laser-cut and
prepared for site delivery.

Workflow 6 (above left). Site
assembly. The primary steel
structure was fabricated with
CNC bending as were the steel
plate ribs. All structural
and cladding components were
fully integrated, allowing a
quick and efficient assembly
sequence on the tight site in
a residential neighborhood.

Workflow 7 (above right).
Completed project. View from
west showing north aperture
at the geometric offset of
the two final surfaces.

Workflow 8 (facing page, above
right). Pangolin.

THE (FUTURE) CONTEMPORARY PRACTICE
—

After an initial period of promise and development in digital design methods and workflow processes, the architectural practice has not advanced markedly but rather has become either desensitized by the immediacy of superficial digital output or debilitated by the learning curve associated with a deeper understanding of the capabilities of the technology. During this same gestation period, industries such as e-commerce, online banking, quantitative sciences and social networking have become pervasive and ubiquitous, infiltrating and reinventing many aspects of modern life through the aggressive and innovative application of essentially the same technology. Within architectural practice, by contrast, a quick satisfaction with the most fundamental of visual output has become apparent. Even more alarming is the complacency towards the ability of digital technology to transform disciplinary boundaries and form a highly integrated working environment.

While the majority of design institutions train students to become thinkers and strategists, the Product-Architecture Lab is educating students to develop a high level of design expertise within digital craft and material resolution. While the traditional architectural practices are migrating towards becoming generalists, the progressive design practices are capitalizing on the opportunities of digital tools and workflows to expand their areas of specialized expertise. The double-edge sword of the unique curriculum and design output being produced at Stevens is that it can be conveniently (and mistakenly) dismissed as a digital trade school focusing solely on execution. However, the efforts described here are about a long overdue re-establishment of an expanded and more meaningful role for the architect within the broader design and construction process.

Recent advances made by architects and engineers in the areas of Building Information Modeling and direct fabrication have initiated the emergence of distinct design specialists. Far from the type of "additive" specialty consultants that inflate design teams today, these design specialists operate at the very core of the increasingly complex digital information exchange that makes up the contemporary design workflow. These specialists have pioneered new models of contemporary practice, both within a larger office structure as well as in the evolving stand-alone design specialty studios. Over the past decade, these specialty firms have grown in size as well as in scope of work and can be broadly organized into the following categories:

– The specialty group within a larger design practice.
– The stand-alone design assistance specialty group.
– The design-build practice.
– The embedded design services within a fabrication practice.

Coinciding with the growing concerns that architects are becoming generalists and shedding the responsibility of building to the emerging design specialist, many of the progressive practices of these kinds have experienced tremendous growth and creative maturity. It remains to be seen if traditional practices are willing to evolve in response to these technological pressures and opportunities. The effects of this digital and technological revolution on the standard practice might be limited to a modest enhancement in drawing production and coordination abilities. If this is the case, then the practice of architecture may have missed out on an opportunity to correct an ongoing downward trend diminishing its role and value in the AEC industry. However, if the work of architects who have welcomed these new tools and methods into their practices are an indication of future trends, a true industry transformation could be just around the corner. [Figure 8]

The Product-Architecture and Engineering Lab **Student Placement and Ongoing Growth**

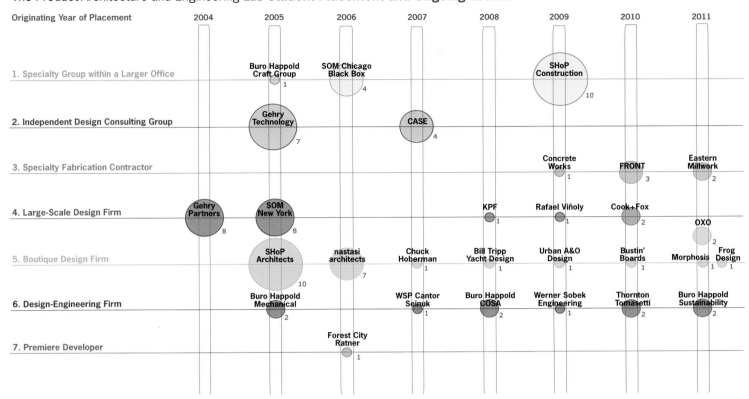

Figure 8. PAL Industry Collaborators
and Student Placement Chart.

EDUCATING INDUSTRY

—

EDITOR'S NOTES

Professional disciplines like architecture and engineering have never coexisted well within traditional academic institutions. The academy is positioned as distinct from professions, with the ability to conduct research and theorize alternative futures unhindered by the established rules of professional protocols. On the other hand, professions (and their associated industries) see themselves as embodying the highest level of accomplishment within a given discipline—where the theory of the academy is made "real". There is undoubtedly a value in this separation that, in the best cases, results in a productive relationship where each progresses in response to the developments of the other. More often, however, architecture and engineering schools take one of two approaches. In one, they defer to industry and limit their curricula to meet the skills and professional development requirements of conventional practice, embodied for instance in the NAAB (National Architectural Accrediting Board)

process for architecture schools and the ABET (Accreditation Board for Engineering and Technology) for engineering schools. Alternatively, schools (perhaps architecture schools more than engineering schools) discount industry, taking a more critical position towards professional standards and expanding their curricula in response to broader social and cultural issues.

The Product-Architecture Lab (PAL) at Stevens Institute of Technology, founded by John Nastasi in 2004, represents the seed of a new educational model for architecture and engineering. The PAL is predicated on a new type of relationship between the academy and industry that combines the best attributes of the two representative examples described above. Importantly to the topic of this book, it does this largely through the potentials of new digital workflows. It avoids the pitfalls of academic trends of using digital tools primarily for form generation—which Nastasi

sees as a gross under-utilization of the power of computation for design—and of industry trends of using performance-driven design tools in an overly deterministic manner. The work of PAL takes a more inclusive approach to the use of technology to merge the qualitative goals of formal complexity with the quantitative goals of data measurement into a continuous workflow. Working between multiple software platforms with an emphasis on interoperability, the curriculum encourages students to expand design problems—searching for atypical yet relevant data to link into the design workflow. These data can range from the detailed behavior of new material composites not commonly used for building applications to real estate values in high-rise housing as they relate to views and orientation. The ability to capture a wide range of data into digital design workflows will become increasingly important for architects and engineers, as buildings become more complex and owners demand more responsive design solutions.

The PAL anticipates these industry changes and has developed a unique curriculum to position its students as leaders in this effort.

Nastasi's concept of the Fluid Desktop envisions a representational model appropriate to the multi-dimensional data feedback of a true digital design workflow environment. It is simultaneously an analysis and design tool that takes any current user interface with a computer screen to a new level of responsiveness, where multiple design objectives of a given project can be parametrically defined with measurable output, allowing them to be prioritized based on design intent. One can imagine this desktop occupied not only by data extracted from the architect's design model but also data from external resources, related to materials or products being used in the design. The Fluid Desktop could also become the platform to incorporate non-technical design criteria related to the social metrics of the building process outlined by

Paolo Tombesi.[1] If one further imagines this type of interactive interface as the topic of a course on architectural representation, it becomes evident how much has to change in architectural education to begin addressing future innovations in industry.

The pervasive professional complacency towards the potentials of digital workflows, noted by Nastasi, has resulted in the current generation of practicing architects taking a wait-and-see attitude. This will only change when a new generation can envision new opportunities. With an industry as divided as the AEC industry, these opportunities will not lie within a single discipline but rather with a realignment of all of its primary constituents—architects, engineers, contractors and owners. Nor will they be found within conventional working processes. Nastasi is committed to this realignment and is convinced that the design, engineering and collaborative potentials of digital workflows will be a predominate driver. The conservatism of the AEC industry often steers the most ambitious architecture students to other industries that are more welcoming of new and innovative ideas. This is a challenge for architecture schools: to find a position between deferring to industry and discounting industry and to identify areas of opportunity that inspire students to not only design innovative new buildings but also to design a new industry.

—

1. See Paolo Tombesi's "What Do We Mean By Building Design?" in this volume.

ON THE SPONSOR
—

Digital workflows encompass a wide range of processes at Turner Construction Co. During construction, digital workflows support the manufacturing, procurement and tracking of material, the integration of complex building systems, and the management of building sequences, quantity, and cost information. Information about building elements is extracted from digital models. The elements are prefabricated with a high level of precision and installed using coordinate points in the model to locate the elements in the field. Design and construction teams use detailed markers or barcodes to identify the trade and item associated with a particular layout point or to track the installation status in the model. Survey points from built conditions are imported into the model to validate that the elements are installed as designed.

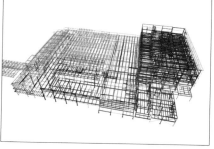

Figure 1 (top). Site logistics and sequencing model of a five story 70,000 square foot co-generation plant for an urban hospital campus.

Figure 2 (bottom). Steel tracking model for a 1,000,000 square foot building consisting of classrooms, gymnasiums, and a central utility plant.

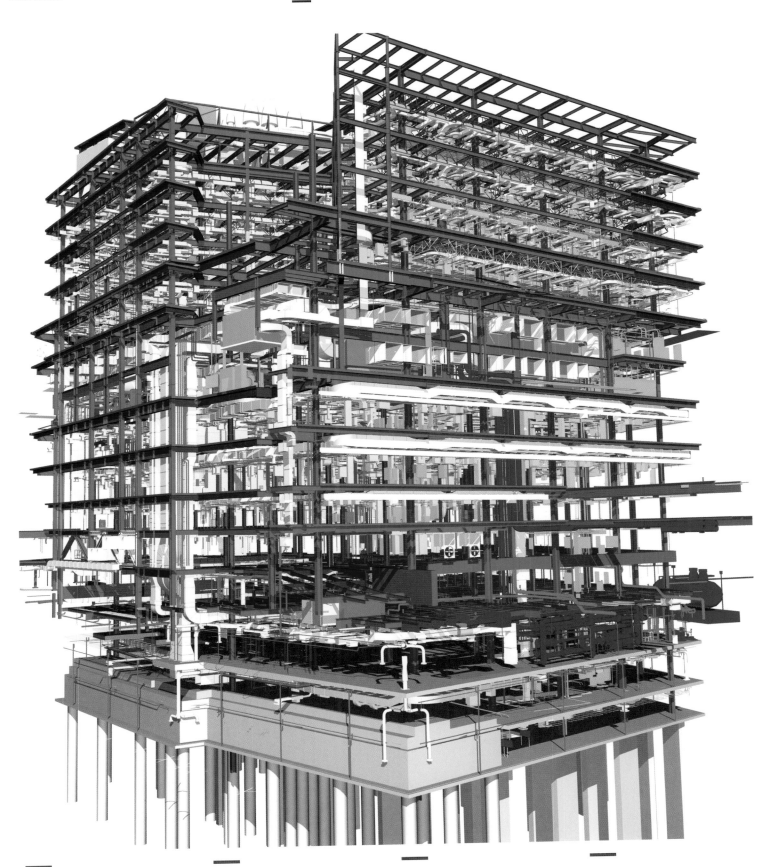

Figure 3. Detailed 3D trade Coordination Model for a 14-story, 150-bed medical oncology, neuro-intensive care, and neuroscience patient facility. The project includes extensive MEP systems including 13 AHU's weighing 467,000 pounds, 32,000 linear feet of mineral insulated copper clad cable in the building, and seven miles of pipe on the fifth floor alone.

ON THE EDITOR

SCOTT MARBLE

Scott Marble is a Founding Partner of Marble Fairbanks Architects and Director of Integrated Design at the Columbia University Graduate School of Architecture, Planning and Preservation (GSAPP). With over 20 years of teaching and practicing architecture, he is continually pursuing new relationships between architectural education and industry by maintaining an active connection between his academic research and the work of his practice. Marble Fairbanks is the recipient of over 25 local, national and international design awards including AIA awards, American Architecture Awards, a PA Award, an ID Award, an ar+d Award for Emerging Architecture from Architecture Review Magazine and an Excellence in Design Award from the Art Commission of New York City. The work of Marble Fairbanks is published regularly in journals and books and has been exhibited around the world including at the Architectural Association School of Architecture in London, the Nara Prefectural Museum of Art in Japan and the Museum of Modern Art in New York, where their drawings are part of the museum's permanent collection. In 2008, the MoMA commissioned their project, Flatform for the exhibition Home Delivery: Fabricating the Modern Dwelling.

Scott is currently Director of the Integrated Design Studios for The Columbia Building Intelligence Project (CBIP), a three-year research pilot project that explores future workflow models using parametric tools to combine the flexibility of service-based industries with the economy of scale of product-based industries. He lectures and participates in conferences around the world including the 2010 ACADIA conference in New York and the CBIP Think Tanks in London, Tokyo and Stuttgart. He has been a visiting design instructor at several universities, most recently at the University of Houston, where the work produced won first prize in the AA|Fab Award sponsored by the Architectural Association in London. He and his partner, Karen Fairbanks, were the Michael Owen Jones Memorial Lecturers at the University of Virginia and the Charles and Ray Eames Lecturers at the University of Michigan, and the book, *Marble Fairbanks: Bootstrapping*, was published by the University of Michigan on the occasion of that lecture. His recent essay, "Imagining Risk" appeared in *Building (in) the Future, Recasting Labor in Architecture* (Yale School of Architecture and Princeton Architectural Press, 2010). Scott received a B.E.D. from Texas A&M University and an M. Arch. from Columbia University.

ON THE AUTHORS

FRANK BARKOW & REGINE LEIBINGER

Frank Barkow and Regine Leibinger founded the Berlin-based practice Barkow Leibinger Architects in 1993. Characterized by the interaction of practice, research and teaching, the firm's "interdisciplinary, discursive attitude allows its work to expand and respond to advancing knowledge and technology". Pursuing their interest in digitally tooled material, Barkow Leibinger's recent research projects investigate revolving laser cutting and CNC-cut translucent concrete formwork with an application to façade systems, precast concrete and ceramic elements. The work of Barkow Leibinger has been published and exhibited worldwide; drawings and other practice materials are included in collections at the Centre Pompidou, Deutsches Architekturmuseum and the Heinz Architectural Center, among others. The firm has won numerous AIA Honor Awards and was nominated in 2004 for the Mies van der Rohe Award for the Customer and Administration Building Ditzingen. Frank studied architecture at Montana State University and the Harvard University Graduate School of Design. Regine studied Architecture in Berlin and the Harvard University GSD. She is currently Professor for Building Construction and Design at the Technische Universität Berlin.

DAVID BENJAMIN

David Benjamin is Co-Founder of the architecture firm The Living and Director of the Living Architecture Lab at Columbia University Graduate School of Architecture, Planning and Preservation. His work experiments with new technologies through open-source, collaborative, hands-on design, applying techniques such as evolutionary computation and ubiquitous computing to the exploration of wide design spaces. Recent projects include creating prototypes of living building envelopes, building public interfaces to monitor and display environmental quality, developing new software tools for design with synthetic biology, and developing novel composite building materials through the self-assembly of bacteria. David is currently Assistant Professor of Architecture at Columbia University GSAPP.

BEN VAN BERKEL

In 1988 Ben van Berkel and Caroline Bos established an architectural practice, Van Berkel & Bos Architectuurbureau, in Amsterdam. Ten years later, they established a new firm, UNStudio (United Net), organized as a network of specialists in architecture, urban development and infrastructure. With UNStudio, Ben has realized many internationally recognized projects including the Mercedes-Benz Museum in Stuttgart, a façade and interior renovation for the Galleria Department Store in Seoul and a private villa in Upstate New York. Ben has lectured and taught at architectural schools around the world and in 2011, was awarded the Kenzo Tange Visiting Professor's Chair at Harvard University GSD. He is currently Dean at the Städelschule in Frankfurt am Main. Ben studied architecture at the Rietveld Academy in Amsterdam and at the Architectural Association in London. He recently became a member of the Strategic Alliance advisory board for Gehry Technologies.

PHIL BERNSTEIN

Phil Bernstein is an architect and a Vice President at Autodesk, Inc., where he leads industry strategy and relations for the architecture, engineering and construction division. At Autodesk he is responsible for setting the company's future vision and strategy for technology serving the building industry, as well as cultivating and sustaining the firm's relationships with strategic industry leaders and associations. Prior to joining Autodesk, Phil was an Associate Principal at Pelli Clarke Pelli Architects. He writes and lectures extensively about practice and technology issues. Phil is a trustee of the Emma Willard School of Troy, New York, a senior fellow of the Design Futures Council, an AIA Fellow, and former chair of the AIA National Documents Committee. With Peggy Deamer, he coedited *Building (in) the Future: Recasting Labor in Architecture*, published by Princeton Architectural Press. Phil received a B. A. and an M. Arch. from Yale University.

SHANE M. BURGER

Ohio-born, Iowa-raised, and educated as an architect, Shane moved to New York City in 2003 and joined Grimshaw Architects. His early work at Grimshaw involved directing geometric and fabrication development on the Experimental Media & Performing Arts Center in Troy, New York. Subsequent research into design computation methodologies were manifested in light-reflecting dome studies for the Fulton Street Transit Center in New York City and the fabrication of a folded plate structural steel roof and dynamic louver system at the Museo del Acero in Monterrey. In 2007, Shane founded the Computational Design Unit at Grimshaw where he directed the research and application of environmental analysis, form and component development for fabrication and embedded design systems. A long-time contributor to the global design computation non-profit organization SmartGeometry, Shane was named Director of the organization in 2010. Shane recently became Director of Design Technology at Woods Bagot in New York City.

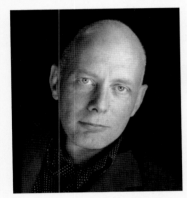

Regine Leibinger & Frank Barkow
David Benjamin
Ben van Berkel
Phil Bernstein
Shane M. Burger

Neil Denari
Marty Doscher
Ian Keough
James Kotronis

Adam Marcus
Thom Mayne
John Nastasi
Jesse Reiser

Nanako Umemoto
Fabian Scheurer
Craig Schwitter
Paolo Tombesi

NEIL DENARI

Neil Denari is Principal of NMDA, Neil M. Denari Architects and a Professor of Architecture at UCLA Department of Architecture & Urban Design. His was the Director of SCI-Arc from 1997 to 2001. Neil was the recipient of the Los Angeles AIA Gold Medal in 2011. In 2009, he was awarded the California Community Foundation Fellowship from the United States Artists and in 2008 he received an Architecture Award from the American Academy of Arts & Letters. NMDA has been awarded the 2005 and 2007 National AIA Awards, 2005 Progressive Architecture citation, and eight Los Angeles AIA Honor Awards, among others. Neil lectures worldwide and is the author of *Interrupted Projections, Gyroscopic Horizons,* and *Speculations On,* forthcoming in 2012. He received his B. Arch. from the University of Houston and an M. Arch. from Harvard University GSD.

MARTY DOSCHER

As Technology Director at Morphosis Architects from 2002 to 2010, Marty provided the leadership that distinguished the firm as an industry leader in technological innovation. He continues to advise and direct the firm's design technology initiatives and oversees digital collaboration to optimize project delivery. Leveraging over 15 years of experience and expertise as an industry innovator, Marty recently founded SYNTHESIS Technology Integration to support and cultivate technologically adept practices to evolve next-generation workflows in the design and construction industry. He is a frequent lecturer at universities and industry conferences, and serves on the AIA's Technology in Architectural Practice Advisory Group. Marty received a B.S. in Architecture from Georgia Institute of Technology and M. Arch. from Southern California Institute of Architecture (SCI-Arc).

IAN KEOUGH

Ian Keough's work with Buro Happold has focused on the implementation of Building Information Modeling (BIM) and the design of software for linking modeling and analysis applications. He has lectured widely on BIM, design automation and computational design at such venues as the SIGGRAPH, the Columbia Building Intelligence Project (CBIP) and ACADIA. While teaching at the Columbia University GSAPP, he developed the software "CatBot", to link parametric modeling and structural analysis through iterative optimization. His current research includes mobile computing in architecture and the development of parametric design tools. His software "goBIM" is the first BIM viewing application for the iPhone and iPad and his tool "Dynamo" for Revit enables visual programming using the Revit geometry API. Ian recently moved to Vela Systems to manage their Field BIM Interactive product development.

JAMES KOTRONIS

James Kotronis has over 20 years experience in the direct application of relational parametric tools in the fields of design, architecture, construction and fabrication. His work focuses on improving design performance through the synthesis of design, construction and fabrication thinking across disciplines and stakeholder boundaries. He currently holds the position of Managing Director at Gehry Technologies in New York City and has led interdisciplinary digital delivery initiatives on projects such as Lincoln Center's Alice Tully Hall, YAS Island Hotel, the Burj Khalifa Office Lobby and the World Trade Center Redevelopment - Lower Manhattan Construction Command Center.

ADAM MARCUS

Adam Marcus is an architect and educator currently based in Minneapolis, Minnesota. He is the Cass Gilbert Design Fellow at the University of Minnesota School of Architecture, where he teaches design studios that focus on new methods of integrating technology into both architectural practice and education. He was previously an Adjunct Assistant Professor at the Department of Architecture of Barnard+Columbia Colleges, where he taught seminars and workshops on parametric design and digital fabrication. From 2005 to 2011, he was a project designer with Marble Fairbanks in New York City, where he managed a number of award-winning educational and institutional projects. He is a graduate of Brown University and Columbia University Graduate School of Architecture, Planning and Preservation.

THOM MAYNE

Thom Mayne founded Morphosis in 1972 as an interdisciplinary and collective practice involved in experimental design and research. Thom is Co-Founder of the Southern California Institute of Architecture (SCI-Arc) and is currently Distinguished Professor at UCLA Architecture and Urban Design. He was elected to membership in the American Academy of Arts and Letters in 2010, appointed to the President's Committee on the Arts and Humanities in 2009, and honored with the Los Angeles AIA Gold Medal in 2000. With Morphosis, Mayne has been the recipient of the 2005 Pritzker Architecture Prize, 26 Progressive Architecture Awards and over 100 AIA Awards. The firm has been the subject of numerous exhibitions and 25 monographs.

JOHN NASTASI

John Nastasi is principal of a design-build practice in Hoboken, New Jersey and Founding Director of The Product-Architecture Lab at Stevens Institute of Technology. Highly influenced by technology in architecture, John has been at the forefront of research into the integration of emerging methods of computation in design and fabrication for the past decade and his work has been published both nationally and internationally. In 2004, John founded The Product-Architecture Lab with the primary mission of dissolving boundaries between design and engineering in both practice and the academy. The program has pioneered many advanced computational techniques that are just beginning to impact the design and construction industry. John received an M. Arch. from Harvard University GSD.

JESSE REISER & NANAKO UMEMOTO

Jesse Reiser and Nanako Umemoto have practiced in New York City as Reiser+Umemoto since 1986, and their work has been widely published and exhibited for over 20 years. They are an internationally recognized architectural firm and have built projects at a wide range of scales: from furniture design to residential and commercial structures, up to the scale of landscape design and infrastructure. They were awarded the Chrysler Award for Excellence in Design in 1999, the Academy Award in Architecture by the American Academy of Arts and Letters in 2000, and the Presidential Citation from the Cooper Union for outstanding practical and theoretical contributions to the field of architecture in 2008. Jesse is a Professor of Architecture at Princeton University School of Architecture and Nanako teaches at Penn Design and Columbia University GSAPP.

FABIAN SCHEURER

Fabian Scheurer is Founding Partner of designtoproduction and leads the company's office in Zurich. After graduating from the Technische Universität München with a degree in computer science and architecture, he worked as assistant for the university's CAAD group, as software developer for CAD-provider Nemetschek and as new media consultant for Eclat in Zurich. From 2002 until 2006 he studied the use of artificial life methods in architectural construction as a member of Ludger Hovestadt's CAAD group at the ETH Zurich and managed to transfer the results to a number of collaborative projects between architects, engineers and fabrication experts. In 2005 he co-founded designtoproduction as a research group to explore the connections between digital design and fabrication and since then has implemented digital production workflows for a number of renowned projects including the Mercedes-Benz Museum in Stuttgart, the Hungerburg Funicular Railway stations in Innsbruck and the EPFL Rolex Learning Center in Lausanne.

CRAIG SCHWITTER

Craig Schwitter is a leader in the engineering design of complex buildings and large-scale developments that include educational, performing arts, cultural, civic, stadia,

transportation and master planning projects. Craig founded the first North American office of Buro Happold Consulting Engineers in 1999 with a focus on integrated engineering and the use of task-appropriate technology. He has played a hands-on role in ensuring the high quality in Buro Happold's projects and breakthrough innovations on recent high-profile engineering commissions with the firm. The firm's work in low-energy and high-performance buildings has been a key area of technology development that Buro Happold continues to pursue across its worldwide portfolio of projects. Under his direction the firm has developed the Adaptive Building Initiative and G. Works, both related industry efforts in North America that address today's critical low-carbon and high-performance building design issues.

PAOLO TOMBESI

Trained as an architect in Italy, Paolo Tombesi is the Chair of Construction at the University of Melbourne. A former Fulbright Fellow, he has a Ph.D. on the division of labor in architecture from UCLA. In 2000, his article "The carriage in the needle", on the industrial restructuring of the architectural sector, won the Journal of Architectural Education Award. In 2005, he received the Royal Australian Institute of Architects' Sisalation Research Prize. The resulting book, *Looking Ahead: Defining the Terms of a Sustainable Architectural Profession*, was published in 2007. He has held visiting positions at the École Polytechnique in Lausanne, Harvard University, the Politecnico di Torino, the University of Minnesota, the University of Moratuwa in Sri Lanka, the University of Reading and Yale University.

ILLUSTRATION CREDITS

All illustrations are from the authors, unless otherwise noted.

"Beyond Efficiency"
David Benjamin
Figure 1. Pareto, V. (1906) *Manuale di economia politica*. Milano, Societa Editrice, p. 57.
Figure 2. Bombardier
Figure 3. Jordan Pollack at Brandeis University
Figure 4. David Benjamin, created using ModeFrontier by Esteco
Figure 5. Hod Lipson at Cornell University
Figure 6. Casey Reas
Figure 7. Processing.org
Figure 8. AnyBody Technology
Figure 9. Buro Happold
Figure 10. Zhendan Xue
Figure 11. Landrum & Brown
Figure 12. Landrum & Brown
Figure 13. Derek Moore, SOM
Figure 14. Landrum & Brown
Figure 15. John Locke
Figure 16. Danil Nagy
Figure 17. Patrick Cobb, Aries Liang, Muchan Park and Miranda Romer

"Precise Form for an Imprecise World"
Neil Denari
Figure 4. Desimone Consulting Engineers
Workflow 16-18. Front Inc.

"Workflow Patterns"
Adam Marcus
Figure 1. Hana Ogita
Figure 2. Marc Teer
Figure 3. FAT
Figure 4. Wikicommons
Figure 5-7. Marble Fairbanks
Workflow 3-7. Mark Collins & Toru Hasagawa
Workflow 15-19. Will Corcoran, Jonatan Schumacher, Oleg Moshkovich

"Intention to Artifact"
Phil Bernstein
Figure 1. Robert Smythson, Royal Institute of British Architects Library
Figure 2. Zaha Hadid Architects
Figure 3. CCDI Group
Figure 4. U.S. General Services Administration
Figure 5. Tocci Building Group
Figure 6. Autodesk, Inc.

"Diagrams, Design Models and Mother Models"
Ben van Berkel
Headshot: Inga Powilleit

"Designing Assembly"
Frank Barkow & Regine Leibinger
Figures 1, 6a, 7, Headshot. Corinne Rose
Figure 4. Barkow Photo, Brooklyn, New York
Figure 6b. Zooey Braun Fotografie
Workflow 11: Christian Richters

"Digital Craftsmanship"
Fabian Scheurer
Figure 3a. Eoghan O'Lionnain
Figure 4. Trebyggeriet AS
Figure 6. Blumer-Lehmann AG
Workflow 5. SJB Kempter-Fitze AG
Workflow 7. Trebyggeriet AS
Workflow 8-9. Hans Olav, Omnes, AF Gruppen

"Algorithmic Workflows in Associative Modeling"
Shane M. Burger
All images courtesy of Grimshaw, unless otherwise noted.
Figure 3. Jo Reid & John Peck
Figure 4. Robert Aish and Bentley Systems
Figure 6. Peter Cook
Figures 9-10. Grimshaw Industrial Design NY
Workflow 12-13. Paúl Rivera, archphoto

"Workflow Consultancy"
James Kotronis
All images courtesy of Gehry Technologies unless noted.
Erwin Hauer Wall
 Workflow 1-2. Erwin Hauer
Burj Khalifa Tower
 Workflow 2. SOM
 Workflow 5, 8a, 8b. Imperial Woodworking
 Workflow 10a. ICON Integrated Construction
 Workflow 13a. Imperial Woodworking
Broad Museum
 Workflow 1. Original rendering by Diller Scofido + Renfro

"The Scent of the System"
Jesse Reiser & Nanako Umemoto
Figure 11. Torsten Seidel Photography

"What Do We Mean by Building Design?"
Paolo Tombesi
Figure 1. From Turin, D. A. (2003) Building as a Process. *Building Research & Information*, vol. 31, iss. 2.
Figures 3a-3b. From an assignment in the Political Economy of Design subject, Melbourne School of Design, 2009. Students: Kok Hui Mah, Judy Chan, Kai Lun Chua, Cheng Li
Figure 4. Caterina Mauro, *The innovation potential of public buildings: the case of the Casa da Musica, Porto*. Final Thesis, Master in Architecture, Polytechnic of Turin, 2009
Figure 5-6. Thierry Duclos, *The innovation potential of public buildings: the case of the Sage Gateshead Music Centre*. Final Thesis, Master in Architecture, Polytechnic of Turin, 2007
Figure 11a. Diagram adapted from: Gray, C.; Hughes, W.; and Bennett, J. (1994) *The Successful Management of Design*. CSSC, University of Reading.
Figure 11b. Diagram adapted from: Nicolini, D.; Holti, R.; and Smalley, M., Integrating project activities: the theory and practice of managing the supply chain through clusters. *Building Research & Information*, 19 (2001), 37-47

"Shift 2D to 3D"
Thom Mayne
Headshot: Reiner Zettl
Figure 1. Michael Powers
Figure 2. Morphosis Architects

"Disposable Code; Persistent Design"
Marty Doscher
All images courtesy of Morphosis Architects.

"Continuous Integration"
Craig Schwitter & Ian Keough
All images courtesy of Buro Happold, unless otherwise noted.
twofour54
 Workflow 1. UNStudio
Crystal Bridges Museum
 Workflow 1. Safdie Architects

Echelman Net Sculpture
 Workflow 1: Janet Echelman & Philip Speranza
 Workflow 10: Stuart Peckham

"Designing Education"
John Nastasi
Figure 2. Marble Fairbanks
Figure 3. SHoP Architects
Ali Al-Sabah Military Academy
 Workflow 1-2. SOM
Apse Church Addition
 Workflow 6. Caliper Studio

INDEX OF NAMES